History and Material

Sources are the raw material of history, but whereas the written word has traditionally been seen as the principal source, today historians are increasingly recognizing
the value of sources beyond text. In *History and Material Culture*, Karen Harvey
embarks upon a discussion about material culture – considering objects, often those
found surrounding us in day-to-day life, as sources, which can help historians
develop new interpretations and new knowledge about the past.

Across ten chapters, different historians look at a variety of material sources
from around the globe and across centuries to assess how such sources can be used
to study history. While the sources are discussed from 'interdisciplinary' perspectives, each contributor examines how material culture can be approached from an
historical viewpoint, and each chapter addresses its theme or approach in a way
accessible to readers without expertise in the area.

In her introduction, Karen Harvey discusses some of the key issues raised when
historians use material culture, and suggests some basic steps for those new to these
kinds of sources. Opening up the discipline of history to new approaches, and
introducing those working in other disciplines to historical approaches, this book is
the ideal introduction to the opportunities and challenges of researching material
culture.

Karen Harvey is Senior Lecturer in Cultural History at the University of Sheffield.
Her publications include *Reading Sex in the Eighteenth Century: Bodies and
Gender in English Erotic Culture* (2004) and *The Kiss in History* (2005).

Routledge guides to using historical sources

Routledge guides to using historical sources is a series of books designed to introduce students to different sources and illustrate how they are used by historians. Each volume explores one type of primary source from a broad spectrum and, using specific examples from around the globe, examines their historical context and the different approaches that can be used to interpret these sources.

Reading Primary Sources
Miriam Dobson and Benjamin Ziemann

History Beyond the Text
Sarah Barber and Corinna M. Peniston-Bird

History and Material Culture
Karen Harvey

History and Material Culture

A student's guide to approaching alternative sources

Edited by Karen Harvey

Routledge
Taylor & Francis Group

LONDON AND NEW YORK

First published 2009 by Routledge
2 Park Square, Milton Park, Abingdon, Oxon OX14 4RN

Simultaneously published in the USA and Canada
by Routledge
711 Third Avenue, New York, NY 10017

Routledge is an imprint of the Taylor & Francis Group, an informa business

Typeset in Times New Roman by Swales & Willis Ltd, Exeter, Devon

British Library Cataloguing in Publication Data
A catalogue record for this book is available from the British Library

Library of Congress Cataloging in Publication Data
History and material culture / edited by Karen Harvey.
p. cm.—(The Routledge guides to using historical sources)
Includes index.
1. Material culture—Research—Methodology. 2. History—Research.
I. Harvey, Karen, 1971–
GN406.H58 2009
930.1072—dc22
2008042321

ISBN 10: 0–415–46849–3 (hbk)
ISBN 10: 0–415–45932–X (pbk)

ISBN 13: 978–0–415–46849–7 (hbk)
ISBN 13: 978–0–415–45932–7 (pbk)

Contents

List of illustrations   vii
List of contributors   ix
Acknowledgements   xii

Introduction: practical matters   1
KAREN HARVEY

1 Things that shape history: material culture and historical narratives   24
GIORGIO RIELLO

2 Ornament as evidence   47
ANDREW MORRALL

3 Back yards and beyond: landscapes and history   67
MARINA MOSKOWITZ

4 Draping the body and dressing the home: the material culture of textiles and clothes in the Atlantic world, *c*.1500–1800   85
BEVERLY LEMIRE

5 Using buildings to understand social history: Britain and Ireland in the seventeenth century   103
ANNE LAURENCE

6 Object biographies: from production to consumption   123
KARIN DANNEHL

7 Regional identity and material culture   139
HELEN BERRY

8 Objects and agency: material culture and modernity in China   158
FRANK DIKÖTTER

vi   *Contents*

 9 Mundane materiality, or, should small things still be forgotten?
    Material culture, micro-histories and the problem of scale   173
    SARA PENNELL

10 The case of the missing footstool: reading the absent object   192
    GLENN ADAMSON

    Index   208

Illustrations

1.1	Early eighteenth-century stomacher and X-radiography showing strips of whalebone	27
1.2	Diagram showing common locations of concealed objects found in sites in the United Kingdom	28
1.3	Sources for historical enquiry	29
1.4	The relationship between sources, narratives and methodologies	32
1.5	Wan Li porcelain wine cup, *c.* 1610, rediscovered in Jamestown, Virginia	34
1.6	'The Aerial Steam Carriage', newspaper cutting, *c.* 1840–45	38
1.7	'The Aerial Transit Company: By Permission of the Patentees', 1843	40
1.8	'The Flying Steam Company, to China in Twenty-Four Hours Certain'	42
2.1	Heinrich Vogtherr the Elder, Capitals, page from *Ein frembdes und wunderbarliches Kunstbüchlin ...* (1538)	50
2.2	Peter Flötner, design for a *Pokal*, Paris	51
2.3	Cornelis Anthonisz, *The Wise Man and the Wise Woman*, *c.* 1540	58
2.4	Anon., *Family of Hans Conrad Bodmer*, Landvogt von Greifensee, 1643	60
3.1	Lucy Salmon back yard	68
3.2	Photographic postcard showing aerial view of Winona, Kansas, *c.* 1930	79
4.1	Bed curtain, *c.* 1700	87
4.2	Pair of tie-on pockets, 1700–1725	94
4.3	Diamond quilted silk petticoat	97
5.1	Beaulieau House, near Drogheda, Co. Louth	107
5.2	Monea Castle, Co. Fermanagh	109
5.3	Coppinger's Court, Co. Cork	110
5.4	Woodhouses bastle house, Northumberland	112
5.5	Mervinslaw pele tower, Roxburghshire	112
5.6	Kirkheaton House, Northumberland	113
5.7	Amisfield Tower, Dumfriesshire	114
5.8	Kellie Castle, Fife	116

7.1   George Balmer, *Sunderland. The Bridge from the Westward*
      (undated, early nineteenth century)   146
7.2   Beilby goblet (*c.*1770)   148
9.1   Iron pastry cutter, Italian, seventeenth century   173
9.2   Iron pastry cutter, English, 1723   174
9.3   Skillet, English late seventeenth century   181
10.1 William Hogarth, *Marriage a La Mode*, Plate II. 1745   193
10.2 Armchair, England, 1675–1700. Oak and elm   197
10.3 George Hepplewhite, *The Cabinet-Maker & Upholsterer's*
      Guide, 1787, Plate 15   199

Contributors

Glenn Adamson is Head of Graduate Studies and Deputy Head of Research at the Victoria & Albert Museum, London. In that capacity, he teaches on the History of Design graduate course run collaboratively with the Royal College of Art. His research ranges from modern craft and industrial design to English and American decorative arts during the seventeenth and eighteenth centuries. He is the author of *Industrial Strength Design: How Brooks Stevens Shaped Your World* (Milwaukee Art Museum/MIT Press). Adamson's monograph *Thinking Through Craft* (V&A Publications/Berg Publishers) was published in October 2007. He also co-edits the new *Journal of Modern Craft* (Berg Publishers) with Tanya Harrod and Edward S. Cooke, Jr. Currently, he is at work on a project about postmodernism for the V&A, to be on view in 2011.

Helen Berry is Reader in Early Modern History at Newcastle University, UK. She is the author of *Gender, Society and Print Culture in Late-Stuart England* (Ashgate, 2003), co-editor with Elizabeth Foyster of *The Family in Early Modern England* (Cambridge, 2007) and co-editor with Jeremy Gregory of *Creating and Consuming Culture in North-East England, 1660–1830* (Ashgate, 2004). The author of numerous articles and book chapters on a wide range of late-seventeenth-century and eighteenth-century topics such as print culture, coffee houses and the history of shopping, she is currently exploring the links between consumption and sexual identity through the history of *castrato* singers.

Karin Dannehl is a research fellow with the History and Governance Research Institute at the University of Wolverhampton, UK. Her research interests are in the areas of eighteenth-century consumption, retailing and trade, with a focus on material culture and its objects and materials as a source of knowledge. She is particularly interested in examining factors influencing value(s) attributed to everyday objects. She works closely together with Nancy Cox and the two have jointly published the online edition of *The Dictionary of Traded Goods and Commodities*, c.*1550–1820* and the monograph *Perceptions of Retailing in Early Modern England*.

Frank Dikötter is Professor of the Modern History of China at the School of Oriental and African Studies, University of London, and Chair Professor of

Humanities at the University of Hong Kong. He is the author of a series of microstudies that trace the contingent ways in which ideas, objects and institutions from abroad were selectively appropriated in China. These studies include, among others, *The Discourse of Race in Modern China* (Stanford University Press, 1992) and *Exotic Commodities: Modern Objects and Everyday Life* (Columbia University Press, 2007). He is now working on a social history of communist China.

Karen Harvey is Senior Lecturer in Cultural History at the University of Sheffield, UK, whose research focuses on the British long eighteenth century. Her published works include *Reading Sex in the Eighteenth Century: Bodies and Gender in English Erotic Culture* (Cambridge University Press, 2004) and *Domesticating Patriarchy: Male Authority in the Eighteenth-Century English Home* (Oxford University Press, forthcoming). Karen has ongoing research interests in masculinity and 'impoliteness', and in this context has published on the material culture of drinking. She has also collaborated with museums and galleries in teaching and research, one outcome of which is the DVD *Studying Material Culture for Historians*.

Anne Laurence is Professor of History at the Open University. Her current research interests are women, wealth and patronage in the period 1550–1760. She has extensive experience of using material culture to teach social history, and in developing methods of using DVD for this.

Beverly Lemire has had a long-time fascination with objects, particularly historic textiles and clothing, and has incorporated material culture study in a number of her works. She is Professor and Henry Marshall Tory Chair at the University of Alberta, and founding Director of the Material Culture Institute. Among her publications are *Fashion's Favourite: The Cotton Trade and the Consumer in Britain, 1660–1800* (Oxford University Press, 1991), *Dress, Culture and Commerce: the English Clothing Trade before the Factory* (Palgrave Macmillan, 1997) and, most recently, *The Business of Everyday Life: Gender, Practice and Social Politics in England, c.1600–1900* (Manchester University Press, 2005). Beverly has worked with collections in major museums in North America, Europe and India, and is currently engaged in a book project on the global history of cotton, in a series entitled 'Textiles that Changed the World'.

Andrew Morrall is Professor, Bard Graduate Center, New York. His publications include: *Jörg Breu the Elder. Art, Culture and Belief in Reformation Augsburg* (Ashgate, 2002), and numerous articles on aspects of Northern European Renaissance art and material culture, aesthetics, the theory of representation, art and Reformation society, and the history of collecting. He is currently completing a book-length study of the history and theory of Renaissance ornament.

Marina Moskowitz is Reader in History and American Studies at the University of Glasgow. She is the author of *Standard of Living: The Measure of the Middle Class in Modern America* (Johns Hopkins, 2004) and co-editor of *Cultures of Commerce:*

Representation and American Business Culture, 1877–1960 (Palgrave, 2006). Her recent research on the American seed trade in the nineteenth century has been supported by several fellowships and grants, including the ESRC-AHRC Culture of Consumption Programme and the Kluge Center of the Library of Congress, Washington DC.

Sara Pennell is Senior Lecturer in Early Modern British History in the School of Arts at Roehampton University, London. She teaches undergraduate and postgraduate courses on the social, cultural and economic history of Britain in the seventeenth and eighteenth centuries, with a focus on material cultural and other interdisciplinary approaches. Her current research is concerned with the material culture of the non-elite domestic interior in this period, and she has recently written on early modern consumption, food practices and artefacts in the context of the historical 'everyday', and recipe books and culinary knowledge.

Giorgio Riello is Assistant Professor in Global History at the Department of History of the University of Warwick, UK. He has written on early modern material culture, textiles, dress and fashion in Europe and Asia. He is the author of *A Foot in the Past: Consumers, Producers and Footwear in the Long Eighteenth Century* (Oxford University Press, 2006), and co-editor of *Shoes: A History from Sandals to Sneakers* (Berg, 2006), *The Spinning World: A Global History of Cotton Textiles, 1200–1850* (Oxford University Press, 2008) and *How India Clothed the World: Textiles in the Indian Ocean, 1500–1850* (2009, forthcoming). Giorgio is currently writing a monograph entitled *Worldwide Wefts: Cotton Textiles in World History, 1200–1800*.

Acknowledgements

The editor would like to thank Annamarie Kino and Alison Yates at Routledge, and also Caroline Watson, Lynn Brown and Julie Willis, for their work on the volume. Special thanks are reserved for Eve Setch at Routledge, who not only commissioned the book, but also gave generous and critical editorial comments in helping me define its shape. I have greatly appreciated her patience, energy and intellectual input.

Figure 1.1: Early eighteenth-century stomacher found at a cottage in Nether Wallop, Hampshire, United Kingdom, and an X-radiography showing strips of whalebone. Deliberately Concealed Garments Project, Winchester School of Art, University of Southampton CG8.a. © The Textile Conservation Centre, University of Southampton and Sonia O'Connor, University of Bradford.

Figure 1.2: Diagram showing common locations of concealed objects found in sites in the United Kingdom. © The Textile Conservation Centre, University of Southampton.

Figure 1.5: Wan Li porcelain wine cup, c.1610: porcelain thinly glazed with under-glaze blue with a scroll design above the footring, width 5.41 inches, height 4.64 inches. Rediscovered in Jamestown, Virginia, Pit 4. © APVA Preservation Virginia.

Figure 1.7: 'The Aerial Transit Company: By Permission of the Patentees'. Colour print, London, published by Ackerman & Co., the Strand, 28 March 1843. Science Museum, London, inv. 1938–0296.

Figure 1.8: 'The Flying Steam Company, to China in Twenty-Four Hours Certain'. Cotton handkerchief with sepia brown ink. Science Museum, London, inv. 1938–0295.

Figure 2.1: Heinrich Vogtherr the Elder, Capitals, page from *Ein frembdes und wunderbarliches Kunstbüchlin* ... (Strassburg, 1538), woodcut, 18 x 13 cm, Warburg Institute, London University.

Figure 2.2: Peter Flötner, Design for a *Pokal*, pen and ink with yellow wash, 75 x 27.5 cm, Paris, Bibliothèque Nationale de France, Cabinet des dessins, inv. no. RES AA5.

Figure 2.3: Cornelis Anthonisz, *The Wise Man and the Wise Woman, c.*1540, hand-coloured woodcut, 28 x 40 cm, Amsterdam, Rijksprentenkabinet, P-RP-P-1932–127.

Figure 2.4: Anon., *Family of Hans Conrad Bodmer*, Landvogt von Greifensee, 1643, oil on canvas, Zürich, Schweizerisches Landesmuseum, Dep. 3721, on loan from a private collection.

Figure 3.1: Lucy Salmon back yard. The back yard of Lucy Maynard Salmon's home in Poughkeepsie, New York, early twentieth century (Lucy Maynard Salmon Collection, Archives and Special Collections, Vassar College, Poughkeepsie, NY).

Figure 3.2: Photographic postcard showing aerial view of Winona, Kansas, *c.*1930. The left side of the image demonstrates how the town developed within the grid of the United States National Survey, and the right shows how the railroad line and Highway US-40 serve as boundaries for the town. © SS. Collection of the author.

Figure 4.1: Bed curtain, *c.*1700, painted, dyed cotton (chintz), Coromandel Coast, India, for European market. IS. 121–1950. Courtesy of Victoria and Albert Museum, London.

Figure 4.2: Pair of tie-on pockets, 1700–1725. Linen hand sewn with linen thread. Embroidered with wool and attached to linen tape. T. 697: B, C-1913. Courtesy of Victoria and Albert Museum, London.

Figure 4.3: Diamond quilted silk petticoat, lined with wool, hand sewn, 1740–1750. T. 306–1982. Courtesy of Victoria and Albert Museum, London.

Figure 5.1: Beaulieu House, near Drogheda, Co. Louth. The house was probably built by Sir Henry Tichbourne (*c.*1581–1667), during the 1660s, but what we see may be the rebuilding of his grandson, another Sir Henry. © The Open University.

Figure 5.2: Monea Castle, Co. Fermanagh, built in 1618 in the Scottish style by the Rev. Malcolm Hamilton, a Scottish planter, Rector of Devenish and Church of Ireland Archbishop of Cashel 1623–9. © The Open University.

Figure 5.3: Coppinger's Court, Co. Cork, built *c.*1618 by Sir Walter Coppinger, a member of an Old English family from Cork city who had bought the land from penurious Gaelic Irish families. © The Open University.

Figure 5.4: Woodhouses bastle house, Northumberland, 1602. © The Open University.

Figure 5.5: Mervinslaw pele tower, Roxburghshire, late sixteenth century. © The Open University.

Figure 5.6: Kirkheaton House, Northumberland. Late medieval tower; early seventeenth century house. © The Open University.

Figure 5.7: Amisfield Tower, Dumfriesshire, 1600. © The Open University.

Figure 5.8: Kellie Castle, Fife, a fifteenth-century tower house joined to a sixteenth-century tower by Lord Oliphant's new range c.1603–7. The 3rd Earl of Kellie remodelled the interior apartments in the 1670s using craftsmen working on Charles II's new palace at Holyrood. James Lorimer restored the house in the 1870s. © The Open University.

Figure 7.1: George Balmer (1806–1846), *Sunderland. The Bridge from the Westward* (undated), ref. J6820. The view shows the River Wear upstream of the cast-iron Wear Bridge (built 1793–96) On the right are the cone-shaped kilns of glassworks. By kind permission, Tyne and Wear Museums, Newcastle upon Tyne.

Figure 7.2: Beilby goblet (c.1770), ref. 99.17BEIL. Bucket-shaped bowl and double series opaque twist in stem, white enamel upon Newcastle light baluster glass. By kind permission Huntington Library Art Collections, San Marino, California.

Figure 9.1: Iron pastry cutter, Italian, seventeenth century, inscribed on other side 'Allerina', V&A Museum no. 105–1884 ©V&A Images/Victoria and Albert Museum, London.

Figure 9.2: Iron pastry cutter, English, dated in inscription 1723, inscribed 'Ann', Colonial Williamsburg Foundation accession no. G1970–3. By permission of the Colonial Williamsburg Foundation. Gift of Mrs Daniel Baker, Jr.

Figure 9.3: Skillet, English late seventeenth century, with handle cast with 'Ye wages of sin is death', Hugh Roberts collection, Bath Preservation Trust, on loan to The Merchants House Trust, Marlborough, Wiltshire. Reproduced by permission of No.1 Royal Crescent, Bath © Bath Preservation Trust.

Figure 10.1: William Hogarth, *Marriage a La Mode*, Plate II. 1745. Etching and engraving on paper. H 38.1 cm × W 46.3 cm. V&A F.118:21; Forster Bequest. Courtesy of Victoria and Albert Museum, London.

Figure 10.2: Armchair, England, 1675–1700. Oak and elm, with carving and turning. H 115 cm × W 57 cm × D 55.5 cm. V&C CIRC. 214–1911. Courtesy of Victoria and Albert Museum, London.

Figure 10.3: George Hepplewhite, *The Cabinet-Maker & Upholsterer's Guide*, 1787.

Introduction
Practical matters[1]

Karen Harvey

A cursory glance across the metres of book shelves on decorative art in bookstores and libraries, a visit to a museum, a trip to a historic building, or even a walk down your street, reveals a mass of data that would – were it not for its material form – be considered a gold mine of primary sources for historians. For some time, this mass of historical evidence was often overlooked or sidelined, considered not the proper raw materials of a historian. As a staple of historical training, material culture has generally been absent from most university history programmes. Increasingly, though, historians regard objects as a useful, even necessary, component of their study of the past. In this context, this book raises two central questions: 'How can objects be used in history?' and 'What can objects offer the historian?'

These are deceptively straightforward questions that invite us to explore a series of substantial methodological and epistemological issues, concerning what we do and how we know. What do historians aim to achieve? How do they go about this? On what do they base their claims to knowledge about the past? In this Introduction I will begin the discussion of these issues, a discussion that continues through the essays that follow. In turn, I will examine (a) some of the important and well-established approaches to 'material culture', and their implications for historians, and (b) the opportunities and challenges of researching 'material culture' for historians, and the specific issues that arise when historians attend to material culture. The two appendices that follow this Introduction are designed as practical guides for those starting the process of researching and writing about material culture.

My aim in the Introduction is not to provide a comprehensive step-by-step 'how to' guide on the method historians should adopt in their analysis of objects – the essays that follow fulfil that role ably, and in their very detail and diversity demonstrate how the maturity of these approaches would render such a 'how to' piece superficial and reductive. Rather, this Introduction will provide a context for the essays that follow. Collectively, these essays insist that history is impoverished without attention to material culture, and one by one and in different ways they demonstrate the gains to be won. The book seeks to open up the discipline of history to new approaches, new sources, new interpretations and new knowledge about the past. As such, it is intended to serve as a guide to those increasing numbers of students of history needing and wanting to integrate material culture into their study of the past. But, crucially, this book has a second ambition. Objects are valuable to historians, but historians have skills and knowledge that can enrich the study of material culture. In this Introduction, I will consider both what historians might learn from material culture and also what students of material culture might learn from the diversity of historians' approaches to objects.

Approaches to material culture

As several of the contributors to this book make clear, historians are not the first to integrate objects into their research. Archaeologists, literary historians, art historians, sociologists, anthropologists – and others – have taken different approaches to objects, and historians have much to learn from these studies. To shape this brief discussion of work on material culture, and to raise issues of particular relevance to historians, I will introduce some basic differences in emphasis by adopting a distinction made by Bernard Herman, author of many studies of material culture. Herman makes a distinction between studies that are 'object-centred' and those that are 'object-driven'.

Object-centred projects tend to look at technological development, typologies, and the aesthetic qualities of taste and fashion.[2] Building on Herman's bi-partite model, we can usefully split this object-centred approach into two main forms. The first focuses closely on the physical attributes of an object, either with single objects (as often in decorative arts) or a series or group of objects (most notably in the assemblage finds or constructed series of archaeology). Here, there is a high premium on connoisseurial expertise, on the detailed knowledge about the material features of the object. The second kind of object-centred analysis is one rooted in an art historical approach, in which the focus moves from the object to what we might regard as the emotional or psychological dimensions of material culture. One example of such an approach is that given by Jules David Prown. His three-stage method is as follows: first, the researcher engages in precise *description*, focusing on the internal evidence of the object; second, the researcher engages in *deduction*, exploring the possible connections between object and people based on both intellectual but also emotional responses; third, the researcher engages in *speculation*, using external evidence but also 'creative imagining' to understand why the object is the way it is, or provokes the way it provokes.[3]

Studies of material culture that are 'object-driven' regard 'objects as evidence of other complex social relationships'.[4] Working in this vein, Herman seeks to 'reconnect objects to their historical contexts' by undertaking 'the construction of collective biographies of objects and sites through a process of thick description'.[5] Using many written sources, as well as material ones, Herman peels off past layers of meaning around objects, and in doing so finds out things about the people that made, used and lived with those objects. Already we can observe the complex nature of work on material culture, because Prown's method edges towards Herman's 'object-driven' approaches. While the emphasis on thick description – a reference to the method of reading culture developed by the anthropologist Clifford Geertz[6] – links to some extent with Prown's attention to close and repeated engagement of the researcher with the object and its meanings, though, Herman's emphasis is more on people and lives.

Another scholar working in the field of material culture studies – Henry Glassie – moves away from written sources. In his characteristically poetic style, the American 'folk historian' reminds his readers of the gain to be had from studying things as well as words:

> studies focused on words, whether written or spoken, omit whole spheres of experience that are cumbersomely framed in language but gracefully shaped into artifacts. We miss more than most people in recent times, and everyone in the most ancient days, when we restrict historical research to verbal documents. We miss the wordless experience of all people, rich or poor, near or far.[7]

Glassie's stress on wordless experience is a considerable challenge for history, a discipline that draws predominantly on written documents. But while his work examines the intricate details of form, style, construction and materials, Glassie moves repeatedly away from the object, to context. For Glassie, objects 'are texts, sets of parts, to which meaning is brought by locating them in contexts'.[8]

Though different, the statements of Herman and Glassie share a concern with context, people and experience. In this they are characteristic of the field of 'material culture studies', particularly prominent and well developed in North America. Part of the distinctiveness of this field is its very interdisciplinarity: Ann Smart Martin, another important scholar in this area, has remarked on the diverse roots of this blended field: from anthropology it has garnered that material culture 'expresses and mediates human and social relationships', from social history it has inherited an interest in the non-elite, and from art history and the decorative arts, the field has developed close attention to aesthetics.[9] In addition to these foci, practitioners in the field adopt a rather specific definition of material culture. According to Martin, objects are a text (in and through which meanings are constructed, and power is created and maintained), and this text has 'its own grammar and vocabulary'.[10] It is important to note what scholars mean by the term 'material culture'. Unlike 'object' or 'artefact', 'material culture' encapsulates not just the physical attributes of an object, but the myriad and shifting contexts through which it acquires meaning. Material culture is not simply objects that people make, use and throw away; it is an integral part of – and indeed shapes – human experience. For historians, there are at least two important and related implications of these definitions of and approaches to material culture: first, material culture is a source type that demands new research practices and skills of the historian; second, objects are active and autonomous, not simply reflective.

All sources need to be handled with appropriate research skills. Objects are no different, and for historians (commonly trained in using written documents), the necessary re-tooling can be substantial. Several scholars have described the rather complex nature of objects as sources. As W. David Kingery has explained:

> No one denies the importance of things, but learning from them requires rather more attention than reading texts. The grammar of things is related to, but more

complex and difficult to decipher than, the grammar of words. Artifacts are tools as well as signals, signs, and symbols. Their use and functions are multiple and intertwined. Much of their meaning is subliminal and unconscious. Some authors have talked about reading objects as texts, but objects must also be read as myths and as poetry.[11]

Such insistence on the multi-faceted nature of material culture, and thus on the necessary range of approaches to be adopted by the researcher, is shared by many others. A study by the UK archaeologist Christopher Tilley – *Metaphor and Material Culture* (1999) – for example, insists on the role of metaphor in people's understanding of the physical world, explaining that metaphor arises out of 'inherent problems in the precise relationship between a world of words and a world of things, events and actions'.[12] Metaphor is inextricably connected to things, then, with (in the case of Yekuana baskets in the Amazon), 'metaphorical meanings of designs … materially present *in* the designs'.[13] Yet researching metaphor takes us into the realm of the 'imaginative faculties … literature … poetry … fiction … emotion and subjectivity', areas deemed 'fundamentally opposed to facts' and to 'a disinterested and objective understanding'. Tilley's impassioned call for social scientists to enter this realm is wise counsel for historians: 'metaphors provide the basis for an interpretative understanding of the world, the goal of the historical and social sciences'.[14] Not all those researching material culture share Tilley's emphasis on metaphor. John Dixon Hunt has questioned whether objects can ever function as metaphors in quite the same way as words, and instead suggests that objects should be regarded as signs that have been encoded, and must then be decoded by researchers.[15] These are significant differences, to be sure. But whether operating as metaphor, sign, symbol or tool – or all of these – the student or researcher needs to be equipped with the appropriate skills to work on such sources.

Arguably it is the 'connoisseurial' skills often deployed when studying material culture that might appear most foreign to historians, particularly in cases of 'art' objects. In Prown's art historical method, the emphasis is on the meaning of the material detail of the object and as such the connoisseurial aspect is given a greater emphasis than when a historian might analyse a written source. Indeed, connoisseurial analyses sit uneasily in the discipline of history, one of the humanities and social sciences rather than the arts, and one that is not object-centred. Historians' training does not predispose them to place aesthetic forms of evidence centre stage. These aesthetic features are certainly regarded as aspects of a source type that need to be acknowledged, but historians then tend to move on to the matter of what the content of the source can tell us about the topic in hand. Yet aesthetic features can serve as illuminating evidence for historians, in particular articulating the often unspoken beliefs and assumptions of a society. This is demonstrated in this book by Andrew Morrall's essay on sixteenth-century Northern European ornament, which takes the latter out of 'its traditional place within art history, … to be understood rather as a potentially important branch of social experience'.[16]

The claim that objects are autonomous and active, rather than merely reflective, is another central tenet of many scholars working under the umbrella of 'material culture studies', as it also is in many 'object-centred' disciplines.[17] This is a more substantial issue than that concerning the relative 'primacy of objects over other documents', a point of debate that has arisen elsewhere in discussions about material culture.[18] The first editorial of the *Journal of Material Culture* (1996) – a leading UK journal in this field – for example, declared that objects were not conduits of information (about the past or anything else) but possessed autonomy: 'Objects tend to be meaningful, rather than merely communicate meaning'.[19] These points are crucial to understanding the challenges of incorporating material culture into history as a discipline. Objects are not simply cultural receptacles that acquire meanings which can then be unearthed and read by the student or researcher. Through their very materiality – their shape, function, decoration, and so on – they have a role to play in creating and shaping experiences, identities and relationships. As Matthew Cochran and Mary Beaudry put it, paraphrasing the position of anthropological material culture studies in the United Kingdom, material culture is 'a potentially active agent in social life'.[20] Cochran and Beaudry go on to tease out the implications of this position in the work of historical archaeologists: 'By acknowledging the active role of objects in everyday life, historical archaeologists avoid the limitations of rigid classificatory schema that segregate objects from people.'[21]

Such a view of objects as active, and the resultant re-balancing of our view of the respective roles of people and things, is particularly important and perhaps contentious for historians. Arguably, it runs counter to the way that historians are invariably trained to view their primary materials: as 'documents', examined from a critical distance, and serving as 'sources' of information about people in the past. By contrast, those scholars who have devised robust methodologies for interpreting objects emphasize that objects are not documents in any simple way. Taking on board these points with regard to objects might lead historians to reassess their view of written documents, seeing them rather more as material objects themselves, perhaps, shaped by materials, design and aesthetics. Historians might even regard written documents as just one available set in a suite of others, rather than the principal source. As Dan Hicks and Mary Beaudry remark in their discussion of historical archaeology, 'written sources represent simply another, albeit distinctive, form of material culture rather than a revolutionary change in the human past'.[22] John Moreland has urged both historians and archaeologists to recognize how people in the past constructed power, identity and social practice out of objects and words, rather than viewing objects and texts as 'simply evidence *about* the past'.[23] Yet there is a further and more substantial issue here, one concerning human agency. There is much theoretical work on human agency, users and things.[24] Interested in people's past lives and experiences, historians are perhaps naturally inclined to emphasize the role of people in making those lives. Yet granting objects agency and power invites a different view of how lives are shaped. In this book, Marina Moskowitz instructs us to acknowledge the geographical, environmental and human impacts on landscape, as well as the interactions between them. Indeed, landscape is a particular kind of material culture, not produced or made in the same way as buildings, spoons or petticoats. Elsewhere in this book, though, a different relationship between people and things is imagined. Frank Dikötter's case study of modern China seeks to underline the ways in which Chinese men and women shaped the uses and meanings of foreign objects. In so doing, this essay rethinks historical arguments concerning the interrelations of globalization and modernity: Western modernity did not wash over Chinese people, dampening indigenous tradition; instead the Chinese actively appropriated modern exports. For historians working on material culture, the agency of material objects is a point of lively debate.

Scholars differ in how they define and describe the kind of source that objects are, and also in the role that objects play in human society. Yet there is an important commonality in all the statements reproduced so far: an emphasis on meaning, on the complex ways in which this is embedded in an object and/or its context, and on the role of the researcher to detect and decipher these meanings. This is crucially important in recognizing the challenges of material culture for historians. Prown's definition of material culture, for example, brings to the fore this emphasis on meanings:

> Material culture is just what it says it is – namely, the manifestations of culture through material productions. And the study of material culture is the study of material to understand culture, to discover the beliefs – the values, ideas, attitudes, and assumptions – of a particular community or society at a given time. The underlying premise is that human-made objects reflect, consciously or unconsciously, directly or indirectly, the beliefs of the individuals who commissioned, fabricated, purchased, or used them and, by extension, the beliefs of the larger society to which these individuals belonged. Material culture is thus an object-based branch of cultural anthropology or cultural history.[25]

With such a definition of material culture, it is little surprise that the latter two stages of Prown's methodology stress the extent of discovery and understanding on the part of the researcher, what we might view as a large space of interpretation between the object and the scholar. This emphasis on interpretation is common. Indeed, Hunt regards objects as offering unique attractions in this regard: 'the object appeals because within its sign is coded a richer range of meanings. It allows us more opportunities to perform as historians.'[26] Objects are particular kinds of sources, that might be agents as well as documents, and they demand that we acquire appropriate skills to understand them. But objects also offer an exciting opportunity for those interested in the past, because they allow the historian space to engage creatively with new sources in new ways, detecting and reconstructing objects' roles and meanings. They make the job of the historian first and foremost one of interpretation.

The discipline of history was perhaps once an inhospitable home for material culture studies. If history has been predominantly concerned with finding out what happened when and why, then studies of the meanings of objects might seem marginal to the central endeavour. History is increasingly interdisciplinary, though, and some historians are – and have long been – open to different approaches. Yet while the historical study of material culture has certainly been a growth area in recent years,[27] Adrienne Hood has detected a recent backtracking and a notable absence of work by historians on objects.[28] Such an absence is in part a result of historians' training in written documents. But it also reflects (especially in the UK, perhaps, where historiographical approaches to material culture spring more from social history than from anthropology or ethnography) the socio-economic-inflected approach of the discipline. Material culture certainly chimes with cultural history, a now well-established element of the discipline, but it is not of universal appeal to all historians. Concerns about the cultural emphasis in historians' work on objects have been expressed by Richard Grassby, for example, who bemoans what he sees as too great an emphasis on the 'symbolic characteristics of objects' and 'the cultural interpretation of material life'. He calls for historians to 'test' the inferences made from objects against written documents, and to 'supplement' documentary evidence with archaeological finds; this, he argues, will enable historians to reconstruct a culture from evidence of people's own 'statements of intention' and people's 'actual behaviour'.[29] Here we have a rather different assessment of the nature and value of objects as sources than found in material culture studies, one that is doubtful about the self-sufficiency of objects as sources, and inclined to see them as enhancing findings from elsewhere.

It is instructive to reflect on such doubts, but to do this we must consider what it is that unites historians. Being wise to the concerns at the core of an academic discipline allows us to be self-reflective about the questions we are asking, and also those questions we are not asking. History is not at heart an 'object-centred' discipline. Guides to the object-centred analysis of material culture as historical texts are useful, but the contributions to this volume suggest that historians will rarely wish to place objects centre stage in quite this manner. While this does not mean paying any less attention to the 'thingness of the thing', it does mean using the results of this enquiry in subtly different ways.[30] In other words, historians are not much interested in things or their thingness for their own sake, but as routes to past experience. To reconcile these basic concerns with the study of objects, for material culture to be integrated securely into historical studies, we need to develop approaches that draw on and complement history's status as both a social science and a humanities discipline. We need to attend to how the study of material culture can satisfy social scientific demands for typicality and representativeness, while also reflecting the complex fabric of social relationships and meanings.

In fact, while Grassby rightly detects a cultural emphasis in some historical work on objects,[31] it is important that we hold on to the range of approaches possible when historians work on or with material culture. Certainly in studies of early American material culture, this range has been ever present: as Martin writes, 'At the heart of the undertaking, in all its diverse forms and thrusts, are relationships between human beings and the material world involving the use of things to mediate social relations and cultural behaviour.'[32] Attention to the material stuff and associated practices of everyday life – notable in archaeology and anthropology, for example – shows how the study of material culture facilitates a focus on social lives and experiences. And it is here that material culture can appeal to a broad constituency in history. Like many disciplines, history has been transformed by the 'cultural turn', with its emphasis on the role of language in shaping experiences. Historians have been exploring how their long-standing attention to the social might be reconfigured, restored or revived in this new landscape.[33] Significantly, historians are not alone in this concern – a 'refocusing upon the material dimensions of social life' has been noted across the arts, humanities and social sciences.[34] In history, integrating meaning and practice is just one way that we might conceive of this project.[35] And, as in other disciplines, material culture provides historians with a superb opportunity to sustain a focus on integrated social and cultural practice.

While a discipline may have a core, it will also feature variety, interdisciplinarity and areas of work that are in some tension with one another. When scholars work on material culture, the variety within disciplines – and also the connections between them – becomes plain. As a result, it can be difficult to distinguish between disciplinary approaches to material culture. Yet this is a feature of the field to be celebrated, not beaten down by oversimplified categories. As Lubar and Kingery cautioned readers in *History from Things* (1993), we need to be 'wary of discipline-oriented overviews'; the reality of academic work in this field happily resists easy compartmentalization.[36] The contributors to this collection are all historians of one form or another.[37] And yet, Helen Berry's piece on glass was forged through conversations with archaeologists, Anne Laurence's work on buildings was influenced by collaboration with art historians and TV producers, Andrew Morrall's essay on decoration explicitly employs an art historical method, while Marina Moskowitz's contribution on landscape is rooted firmly in the field of cultural landscape studies. A historian's study will always have particular emphases. These essays make palpable the range of approaches historians might take to material culture, whether object-centred or object-driven, and with a greater or lesser emphasis on cultural meaning or social practice. The volume demonstrates that this range of approaches to material culture can be accommodated within (but also transform) a predominantly text-based view of the past. Authors draw on the distinctive characteristics of the historical discipline, notably stressing context, a range of documents and the agency of social actors, but they simultaneously put into practice approaches and techniques garnered from other disciplines. The result is a collection of blended approaches which resist categorization as cultural or social histories, and which demonstrate that historians have much to gain from the study of material culture. As I now want to discuss, these essays show, too, that historians have a great deal to offer the wider field of material culture studies.

History and material culture

While certainly not a universally accepted aspect of the discipline of history, material culture has received attention from historians for some time. In this section, it is not my intention to provide a comprehensive review of the many works by historians that use or research material culture.[38] Instead, I want to convey the breadth of this work, along with its roots in a socio-economic discipline. We must begin with the history of consumption. Historians' interest in objects has often been one component of a much broader interest in 'consumption', often grounded in the use of probate inventories.[39] The questions asked have often concerned what was new, and particularly the 'the consumer revolution'.[40] There have been limitations to this work. The research questions have perhaps naturally given rise to a focus on change, rather than the persistence of tradition, while the sources themselves mean that the poor are often not represented.[41] Moreover, conceiving of objects as social and/or economic products ('goods') risks failing to recognize the many levels at which humans interact with their material world.[42] But while on the one hand this work was rooted firmly in the well-established socio-economic concerns of the modern historical discipline, at the same time it represented that discipline in flux. Others working on objects had cautioned that attention to objects as units of production and consumption also required attention to cultural meanings. As the archaeologist Matthew Johnson writes, objects have been not only economic entities with monetary value; they 'must be understood in a variety of ways beyond the "economic". These different ways involve the study of the very different meanings, ambiguous, subtle, changing, multiple, that artefacts carried and that were involved in their production and consumption'.[43] Similarly, Kopytoff stressed the need to write a 'culturally informed economic biography of an object [that] would look at it as a culturally constructed entity, endowed with culturally specific meanings, and classified and reclassified into culturally constituted categories'.[44] Dannehl's essay on kitchen stuff in this book (Chapter 6) reveals the ways in which historians can enrich their work by reconstructing the life of an object from production to consumption. 'By itself', Dannehl explains, 'an artefact is a time capsule that allows insight into only a relatively limited time period.' Examining the life of an object can reconstruct context, and 'snap-shots may be turned into a sequence of stills'.[45]

The history of consumption now encompasses a steady focus on the economic, social, political and cultural value of luxury, taste and decoration. Indeed, an earlier focus on everyday objects of the past as 'pots and pans history',[46] is now accompanied by 'cushions and curtains history', with greater attention to style, the elite and the cultural. Throughout, emphases on the links between the economic, social and cultural aspects of objects are retained, with historians moving well beyond the earlier concerns with consumption.[47] Several essays in this book display this complexity characteristic of a mature field of study. In her essay (Chapter 7), for example, Berry uses fine glass made in the north-east of England to challenge the view of that area as both an economic and cultural backwater, thereby also suggesting a revised vision of the geography of eighteenth-century English industry. In related work, the early attention given to the trade context of early Anglo-American consumption has developed into a mature field that places material culture in a global economic and cultural context.[48] In this volume, Beverly Lemire's study (Chapter 4) of the production, materials, trade, use and meanings of textiles and clothes in the context of the Atlantic world demonstrates how these approaches can produce rich and textured accounts, revealing (in this case) interactions between people across large areas of the globe, as well as men's and women's intimate experiences of their clothed bodies. The range of historical work is considerable, and while clearly affected by the 'cultural turn' and the attendant focus on language, 'texts' and 'discourse', much of this work displays a debt to the roots of historians' interest in the economic and social, as well as drawing on approaches from outside history. We can observe the force of these links in another essay in this volume. The three vignettes in Giorgio Riello's piece (Chapter 1) tease out the different ways in which historians can work with or on material culture, sometimes – as in the case of his 'history and things' – seizing the opportunity to use new sources to revise well-established historiographical narratives: in Riello's final example, a nineteenth-century cut image of 'The Aerial Steam Carriage', bought by Riello for 50 pence, leads to the recasting of the nature of the Industrial Revolution.

In other areas, too, the work of historians using material culture is characterized by interdisciplinarity. Research on gender and material culture has been enriched by insights from a range of areas, including design history, ethnography and film theory.[49] An impact of art and design history is palpable in work on the meaning of past styles and designs.[50] Several studies have demonstrated the political resonance of styles in a national context,[51] yet there are many levels at which style and design held important meanings.[52] Regarding architecture and the house, for example, historians' analyses have benefited from work on interpersonal performance and psychology.[53] Anne Laurence's chapter in this volume (Chapter 5) combines the work of architectural historians on style and design with a historian's reading of context: the use of defensive architectural features (such as slit windows and gun ports) in domestic buildings, for example, reflected the political and cultural differences of the populations of England, Ireland and Scotland. The challenge – but also the opportunity – of choosing to work on a body of material that has not conventionally come under the auspices of historical research is one that historians are welcoming with open arms.

In this context, the essays in this volume reflect the achievements of historians, but also indicate routes forward for both historians and others working on material culture. The essays here were commissioned in order to show something of the chronological and geographical range of historians' focus in this area. Most significantly, though, these essays have been selected to convey (a) a range of types of material culture (for example, including 'art' and 'everyday' objects; and those made from different materials, such as metalwork, glass and textile) and (b) a range of methodological positions and analytical frameworks. Of course, the essays that follow cannot possibly exhaust the many types of objects and analytical positions available to historians. Yet, as a guide to how historians can engage with material culture, the contributors cover an extensive amount of ground. Not surprisingly, given the complex nature of the field, the authors address the two key questions ('What can objects offer the historian?' and 'How can objects be used in history?') in different ways. The structure of the book reflects a rough distinction between those authors that focus on a type of object (Chapters 2, 3, 4 and 5), and those that take a specific approach or tackle a problem (Chapters 6, 7, 8, 9 and 10), but these chapters might have been categorized in many different ways. It is clear, though, that some recurring general themes emerge, and I wish to highlight three here: context, the nature of objects as sources, and the historian's identity in engaging with those sources.

'Context' is a keyword of historians; as E.P. Thompson put it, history is 'the discipline of context'.[54] Significantly, context is also a keyword of those 'object-driven' material culture studies discussed above. As Herman explains, 'For us to derive meaning from material culture we must reconnect objects to their historical contexts.'[55] Glassie specifies three 'master contexts' to which the researcher must attend: creation, communication and consumption.[56] Such an approach is particularly accessible to historians. At the same time, though, it indicates the contribution that historians can make to material culture studies by their professional training as (in part) scholars of context. The types of context examined in this volume are numerous: they are spatial, material, textual and ritual. Put simply, the contributors insist that where an object is – in terms of time and geography, for example, as much as its materials or design – makes it what it is. The juxtaposition of Berry and Dikötter's discussions of glass make this palpable: here we can see how the same material meant very different things in eighteenth-century Newcastle and twentieth-century China.

One of the manifestations of these historians' emphases on context is the liberal use of a range of sources. This is part of the second theme to emerge from these essays: the nature of objects as sources for historians. It is notable that no contributor to this book uses objects alone. In fact, one contributor – Glenn Adamson (Chapter 10) – addresses head on the problem of studying a type of object that no longer exists. His is an essay that exemplifies well historians' concern for cultural context, as the author plays detective in searching out the possible meanings of the missing material thing – in this case, eighteenth-century footstools. Even in cases where objects are extant, the 'thingness' of objects is sometimes moved to the background as other sources are brought to the fore. For example, in the essay by Dannehl (Chapter 6), the life stories of objects – so significant in understanding their place in the past – are gathered largely from the discursive material that surrounds the object. Laurence (Chapter 5) is adamant that historians must use documents when working on buildings; she cautions that undocumented buildings can be problematic, in part because they are often not preserved in the systematic way in which some other (written) sources have often been. Laurence thus insists that students should use a range of sources to complement the material objects. This is a recurring theme: Pennell (Chapter 9) stresses the associations of kitchen pastry cutters and pan handles, manifest most clearly in documentary sources, while Lemire (Chapter 4) balances the fine detail of textiles with 'theoretical interpretations and documentary sources'.[57]

Several contributors discuss the role that objects should play in the historian's analysis. The three varieties of historical project outlined in Riello's essay (Chapter 1) might be distinguished by the relative significance the historian grants the objects in their contribution to historical narratives, whether as raw materials for information about the past (history from things), the subject matter of historical enquiry (history of things), or as independently valuable and direct keys to aspects of the past that are otherwise inaccessible (history and things). And we might usefully consider each subsequent contribution against Riello's model. But all these essays demonstrate the often new skills that historians require to research material culture effectively, usually centring on the informed appreciation of physical detail, whether of building style, textile construction or glass manufacture. And new research skills are not limited to the objects themselves. Several contributors here note the importance of recognizing the modern context of historical objects, whether that be a museum or gallery, historic house or archaeological archive. Each context has implications for the historian's interpretation. The point is perhaps made most clearly in the case of landscape where, as Moskowitz (Chapter 3) shows, the material object is 'dynamic', with each generation leaving its trace.[58] We need to be aware of the layers of interpretation that surround objects in our encounters with them, and also of the distinctiveness of such extant objects. Finally, in their discussion of the kind of encounter that historians might have with a physical object, some of the contributors discuss the gains of a hands-on experience, a sensory engagement with the thing, whether this comes from feeling the heat of a fire or holding fragile glass. As Dannehl urges in her contribution: 'The experiences of weight, surface texture, sound and smell are part of the physicality of objects. They are an essential part of what artefacts have to offer the historian and can be experienced with our senses – sight, touch, balance, hearing and smell.'[59] Such sensory engagements are also intellectual ones, and can provide vital information for our work.

Incorporating our own sensory and emotional experiences of objects into our analysis can be valuable, and takes us back to Prown's 'creative imagining'. This takes us to the third general theme, which is the nature of the historian's identity as a researcher as s/he engages with material culture. Is s/he, as Prown put it, a farmer or a cowman? For Prown, farmers are 'hard material culturalists' (interested in science and technology, the physical aspects of an object); cowmen are 'soft material culturalists' (often from social sciences or humanities, interested in culture and objects as part of a language).[60]

> For farmers, reality lies in facts – in the artifact itself as surviving historical event, in written records and comments, in experimental proof, in statistical data. The enterprise is scientific; interpretations are verified by physical or verbal or statistical data. For soft material culturalists, the cowmen, reality resides in neither the physical object nor contextual data, but in the underlying belief structure of the culture that produced the object. To unmask this, the investigator becomes a creator.[61]

The authors in this book discuss a number of issues in the light of these contrasting epistemological positions. Questions are raised, for example, about the number of objects a historian needs in order to render a study valid. The single-object study sits more comfortably in design or art history, perhaps, while it is more common in archaeology to use many objects of the same type – for example, to create a series of objects used to show change over time and allow the dating of finds. Different contributors respond to this issue in different ways. Sara Pennell (Chapter 9) insists on the value of studying a single object or a small group of objects, particularly if we resist the impulse to fit them into an established historical context and begin by examining each as an independent fragment. Contrasting with this is Anne Laurence's study (Chapter 5) of several buildings in Britain and Ireland, along with the reading of these in the context of seventeenth-century politics, economy, society and religion. Taken together, though, these essays show that historians are comfortable moving between these two poles. Historians defy Prown's distinction, being neither farmers nor cowmen.

The contributors to this volume stress context, treat objects as complex sources, and employ a range of research methods and identities. They demonstrate that in its approach to material culture, history is a varied and flexible discipline, with a series of intersections with other disciplines. The gains for historians working on material culture are considerable. As the essays that follow demonstrate, material culture is one important key to unlocking the everyday lives of people in the past; it enables historians to tackle directly the issue of human agency, balancing social and cultural contexts with the physical facts of things; and it can free historians to recast historical narratives, sometimes challenging historical orthodoxy. At the same time, trained in using a wide range of sources together, all placed firmly in or used to recreate a multi-faceted context, historians make an important contribution to the study of material culture as one part of the endeavour to comprehend the complexities of people's lives and experiences.

How to read this book

These essays can be read in various ways. They have been designed first as 'methodological object studies': examples of how to analyse a specific object or type of object, while teasing out the general methodological implications. The writers in this volume imagine themselves leading students as they embark on their own projects on (for example) clothing, buildings or pots. The case studies have been carefully selected to illuminate the more general concepts underpinning that type of approach. While there are many other examples of 'object studies' in print to consider, the methodological implications of these are often implied rather than explicit. And though there are some excellent student guides to historical skills and sources, none deals specifically with the methodological and historiographical issues involved in using objects in history. Indeed, most standard handbooks on historical sources and methodology simply do not address material culture.[62] Thus, each of the chapters that follow introduces students to work already conducted in that area. Yet the relatively youthful state of the field means that we cannot provide full syntheses or lay out clearly marked paths to follow step by step, because those paths are still being laid. Each of these writers teases out general points through an original study, and seeks to acquaint you with work already done on material culture, pointing to new ways forward, and engaging you in ongoing debates in this area of research. Indeed, we hope that the chapters are useful to the navigation of this burgeoning area of historical study, but also in thinking more generally about historical skills, sources and knowledge.

Appendix 1: notes for beginners

This section is designed as a very practical guide for students wanting to research or use material culture. It can be daunting to embark on a new kind of research. In studying material culture, you may need to develop new research skills, both to find sources and to analyse them. Without wanting to reduce the important detail in subsequent contributions, I will provide some brief guidance on finding sources, and also some basic steps to remember in going about your research. Many of your sources will be located, not in libraries and archives, but in museums, galleries and other collections. I will suggest some pointers on how to engage with these objects and their custodians. Finally, the appendix will end with some comments on the presentation of objects in written work. Note that this appendix should not be used in isolation: read and reflect on the foregoing discussion, and the detailed analyses that follow in subsequent chapters.

How to find your sources

There is no universal, regulated and systematic way of keeping historical objects. What survives – wherever that may be – does so for a range of reasons, each of which needs to be considered by the researcher. An object may have been collected by a museum because it was thought to exemplify the very best in design, an object may have survived because the ceramic material did not deteriorate in the conditions in which it was later found by an archaeologist, and a building survived because of local geo-political factors leading to its preservation. Those seeking material culture can certainly use such objects from museum collections and from archaeological digs. I cannot advise here on the full range of source types or repositories available, but hope that the advice that follows gives pointers useful at the start of a range of research projects.

Collected and found objects are held in regional and national museum collections, and are often on display. Visits to museums and historic houses – obvious as that may seem – can be a first step in identifying suitable material. Many archaeological reports – published in journals such as *Post-Medieval Archaeology* – can be valuable, though note that these are generally identified by the site of the excavation, rather than the type of object located.

Details of museum and gallery holdings can be found in a number of ways. Catalogues – of specific exhibitions, of permanent collections or (perhaps most usefully) of a type of object (delftware, for example) found in a number of different collections – are a gold mine for historians, containing hundreds of photographs with accompanying descriptions of varying length, and often valuable introductions and essays by expert curators or decorative art scholars. If you cannot browse the 'decorative art' shelves of a good library, such publications can be found using library or retailers' catalogues using keywords (usually of materials). The internet is a great resource here. Virtual exhibitions, museum websites and collection databases are rich with sources for your work, and some examples are given in Appendix 2.

The process of research

Each of the chapters that follow can be examined for its research process. Berry, for example, moves from general context to local context (Newcastle), from documentary sources to objects (style, materials, decoration), and from the spatial and material context to the ritual context. In the case of each essay, though, the process as it is outlined in the narrative might depart from the process of research as it was carried out. Here I will provide a very brief outline of a research process that historians might follow in studying material culture.[63] Note that this does not amount to a methodological position or analytical framework; these complex issues are dealt with elsewhere in this book. What follows are basic questions that a student may wish to bear in mind in their research, questions that I and my students have found useful. While a study should go through each stage at some point, it is important to remember that the order of the steps might vary, and (as with all research processes) there will be times when we need to return to an earlier stage in the light of new findings. This three-step model is intended as a very simple guide. It omits many steps that some historians would stress, some mentioned above (for example, the modern context in which the object now finds itself) and other discussed in the essays that follow (for example, the importance of tracing the life of an object from production to consumption). But it is based on years of teaching very able history undergraduates as they embark on their first attempts to study material culture.

1   We should attempt a description of the object itself, its physical attributes. Assess what the object is made of, how it was made and (of course) when; production methods and manufacture, materials, size, weight, design, style, decoration and date are some of the key issues to address here, though different forms of material culture will require different questions. If possible, find out how much such an item would cost for contemporaries.
2   We can place the object in a historical context, primarily by referring to other evidence. Here we can explore who owned this (or similar) objects, when, and what they were used for. Some of this can also be gleaned from handling or experiencing the objects themselves, an important part of the research process, and to be undertaken if possible. Knowledge about the physical attributes of an object, combined with external information, should help us understand how it was used.
3   Finally, we can explore more fully the place of the object (or its type) in the socio-cultural context, perhaps including 'documentary' and 'imaginative' written documents, as well as visual references. At this stage, and indeed throughout, the researcher will continue to engage with and reflect on the material nature of the object.

Using museum, gallery or other collections[64]

One of the daunting features of material culture for history students can be the need to enter new spaces. Many students use objects in museum, gallery and other collections, and the following hints should serve as a useful guide to researching at such venues.

- You can use the online and published resources to locate objects in collections, but many collections (perhaps smaller ones) do not have these. You can visit displays, but also write or email staff at the collections (or you might ask a teacher to do this for you). The curators – rather than administrative or education staff – are the experts on the collections, so try to address queries to them if you can. Note that museums are often organized in ways that might not map onto your own concerns. For example, they are often organized into departments by materials (metalwork, textiles, etc.), or other foci (decorative art, archaeology, social history, etc.), with each department having its own curator.
- When you write, give as much detail as possible about what you want and why. If you are trying to set up a visit, give plenty of notice. Remember that – unlike archives and libraries – facilitating visits from students is not the only (or the main) activity of these institutions.
- Try to appreciate the nature of curatorial work. It is not desk-based, is varied and has very intense phases (for example, when an exhibition is about to open).
- Before your visit, do as much research on the objects as you can, so you can make the visit as effective and efficient as possible. Prepare a list of questions to take with you.
- On your visit, take a pencil and paper. Date each set of notes you make. Make full notes on objects, including object numbers and a full description (this helps if you have to match your own photos to your notes).
- You will want to make a visual record of the object. You can make your own drawing, a technique that some researchers find encourages them to look more closely at an object. Alternatively, take a camera, but ask before you use it. Make it clear that the pictures are for private research. You should never use your own photos in any work (on paper or on the web) without the written permission of the owner/custodian/copyright holder of the object.
- Curators are experts on the objects, and often researchers themselves. But do not expect curators to have read the works you have, or to share precisely the same concern with historical context as you do. The curator will hopefully be able to share their knowledge with you. As with any conversation or interview that takes place as part of research, take notes, and if a curator gives you information that you would like to use (perhaps in an essay or dissertation) ask them if they can give you a reference to chase up so you can read more.
- Be aware of the gallery or museum context of the objects you see. If they are in a display, note that choices have been made, and the range of objects you see is not necessarily the sample that a historian would have chosen. Ask the curator about the conservation of the object and if this has had any impact on its appearance.
- If you go on to produce written work arising from or relating to the visits, it is courteous to send a copy to those who have helped. Many curators are pleased to receive analyses of the objects in their care; some museums and galleries

will ask for a copy in return for permission to reproduce images of their objects.

Including images of objects in your written work

It is often helpful or necessary to include images of objects you discuss in your written work, though it can be a time-consuming (and costly) process. First, you will need to obtain the image (from a published book, taken by yourself, or provided by the holder of copyright to the object/image, depending on its intended use). Student essays, dissertations and theses are not usually published, so the inclusion of images without permission to reproduce is normally acceptable. Do check guidelines at your institution, though, particularly if electronic publication is possible. For any published work, all reproductions require permission from the copyright holder. For this, you will need to provide a number of details about the publication (obtainable from the publisher). You may have to pay a fee, and you will be required to reproduce the image with a caption including the specific credit line provided by the copyright holder. The caption should also include the author/maker/designer/artist, title, date, repository/collection, medium, size and any additional description you wish to include.

Appendix 2: some useful internet resources

While hands-on experience of objects is important (and something emphasized by several contributors to this book), it is often difficult to arrange (when, for example, you are writing a small piece of student work and are at some distance from the objects). While there are problems with internet resources, and they should not replace contact with the 'real thing', they can be an invaluable research tool. This is a short and suggestive list, but many museums (national and regional) have very good collections information online. Do conduct your own searches according to your interest.

Museum of London, London, UK
http://www.museumoflondon.org.uk/English/Collections/
From this page you can search the 'London Archaeological Archive and Research Centre online resources', and the extensive 'The Ceramics and Glass Collection', as well as other museum microsites.

Victoria and Albert Museum, London, UK
http://www.vam.ac.uk/collections/index.html
From this page you can search the V&A collections, and also access many microsites.

Geffrye Museum of the Home, London, UK
http://www.geffrye-museum.org.uk/collections/
From this page, you can access a range of visual and material sources from the

microsite 'Life in the living room 1600–2000', with sections on aspects such as floors, furniture and ornaments.

Revolutionary Players of Industry and Innovation
http://www.revolutionaryplayers.org.uk/home.stm
This website focuses on digitized material from libraries, museums and archives across the West Midlands region relating to the development of the Industrial Revolution, for the period 1700–1830. Several articles examine the production and design of objects in this historical context.

Eighteenth-Century Resources – Art
http://andromeda.rutgers.edu/~jlynch/18th/art.html
This page is maintained by Professor Jack Lynch, from the Department of English, Rutgers University (Newark, New Jersey, USA). It is one part of his site 'Eighteenth-Century Resources', and is a very good example of a reputable site set up and maintained by an established professional academic. There are others in other fields and periods.

http://www.history.ac.uk/ihr/Focus/Holocaust/debate.html
Useful article on how to use museum objects in studying history.

'Bissonnette on Costume: A Visual Dictionary of Fashion'
http://dept.kent.edu/museum/costume/index.asp
Produced by Anne Bissonnette, Curator, Kent State University Museum, this useful site on costume allows searches by geography, time or subject, and includes detailed photographs of costume.

ArtServe: Art & Architecture (Australian National University at Canberra)
http://rubens.anu.edu.au/
ArtServe on Rubens is a website established by Professor Michael Greenhalgh, Sir William Dobell Foundation Professor of Art History at the Australian National University. Though not particularly well organized or user-friendly, it does contain a mass of visual images of art and architecture from around the world.

The Ashmolean Museum of Art and Archaeology, University of Oxford, Oxford, UK
http://www.ashmolean.org/collections/
From this page you can search a number of databases, including 'PotWeb: Ceramics Online @ the Ashmolean', described as '2000 years of history in ceramics at your fingertips'.

WorldImages
http://worldimages.sjsu.edu
WorldImages provides access to the California State University IMAGE Project. It is global in coverage and includes a broad range of visual imagery, including (for

example) an indexed section on 'Material Culture and Daily Life'. There is also an advanced search option.

The Fitzwilliam Museum, Cambridge, UK
http://www.fitzmuseum.cam.ac.uk/collections/
From where you can search the collections, or browse the collections, for example in the categories of 'Applied Arts' or 'Paintings, Drawings and Prints'.

The Bridgeman Art Library
http://www.bridgeman.co.uk/
This is a massive collection of 'cultural and historical art images', available online, representing museums, galleries and artists from all over the world.

Digital Library for the Decorative Arts & Material Culture, University of Wisconsin-Madison
http://decorativearts.library.wisc.edu/
A rich source of documents, images and other resources relating to (mainly) American material culture.

Notes

1 For discussing the issues that follow I would like to thank audiences at ASECS 2008, colleagues at the Victoria and Albert Museum (in particular Glenn Adamson and Angela McShane) and also at Museums Sheffield, and the many students on my further and special subjects at the University of Sheffield from 2003 to 2008. I also wish to thank Helen Berry, Mike Braddick, Natasha Glaisyer, Anne Laurence, Ann Smart Martin, Andrew Morrall, Giorgio Riello and Rosemary Sweet for their comments on this chapter. I thank Maxine Berg, Elizabeth Buettner and an anonymous reader for their valuable comments on the book.
2 Bernard L. Herman, *The Stolen House* (Charlottesville and London: University of Press of Virginia, 1992), pp. 11, 4.
3 Jules David Prown, 'Mind in Matter: An Introduction to Material Culture Theory and Method', *Winterthur Portfolio*, 17, 1 (Spring 1982), pp. 7–10. Republished in Jules David Prown, *Art as Evidence: Writings on Art and Material Culture* (New Haven and London: Yale University Press, 2001).
4 Herman, *Stolen House*, pp. 11, 4.
5 Ibid., p. 7.
6 Clifford Geertz, 'Thick Description: Toward an Interpretive Theory of Culture', *The Interpretation of Cultures: Selected Essays* (1973), pp. 3–30.
7 Henry Glassie, *Material Culture* (Bloomington and Indianapolis: Indiana University Press, 1999), p. 44.
8 Ibid., p. 47.
9 Ann Smart Martin, 'Shaping the Field: The Multidisciplinary Perspectives of Material Culture', in Ann Smart Martin and J. Ritchie Garrison (eds), *American Material Culture: the Shape of the Field* (1997), passim, quote at p. 4.
10 Ibid., p. 3. A similar point was made by William B. Heseltine in 'The Challenge of the Artifact', in Schlereth (ed.), *Material Culture Studies in America* (1982), pp. 93–100, where he argued for a major difference between object and literary source, calling for a specific method for extracting meaning from objects for historians.
11 W. David Kingery, 'Introduction', in W. David Kingery (ed.), *Learning from Things:*

Method and Theory of Material Culture Studies (Washington and London: Smithsonian Institution Press, 1996), p. 1.

12   Christopher Tilley, *Metaphor and Material Culture* (Oxford: Blackwell, 1999), p. 6.

13   Ibid., p. 72.

14   Ibid., p. 4.

15   John Dixon Hunt, 'The Sign of the Object', in Steven Lubar and W. David Kingery (eds), *History from Things: Essays on Material Culture* (Washington and London: Smithsonian Institution Press, 1993), p. 297.

16   Andrew Morrall, 'Ornament as Evidence', Chapter 2 in this book, p. 47.

17   There are a number of important journals in this field, including *Winterthur Portfolio*, published by the University of Chicago Press on behalf of the Henry Francis du Pont Winterthur Museum, United States, and the *Journal of Material Culture*, published by Sage. There are also many other specialist journals – for example, on silver, textiles and glass.

18   Quote from Hunt, reporting the conference from which his essay arose. Hunt, 'Sign of the Object', p. 294.

19   'Editorial' by Daniel Miller and Christopher Tilley, *Journal of Material Culture*, 1 (March 1996), p. 8. An important collection of articles also to emerge from the Material Culture Group at University College London in the UK is Victor Buchli's (ed.), *The Material Culture Reader* (Oxford and New York: Berg, 2002).

20   Matthew D. Cochran and Mary C. Beaudry, 'Material Culture Studies and Historical Archaeology', in Dan Hicks and Mary C. Beaudry (eds), *The Cambridge Companion to Historical Archaeology* (Cambridge: Cambridge University Press, 2006), p. 195.

21   Cochran and Beaudry, 'Material Culture Studies', p. 203.

22   Dan Hicks and Mary C. Beaudry, 'Introduction: The Place of Historical Archaeology', in Hicks and Beaudry (eds), *Cambridge Companion to Historical Archaeology*, p. 2.

23   John Moreland, *Archaeology and Text* (2001; Duckworth: London, 2007), p. 119 and passim.

24   Michel de Certeau, for example, focused on the creative practices through which non-elites (or 'common people') operate within an inherited dominant culture, appropriating aspects of that culture, exercising everyday agency to the point of an 'antidiscipline'. Michel de Certeau, *The Practice of Everyday Life*, transl. Steven Randall (1974; Berkeley: University of California Press, 1984), p. v and passim.

25   Jules David Prown, 'The Truth of Material Culture: History or Fiction?', in Lubar and Kingery (eds), *History from Things*, p. 1.

26   Hunt, 'Sign of the Object', p. 298.

27   The world-renowned postgraduate programmes at the Winterthur Museum, BARD Graduate Center and the Victoria and Albert Museum/Royal College of Art (the latter two both represented among the contributors here) are well established, though new courses are being developed rapidly. New centres are also being set up: the 'Chinese Material Culture Research Institute' at Nanjing University, China, and the 'Material Culture Institute' at University of Alberta, Canada, are indicative of a growing global academic interest.

28   Adrienne D. Hood, 'Material Culture: The Object', in Sarah Barber and Corinna Peniston-Bird (eds) *History Beyond the Text: A Student's Guide to Approaching Alternative Sources* (New York and London: Routledge, 2008).

29   Richard Grassby, 'Material Culture and Cultural History', *Journal of Interdisciplinary History*, 35, 4 (Spring 2005), pp. 597, 601, 603.

30   Hood, 'Material Culture', passim.

31   The introduction to a recent collection also takes a culturalist approach. See Jennie Batchelor and Cora Kaplan (eds), *Women and Material Culture, 1660–1830* (London: Palgrave Macmillan, 2007), pp. 1–8. It is worth noting that not all the essays adopt such an approach, though. Barbara Burman and Jonathan White's 'Fanny's Pockets: Cotton,

Consumption and Domestic Economy, 1780–1850', pp. 31–51, insists on the contribution of the essay to social history.

32   Ann Smart Martin, 'Material Things and Cultural Meanings: Notes on the Study of Early American Material Culture', *The William and Mary Quarterly*, 3rd Series, 53, 1 (January 1996), p. 7.

33   This issue provides the focus for Victoria E. Bonnell and Lynn Hunt's (eds), *Beyond the Cultural Turn. New Directions in the Study of Society and Culture* (Berkeley: University of California Press, 1999). A useful review of these issues is Thomas Welskopp, 'Social History', in Stefan Berger, Heiko Feldner and Kevin Passmore (eds), *Writing History: Theory and Practice* (London: Hodder Arnold, 2003), pp. 203–22.

34   Hicks and Beaudry, 'Introduction', p. 6.

35   For a more detailed discussion of these issues, see Karen Harvey, *Reading Sex in the Eighteenth Century: Bodies and Gender in English Erotic Culture* (Cambridge: Cambridge University Press, 2005), pp. 1–3; Karen Harvey, 'Introduction', in Karen Harvey (ed.) *The Kiss in History* (Manchester: Manchester University Press, 2005), pp. 1–5.

36   Steven Lubar and W. David Kingery, 'Introduction', in Lubar and Kingery (eds), *History from Things*, pp. xi, xvii.

37   All except one of the contributors to this book either trained at postgraduate level in history and/or are now teaching in a department of history.

38   There are other works that provide this kind of survey – for example, Hood's 'Material Culture' in particular outlines an array of possible approaches, and wisely advises that 'the important thing is to articulate it clearly and apply it rigorously'.

39   Key works include Mark Overton, Jane Whittle, Darron Dean and Andrew Hann, *Production and Consumption in English Households, 1600–1750* (London: Routledge, 2004); Carole Shammas, *The Pre-Industrial Consumer in England and America* (Oxford: Oxford University Press, 1990); and Lorna Weatherill, *Consumer Behaviour and Material Culture in Britain, 1660–1760* (London: Routledge, 1988).

40   The landmark work is Neil McKendrick, John Brewer and J.H. Plumb, *The Birth of a Consumer Society: The Commercialisation of Eighteenth-Century England* (London: Europa, 1982). But also see the essays in the three volumes: John Brewer and Roy Porter (eds), *Consumption and the World of Goods* (London: Routledge, 1993); Ann Bermingham and John Brewer (eds), *The Consumption of Culture, 1600–1800: Image, Object, Text* (London: Routledge, 1995); and John Brewer and Susan Staves (eds), *Early Modern Conceptions of Property* (London: Routledge, 1995). An important response to this attention to consumption is Sara Pennell, 'Consumption and Consumerism in Early Modern England', *Historical Journal*, 42, 2 (1999), pp. 549–64.

41   A counterpoint to this latter emphasis is provided by Peter King's 'Pauper Inventories and the Material Lives of the Poor in the Eighteenth and Early Nineteenth Centuries', in Tim Hitchcock, Peter King and Pamela Sharpe (eds), *Chronicling Poverty: The Voices and Strategies of the English Poor, 1640–1840* (London: Longman, 1997), pp. 155–91. See also John Styles, *The Dress of the People: Everyday Fashion in Eighteenth-Century England* (New Haven and London: Yale University Press, 2007).

42   Glassie notes that the word 'goods' instead of 'artefacts' reflects a focus on commodities and possessions, rather than the act of production by artisans and workers. See Glassie, *Material Culture*, p. 77.

43   Matthew Johnson, 'Archaeologies of Authority', in *An Archaeology of Capitalism* (Oxford: Blackwell, 1996), p. 179.

44   Igor Kopytoff, 'The Cultural Biography of Things: Commoditization as a Process' in Arjun Appadurai (ed.), *The Social Life of Things: Commodities in Cultural Perspective* (1986; Cambridge, New York, Oakleigh: Cambridge University Press, 1992), p. 68.

45   Karin Dannehl, 'Object Biographies: From Production to Consumption', Chapter 6 in this book, p. 121.

46   See Elizabeth B. Wood, 'Pots and Pans History: Relating Manuscripts and Printed

Sources to the Study of Domestic Art Objects', *American Archivist,* 30 (1967), pp. 431–42.

47 For example, the concerns of the contributors to John Styles and Amanda Vickery (eds), *Gender, Taste and Material Culture in Britain and North America 1700–1830* (New Haven and London: Yale University Press, 2006), are much wider than those of early studies on 'consumption' in this period.

48 See, for example: John E. Wills, 'European Consumption and Asian Production in the Seventeenth and Eighteenth Centuries', in John Brewer and Roy Porter, *Consumption and the World of Goods* (London: Routledge, 1993), pp. 133–48; Nuala Zahedieh, 'London and the Colonial Consumer in the Late Seventeenth Century', *Economic History Review,* 47, 2 (1994), pp. 239–61; T. Barringer and T. Flyn, *Colonialism and the Object: Empire, Material Culture and the Object* (London: Routledge, 1997); James Walvin, *Fruits of Empire: Exotic Produce and British Taste, 1660–1800* (New York: New York University Press, 1997); Maxine Berg, 'In Pursuit of Luxury: Global Origins of British Consumer Goods in the Eighteenth Century', *Past and Present,* 182 (2004).

49 See, for example: Victoria de Grazia and Ellen Furlough (eds), *The Sex of Things: Gender and Consumption in Historical Perspective* (Berkeley: University of California Press, 1996); Katharine Martinez and Kenneth L. Ames (eds), *The Material Culture of Gender, The Gender of Material Culture* (Winterthur, 1997); Alice T. Friedman, 'Architecture, Authority, and the Female Gaze: Planning and Representation in the Early Modern Country House', *Assemblage,* 18 (1992), pp. 41–61.

50 Two works that serve as useful introductions to studying style and design are Judy Attfield, 'The Meaning of Design, Things With Attitude', in Judy Attfield, *Wild Things: The Material Culture of Everyday Life* (Oxford: Berg, 2000); and Adrian Forty, *Objects of Desire: Design and Society since 1750* (London: Thames & Hudson, 1995).

51 Important examples include Leora Auslander, *Taste and Power: Furnishing Modern France* (Berkeley: University of California Press, 1996); John E. Crowley, *The Invention of Comfort: Sensibilities and Design in Early Modern Britain and America* (Baltimore: Johns Hopkins University Press, 2001); and David L. Porter, 'Monstrous Beauty: Eighteenth-century Fashion and the Aesthetics of the Chinese Taste', *Eighteenth-Century Studies,* 35, 3 (2002), pp. 395–411.

52 Browsing the leading journal in this area, the *Journal of Design History,* published by Oxford Journals (Oxford University Press), will give a good overview, as will *Studies in the Decorative Arts* published by the Bard Graduate Center, New York. Some very useful and brief guides to period style are found on the website of the Victoria and Albert Museum: http://www.vam.ac.uk/collections/periods_styles/index.html. See also Anna Jackson, *The V&A Guide to Period Styles: 400 Years of British Art and Design* (London: V&A Publications, 2002).

53 Erving Goffman, *The Presentation of Self in Everyday Life* (1959; Harmondsworth: Penguin, 1974), and Norbert Elias, *The Civilizing Process* (particularly *Volume 1 – The History of Manners* (1939)) have been used extensively by historians. Lorna Weatherill adapted Goffman's front-stage/back-stage distinction for *Consumer Behaviour and Material Culture,* while Mark Girouard's *Life in the English Country House: A Social and Architectural History* (1978; Harmondsworth: Penguin, 1980) has the civilizing process threaded throughout his important study.

54 E.P. Thompson, 'Anthropology and the Discipline of Historical Context', *Midland History,* 1, 3 (1972), p. 45. For further discussion, see Harvey, 'Introduction', in (ed.) *Kiss in History,* p. 4.

55 Herman, *Stolen House,* p. 7.

56 Glassie, *Material Culture,* p. 48.

57 Beverly Lemire, 'Draping the Body and Dressing the Home: The Material Culture of Textiles and Clothes in the Atlantic World, *c.* 1500–1800', p. 85.

58 Marina Moskowitz, 'Back Yards and Beyond: Landscapes and History', p. 67.

59 Dannehl, 'Object Biographies: From Production to Consumption', Chapter 6 in this book, p. 67.

60 Prown, *Art as Evidence*, p. 236.

61 Ibid., p. 239.

62 See, for example, Peter Burke's (ed.), *New Perspectives on Historical Writing* (1991; Cambridge: Polity Press, 2nd edn, 2001); Ludmilla Jordanova's *History in Practice* (2000; London: Arnold, 2006); and John Tosh, *The Pursuit of History: Aims, Methods and New Directions in the Study of Modern History* (1984; Harlow: Longman, 2nd edn, 1991).

63 These steps are reproduced in the short film, *Studying Material Culture for Historians* (written by Karen Harvey, directed by Graham McElearney, University of Sheffield, 2007). This film was made as part of a University of Sheffield Learning and Teaching Development Grant Project, titled 'Using Museum and Gallery Collections in History Teaching' (2006–08). The film is designed to introduce advanced history students to artefacts, museums, curators and a 'material culture' approach to the past.

64 For useful comments from a curatorial perspective on history students entering museums, see Hood, 'Material Culture'.

1 Things that shape history

Material culture and historical narratives

Giorgio Riello

Beds, pans and teacups, mirrors and combs, stools and chairs, sheets, covers, Coca-Cola bottles, Walkmans, cars and old coaches, diamonds, chests of drawers, toilets, stiletto shoes, antiquities, oddities and monstrosities. This is not a summary of items appearing on *The Antiques Roadshow* but a succinct list of things that appear as subject matters dealt with in articles and books written by historians. This list should not mislead us into thinking that historians consider 'things' as either important or interesting per se. In the reading list of material culture, one will not find any of the brilliant old-fashioned antiquarian types of titles such as 'Old English bedsteads' or 'Some early English sea service buttons'.[1] Historians are as or even more interested in a thick conceptual 'sauce' that includes savoury concepts such as gender, class, identity, politics, and the usual carousel of presentations and representations, perspectives, semiotics and theoretical underpinnings.

This essay reflects on the relationship between the methodologies and conceptual categories used by historians and their recent engagement with material culture. My specific concern is the relationship between artefacts and the large concepts that historians constantly mobilize to understand the past – what I call 'narratives' or 'tropes'. Historians are increasingly presented with isolated objects, often de-contextualized, which they seek to fit (alongside other events, facts and analyses) within the broad narratives that preside over history as a subject. The rise of capitalism, the Renaissance, the Industrial Revolution, globalization and the like are all 'big boxes' that even the most astute postmodernist cannot avoid without difficulty. Historians also construct their scholarship in very precise ways, by adopting widely shared methodologies. This chapter asks whether material culture helps historians to do things differently.

I will address these issues by considering three case studies, which I suggest represent three of the ways in which history relates to material culture. I have chosen a rather tatty eighteenth-century stomacher, a seventeenth-century broken wine cup and a nineteenth-century print. However, before looking at this selection of items it is worth reviewing the general approaches historians have employed in the burgeoning field of material culture studies.

Varieties of material cultures

Historians have survived, even thrived, during the last two centuries with little or no engagement with objects. In many ways, it appears that historians do not feel at ease when dealing with material things.[2] Yet, arguably objects reveal history in important ways and, indeed, the study of material culture has significantly influenced the field of history in recent years.[3]

History from *things*

A first way in which historians relate to material culture is by concentrating on its material form and treating it in the same way in which they treat a manuscript, a diary, an inventory or an image: objects as primary sources. In this case, artefacts are important because they can be used as evidence of something that was part of the past. This is what I call *history from things*, in which material artefacts are used as raw materials for the discipline of history and the interpretation of the past. The pay-off for historians is a wider (more numerous but also more varied) collection of sources through which to back their arguments and interpretations.

History of *things*

Historians are not necessarily interested in uncovering another saucepan, or finding out a previously unknown variety of medieval roasting fork. In the subject of history the material finding does not constitute research and will not be given much space in the pages of a historical publication. The development of studies on consumption and the coming of age of design as respectable fields of historical enquiry have meant an increasing interest in material artefacts. Today the bulk of the history of material culture is about *history of things*, that is to say the historical analysis of the relationship between objects, people and their representations.[4]

Things are important in all those areas of history in which they played a relevant part. If a historian is interested in analysing the philosophical thought of Voltaire, he or she will find little help by examining Voltaire's teacup, or any eighteenth-century teacup for that matter. But if one is instead interested in considering the culture of politeness, the examination of tea services, snuff boxes and Hogarth prints might be very relevant. There are many different approaches towards the *history of things*: the finding of deeper personal meanings in individual objects (as magisterially done by Laurel Thatcher Ulrich), or less personal, quantitative analysis of ownership patterns (as found in the scholarship of Lorna Weatherill).[5] In both the object is not a 'prop of research' but the very subject matter of analysis. In this case the pay-off for historians is the capacity to extend their coverage by producing new fields (and new depths) of historical enquiry, often based on a high degree of interdisciplinarity.

Table 1.1 Varieties of material culture, methods and narratives

Variety of material culture	Cases	Things, methodologies and narratives		
History *from* things	1	**Thing** A 'concealed' stomacher	**Methodology** Integration of sources	**Narrative** Choice of a narrative
History *of* things	2	**Methodology** Interdisciplinary research	**Narrative** The consumer revolution	**Thing** Pottery excavated in Jamestown
History *and* things	3	**Narrative** The Industrial Revolution	**Thing** A cut image of a flying machine	**Methodology** Revising positivism

History and *things*

A third way of considering material artefacts is by positioning them outside history altogether. The subject of history has been slow at accepting this more 'democratic' vision of material culture in which material objects are not in a servile position to historical scholarship. Other disciplines, such as sociology, archaeology and anthropology, have developed flexible methodologies of analysis of material artefacts by stating their heuristic independence. History has been slow to recognize the material world's capacity to challenge the overall concept of the analysis of the past by evoking and shaping new processes of gathering, systematizing and presenting ideas. Artefacts have long brought the past to life for wider audiences via museum displays and television documentaries and dramas. They provide both immediacy and a direct way for people to relate to the past, qualities of which professional history has been wary. *History and things* provides a qualitative pay-off for historians: the capacity to unlock more creative and freer ways of conveying ideas about the past that are not necessarily mediated by written language in books and articles produced by professional historians.

The rest of this chapter will 'put into practice' these different approaches. I wish to show how there are different ways in which material culture relates both to the 'big' concepts of history and to the methodologies through which historians construct their scholarship. The following case studies present objects from 1600 to 1850, and are intended not as a guide for 'ideal' historical analysis,[6] but as a reflection on how artefacts have inspired historians to ask new questions, to challenge established paradigms and formulate new interpretations (Table 1.1).

Concealed capitalism: things that money can't buy

Things: a 'concealed' stomacher

In 1980 Mr and Mrs Maynard moved into their new cottage in Nether Wallop, Hampshire, UK. The house was in a state of disrepair, and restructuring soon

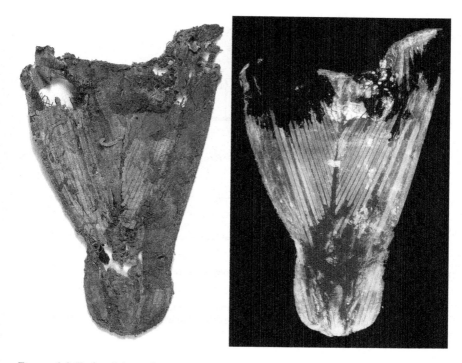

Figure 1.1 Early eighteenth-century stomacher found at a cottage in Nether Wallop, Hampshire, United Kingdom, and an X-radiography showing strips of whale-bone. Deliberately Concealed Garments Project, Winchester School of Art, University of Southampton CG8.a. © The Textile Conservation Centre, University of Southampton and Sonia O'Connor, University of Bradford.

started. During the process, the Maynards uncovered what appeared at first sight to be a bundle of rubbish stuck in the chimney breast. On closer examination, they discovered that the bundle consisted of a velvet waistcoat and a stomacher, wrapped in paper. Once the excitement of this finding waned, the Maynards put all objects in a plastic bag in the old bread oven 'as we didn't quite know what to do with them'.[7] One of the paper fragments is a newspaper dated 1752, thus providing the earliest date when they were left there, though the remaining objects are earlier. The stomacher (Figure 1.1) pre-dates the concealment and was originally a corset. Signs of wear and repair suggest that at some time, probably in the early eighteenth century, it was cut down into a stomacher. The garment is also atypical because the material is stiffened with strips of whalebone.[8]

The Maynards' finding is not unique. What they found was a cache of 'deliberately concealed objects'. The practice of concealing objects, especially garments, in the very fabric of buildings was undertaken from the Middle Ages to the twentieth century in many parts of the world, and especially in Northern Europe, North

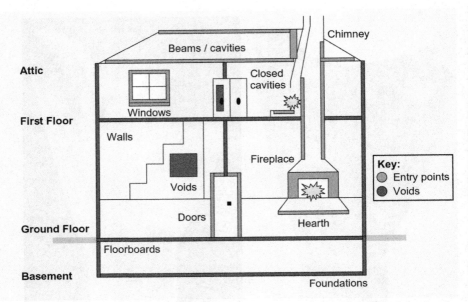

Figure 1.2 Diagram showing common locations of concealed objects found in sites in the United Kingdom. © The Textile Conservation Centre, University of Southampton.

America and Australia.[9] The demolition and restructuring of old buildings has unearthed many such objects. In the late 1960s the Northampton Boot and Shoe Collection started preserving and cataloguing footwear concealed in buildings.[10] Since 1998 the Concealed Garments Project at the Winchester School of Art has been, under the direction of Dinah Eastop, recording, preserving and interpreting concealed garments and other objects found in British buildings.[11]

Why did people decide to hide a shoe or a stomacher in the wall of their house? This question has no definitive answer. Archaeological analyses suggest that they were primarily concealed in junctures between old and new parts of buildings or within points of entry and exit such as doorways, windows and chimneys (Figure 1.2).[12] The fact that their placing was intentional is suggested not just by the numerous findings with similar patterns of concealment, but also by the more puzzling practice of mutilation of such objects. Garments are often found knotted, suggesting that their placing within a wall was supposed to terminate their function as clothing. Historians, anthropologists and experts agree that such objects were hidden with the intent of protecting the house and its inhabitants from malign forces and were placed in the most vulnerable points of connection with the outside world. It also appears that these objects invoke the physical presence of their wearers and owners. In the case of the Nether Wallop finding, even the paper scraps were cut in the shape of garments.

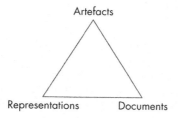

Figure 1.3 Sources for historical enquiry

Methodologies: the integration of sources

What makes the stomacher found in the cottage at Nether Wallop and similar concealed objects so remarkable is that they refer to a practice that has no known documentary evidence. No contemporary letters, diaries or manuscripts have been identified that record such items. Here, then, the idea of the 'object survivor' is more than a simple cliché. It is only through the engagement with the object (but also its location, finding and story) that historical questions over the meaning of protection for householders in the early modern period can be raised.

This specific case is indicative of wider trends in history: what I call the integration of sources. Historians are asked to extend their remit of investigation also to non-documentary evidence, the most important categories of which are artefacts and visual representations (Figure 1.3). The strict boundaries by which historians read documents in dusty archives, while art historians analyse paintings, and museum curators and archaeologists deal with objects have now been superseded. In many cases written records remained the favourite source material and are just accompanied by representations and objects that back the argument created by documentary evidence. The addition of an image or reference to an object is not sufficient to create a dialogue with other sources.

Narratives: how to choose one

History from things should move beyond either the object as example or the object as an easy prop. Objects should not be used as an aid for providing enhanced answers, but for asking better questions. So far, I have located an early eighteenth-century stomacher in terms of its discovery, but I have also purposely contextualized the object within a specific interpretation or narrative: stomacher as a concealed garment. The fact that it was found with other objects and that all circumstantial evidence suggests that it was purposely hidden in a wall cavity, has made us accept that:

1   there is a direct relationship between this object and a specific socio-cultural practice that we find in history
2   this stomacher belongs to a category of objects that we call 'concealed garments'

3   it is a tool for historians to understand and investigate a rather mysterious
     social practice.

These three points derive from the fact the stomacher is part of a cache of objects
and that this cache found in Nether Wallop is similar to hundreds of others. The
meaning given to the stomacher is referenced to a series of objects.

I am not suggesting that the stomacher is not a concealed garment, but only that historians and researchers have decided, beyond reasonable doubt and through a process
of thorough checking, that it is. This has created a narrative for this object that the very
materiality of the object does not support. Such a narrative relates to a socio-cultural
practice in which this object found itself at a certain point in time. If we use
Apparudai's concept of the 'social life of things',[13] the stomacher was something else
at the beginning of its life, was recycled as a garment in the early eighteenth century,
became a concealed garment only some time after 1752, disappeared for nearly 260
years and is now in a storeroom at the Winchester Centre for Textile Conservation
together with other textiles, from precious silks to pockets and large tapestries.

In the overall 'life' of this object, it has been characterized by one specific stage,
that of concealment. We have 'narrativized' this stomacher and scholarship has
created around it further explanations: where and what type of things are concealed,
the possible reasons for concealment, how concealment relates to the wider early
modern belief system, etc. One can use theory and historical scholarship on magic,
folklore and village life to provide an even wider background. The stomacher is
therefore contextualized and can be accessed by any historian who can see the garment, look at other objects, read articles on the concealed garments project, as well
as books on magic, early modern socio-economic practices, and the anthropology
and sociology of similar practices around the world.

My point is that if I had seen this stomacher in a museum display or storeroom,
without any previous knowledge of its story and affiliation, I could have reached
very different conclusions and located the stomacher within altogether different
narratives. Artefacts are multifarious entities whose nature and heuristic value is
often determined by the diverse range of narratives that historians bring with them.
Here are some examples.

A stomacher and the narrative of dress and fashion

The Nether Wallop stomacher is probably one of the earliest examples of printed
linen in England. The textile printing industry developed in the last quarter of the
seventeenth century around London, but few textiles or garments from this period
survive. The printed linen of the stomacher shows the limited expertise on this
branch of textile finishing acquired in England by the early eighteenth century. In
the narrative of textiles, this stomacher is not just a 'perfect example', but also a
very rare one. Particular attention could be given also to the design and colours in
the discussion of the meaning of colours in the early modern period.[14] A stomacher
could be also productively contextualized in the wider narrative of the relationship
between clothing, sexuality and gender.[15]

A stomacher and the narrative of the body and anthropocentrism

The stomacher could also be contextualized in wider historical discussions about the relevance of the body and the senses in historical investigation. Clothing has often been examined in relation to the body. The physicality of the owner is materialized through the survival of textiles and garments.[16] The stomacher was worn by a woman, and was later probably used as a ritual object for its capacity to represent a physical person. Does this mean that an object like a stomacher makes our understanding of social practices more tangible or more 'personal'? Not necessarily. Ewa Domanska comments about the fact that objects support a 'non-anthropocentric history' in which the inorganic (rather than the human) is to be at the centre of attention.[17]

A stomacher and the narrative of bio-diversity

The Nether Wallop stomacher has been thoroughly studied not just by historians, curators and restorers but also by scientists. X-radiography was adopted to study the internal structure and materials of the garment.[18] It confirmed that the stomacher is stiffened with strips of whalebone. DNA analysis showed that the material came from a North Atlantic whale (*Eubalaena glacialis*). Marine biologists had previously thought that the mitochondrial lineage of this species of ballen had remained unaltered over the centuries. However the DNA analysis of the stomacher showed that this 'bio-diversity narrative' was incorrect as the whalebone came from a previously unrecorded species.[19]

A stomacher and the narrative of buildings

Perhaps the object we should be interested in is not the stomacher but the building where it was found. The stomacher could be contextualized within a wider investigation of buildings, as done for instance by Matthew Johnson in his *An Archaeology of Capitalism* (1996). In this case the artefact considered is the building itself that stands as testimony to the ways in which space was articulated in early modern England.[20] One could map the findings of objects against the paradigm of the so-called 'Great Rebuilding' of Tudor and Stuart times. Were concealed objects to be found mostly in the new buildings erected between 1570 and 1640? What do they have to do with the changing layouts of properties? Or perhaps with the appearance of nuclear families? Or simply with the accumulation of new goods? Do they belong to a wider spectrum of household practices?[21]

A stomacher and the narrative of commodification in capitalism

The Nether Wallop stomacher could also be fruitfully used to discuss the relationship between the meaning and economic value of commodities in the early modern period. The stomacher shows that the garment was heavily used and passed through a series of stages in its functional life. It was recycled, as most artefacts were, in a

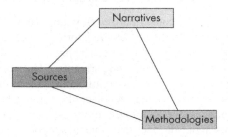

Figure 1.4 The relationship between sources, narratives and methodologies

world of material dearth.[22] Concealed garments, however, seem at odds with tradi-tional narratives of commodification under capitalist regimes, which indicate that during the early modern period artefacts became increasingly part of a commer-cialized culture. Marxist and Marxian interpretations identify an emerging separa-tion between economic value and personal/subjective attributes in relation to the making and use of artefacts. In this case the specific object is adjacent to a large-scale narrative, politically created and since used by historians to describe a general transition towards a 'modern' capitalist world.[23] Concealed objects show instead the endurance of a profound belief system created and structured through processes of de-commodification (symbolized by the mutilation of the clothing).

This case study has supported the idea of a strong integration between sources, nar-ratives and methodologies (Figure 1.4). We have started by considering artefacts as sources (*history from things*), but we have soon discovered that artefacts are given specific narratives and can be 'adopted' in historical research through different methodologies. My second case study concentrates on methodologies and exam-ines the ways in which interdisciplinary artefact-based research might challenge historical narratives.

A global consumer revolution: broken all in pieces

Methodologies: the power of interdisciplinarity

The last three decades have seen the emergence of a new field of historical enquiry that has been defined as 'history of consumption'.[24] The main interest of history of consumption is the examination of the pattern and meanings of consumption through history. Central to the field of history of consumption has been an interest in the very material objects that were produced, bought and consumed to satisfy people's physical, but also relational, psychological and moral needs. History of consumption is quintessentially a *history of things*, as what it wishes to explain is why, how and what becomes part of the material world that surrounds human beings.[25]

The success of history of consumption has been based on multi/interdisciplinarity.[26] Basic historical narratives have been created, revised, criticized and sometimes dismissed not so much through in-depth primary research, but by forging alliances across disciplines through the medium of objects.[27] If one concentrates on the eighteenth century and the so-called 'birth of a consumer society', it is evident how material culture has created a fertile terrain for discussion and confrontation. It is not uncommon to find in explanations of the eighteenth-century consumer revolution references to anthropologists such as Mary Douglas and Daniel Miller, sociologists such as Arjun Appadurai, Ben Fine and Ellen Leopold, and Grant McCracken, and philosophers such as Pierre Bourdieu and Michel Foucault.

Narratives: shifting the consumer revolution

History of consumption came to the fore in 1982 with the publication of *The Birth of A Consumer Society* by Neil McKendrick, John Brewer and Jack Plumb.[28] Their narrative was constructed around the idea of a consumer revolution in eighteenth-century Britain based not just on an increasing income and wider supplies of cheap consumer goods, but also on emulative forces of a Veblerian nature.[29] This original formulation was heavily criticized but sparked a series of further studies on eighteenth-century consumption.[30] Lorna Weatherill shifted the agenda to the more personal meanings of possession by drawing on Goffman's theories of front- and backstage.[31] Other historians considered consumption and the possible emergence of a consumer society from specific angles that included gender, domesticity, politeness, urban living, the press, clothing, luxury, and even more traditional perspectives such as the political economy, manufacturing and the history of specific commodities. The consolidation and expansion of the field of history of consumption did not mean a separation from other disciplines, rather the opposite. Recent works show a surprising intensification of interdisciplinarity not just by historians dialoguing with other disciplines but also through the direct participation of sociologists, anthropologists, historical geographers and literary scholars in what were previously seen as quintessentially historical debates.

Three developments have characterized the narrative of the consumer revolution during the last decade. First, the move towards a deeper and more sophisticated analysis of artefacts. Joint conferences, workshops and research projects between museums and universities are cementing a more direct engagement for historians with material objects. Second, the paradigm of the consumer revolution has been challenged and its chronologies recast. Research on consumption has gone back in time to the Middle Ages and forward into the nineteenth and twentieth centuries. Attempts have been made to construct a wider explanation of change over the *longue durée*. Finally, the remit of research has become geographically broader. The Anglocentric formulation of a consumer revolution has expanded with studies on Europe and North America in the 1980s and 1990s. More recently, historians have fully embraced a more global agenda. One of the key topics has been how much consumption can explain Western economic and social dominance over the last two or three centuries, and how it connects with the concept of globalization.[32]

Figure 1.5 Wan Li porcelain wine cup, *c*.1610: porcelain thinly glazed with underglaze blue
with a scroll design above the footring, width 5.41 inches, height 4.64 inches.
Rediscovered in Jamestown, Virginia, Pit 4. © APVA Preservation Virginia.

Things: broken pieces from/of china

This scholarship in 'global consumption' is interested in objects such as the cup in
Figure 1.5. More than a dozen of these cups have been found on Virginian archaeological sites. They are thinly glazed wine cups of high quality and have been found
as part of the extensive archaeological survey of Jamestown carried out over the last
three decades. They are some of the more than 150,000 objects recovered in digs
that unearthed tools, coins, parts of furnishings, decorative items, residues of food,
potteries and ceramics. Nearly half the objects date to the first years of English settlement in 1607–10.[33]

Ceramics, and porcelain in particular, have played an important part in the study
of history of consumption and the consumer revolution in Europe. They figured
highly among the different consumer items that enjoyed widespread success in
eighteenth-century Europe. Any eighteenth-century conversation piece (portraits
of upper- and middle-class families in informal situations) shows the presence of
the necessary tools of polite sociability, such as porcelain cups and saucers and

teapots. Pewter plates were also replaced by ceramic and porcelain ones. While porcelain items were still relatively uncommon in the early seventeenth century, by the end of the century they had entered all prosperous households and, during the following century, came within reach of the lower strata of society. Porcelains are therefore 'perfect examples' for a 'consumer revolution' as they were not just new commodities sought after by consumers, but also explain the search for substitutes in Europe (from Majolica to different types of glazed earthenware), and the importance of global trade in the early modern period.

The broken wine cup found in Jamestown was not a locally produced artefact. It was not even a European object as the old continent learned the secret of porcelain production only in the early eighteenth century. The underglaze blue motif and porcelain body identify it as a Chinese 'Wan Li' porcelain.[34] One can only be surprised to learn that in the early years of settlement of North America, the 225 English colonists had at their disposal high-quality consumer goods coming from the other side of the world. They could have brought these Chinese porcelains with them from England or received them from European merchants.

What is certain is that these items were the latest fashion. Before 1600, little Chinese porcelain entered Europe. It was with the setting up of the Dutch and English East India companies trading with Asia at the very beginning of the seventeenth century that trade in these commodities started in earnest. In 1602 the Dutch seized two Portuguese vessels trading in the Indian Ocean. One of them contained 10,000 pieces of Chinese porcelain. During the following couple of years the sale of these porcelains created a china-mania in Holland.[35] Evidence of the fact that Chinese porcelains were highly sought after can be found by looking at figures. It is estimated that, between 1600 and 1800, the Dutch East India Company imported 43 million pieces of porcelain from Asia. This was in addition to 30 million pieces imported by the English, French, Swedish and Danish companies.[36]

The study of the global trade in porcelain – but also in cotton textiles and other exotic products such as lacquerware, ornamental bronze and brassware, ivory, jade and other precious materials – is part of the re-configuration of the Anglocentric narrative of a consumer revolution into a much wider, often global setting.[37] It has been argued that such products were part of 'global commodities' that changed the consumer tastes not just of Europeans, but also Africans, as well as indigenous and new populations in the Americas. They have also been taken as evidence of an early modern phase of globalization with increasing trade, but also cultural and material connections across vast parts of Eurasia, Africa and the Americas.

The finding of a Chinese wine cup in an early North American settlement clearly confirms, if not even strengthens, this narrative. The cosmopolitan nature of trade is materialized not just through this specific artefact, but also through another hundred types of potteries and ceramics found in Jamestown.[38] Apart from Wan Li, there are at least another two varieties of Chinese porcelains present in Jamestown: the Swatow and the Kraak types.[39] The remaining ceramics and potteries have been identified as coming from England, France, Germany, Italy, the Netherlands, Spain and Portugal, as well as locally produced wares.[40] The global richness of the material culture of a rather remote place in the early seventeenth century can be taken as an indicator of the high degree of interconnectedness of the early modern world. In its early years of European settlement, North America was already part of a web of global connections and a process that we call globalization.

Extending narratives and revising methods

The ceramics unearthed at Jamestown are significant findings as they have helped historians to shift the narrative of consumption within a more global framework. They act as connecting elements between debates over globalization, the relevance of the exchange of goods and the historical significance of consumer choices.[41] I have briefly contextualized a Wan Li wine cup within a series of other ceramics present in Jamestown in 1607–10 and coming from several parts of the world. I have also presented figures on the European trade in Chinese porcelain over a longer period, which has allowed us to explain the 'scale' of the phenomenon. Although this cup is quite unique, it is also just one of a million similar cases, most of which have left no material trace.[42] The historian of material culture is asked to assess how common or how unique a specific artefact might be.

Second, the Wan Li wine cup shows a problem in connecting objects and narratives. Objects are more static than narratives: the broken pieces of porcelain found in Jamestown tell us a great deal about the sophistication of the consumer culture of this place and its world connections at the very beginning of the seventeenth century, but they tell us nothing about the overall evolution (the dynamic) aspect of either the consumer revolution or globalization. They are unable to tell us, for instance, if the world in 1750 was more or less globalized. This is because individual objects are often, though not always, the fruit of a specific time and place when/where they are produced, exchanged and consumed. This is why there are questions and problems that cannot be solved just by considering artefacts from one space/time.

The Jamestown ceramics tell us that this was a rather 'cosmopolitan' and 'global' place, but what does it say about the process of globalization? Nearly everything published by economists, sociologists and historians on globalization implies that this is a cumulative and progressive process. But was the world of Virginia even more cosmopolitan in the eighteenth or nineteenth centuries? The answer is no. As archaeologists at Jamestown observed: 'As England attained commercial control of North America in the late 17th century, the material record becomes more homogenous and more predominantly English.'[43] The European discovery of the process of porcelain production and, more importantly, the increasing power of Britain in the geo-politics of the Atlantic Ocean, shows a shift of Virginian material culture into the orbit of English consumer culture, with Staffordshire ware replacing Chinese, German or Italian artefacts.

By comparing objects across time, researchers can cast doubt on the idea that the process of commercial globalization is linear and incremental. By connecting different narratives, such as the consumer revolution and globalization, a classic example of the history of things has been transformed into a powerful tool to re-think wider narratives in global history.

The Industrial Revolution: the greatest invention of all times

Narratives: the Industrial Revolution

The final case study focuses on a well-known historical narrative: the Industrial Revolution. The Industrial Revolution is not a precise event in time, but a series of historical changes, geographically located in the British Isles between the 1770s and the 1840s. Historians like to define the Industrial Revolution as a process of self-sustained and continuative economic growth joint with social transformation, urbanization, the intensification of labour and, above all, capital-intensive technological innovation. This is a rather technical definition, especially if we consider that, together with the French Revolution and the Renaissance, the Industrial Revolution is a historical narrative that transcends the confines of the subject of history. It is a label commonly used by the media and in everyday speech.

In its more popular version, the Industrial Revolution can be summarized by a series of images that we have in our minds that include locomotives, great inventors, factories, long working hours, cotton mills and machinery. The historical narrative is broken down into 'vignettes', some of which refer to specific artefacts such as a factory in Manchester, a spinning machine at the Science Museum, or the portrait of Richard Arkwright. The narrative that is widely accepted – perhaps not by historians, but more importantly by everyone else – is actually formed not by books in libraries, or figures and graphs, but by images and objects. In 1947 Klingender published a book entitled *Art and the Industrial Revolution*, in which he united narrative, object and representation, though his remit of art was just flat representational forms such as paintings and prints. His book remains the best visual catalogue of what we define as the Industrial Revolution.[44]

Since 1947 the concept of the Industrial Revolution has been the subject of criticism, especially from postmodern scholarship, claiming that the Industrial Revolution never really happened: one can find economic growth, urbanization, technological innovation, but the bestowing of a systemic meaning on these events remains rather controversial.[45] The de-constructivist mood of much postmodernism underlines how the more one starts questioning the relationship between the sources (events, people, figures, documents, but also representations and artefacts) that support the narrative of the 'Industrial Revolution', the more the narrative disintegrates. One might argue that this is a good thing, though it does not help us in at least two ways. First, while the narrative might be thought unsound, it may remain useful (and this is probably why it was constructed in the very first instance). The Industrial Revolution might have never existed, but we find it useful to refer to it as a 'ready-made' label. Second, the more materials one takes away, the less one can grasp the contours of the 'bigger picture'.

Things: a cut image of a flying machine

What happens when, instead of subtracting, we add a new element? This is what many historians are asked to do: to uncover missing or previously unknown materials. Our engagement with primary sources is not the result of a profound love for dusty archives (or cold museum storages for the historians of material culture), but generates from the idea that what we find there is the 'gem', something that can become a new piece in the puzzle.

My new piece is an artefact: a two-dimensional representation of what the included text calls 'The Aerial Steam Carriage' (Figure 1.6). This is, first of all, an 'image' or a representation. But at the same time it is an artefact, a material object that in this case is glued to a heavy paper support (something that cannot easily be conveyed through this text). Such support suggests that it was part of a larger folio, possibly a scrapbook, a collection of cut images produced especially by young ladies in Victorian times as a hobby. It is not a print, but rather a cut image. This is evident by the fact that one can distinguish the lettering on the back. Considering the quality of the paper, one can say it is a newspaper page, though I have still to identify from which newspaper it comes or its precise date. I bought it some years ago for the princely sum of 50 pence simply because it was a mysterious (and alarmingly cheap) object.

This print presented me with two problems. First, airplanes did not exist in Victorian times. It is well known that it was the Wright brothers in the early twentieth century (not in Victorian times) in the USA (not in England) that performed the first flight. Second, the very technology used (combustion engines) had not been invented in the early Victorian age. As I was pretty sure that airplanes did not feature at the time of Industrial Revolution, my print was framed and displayed in my office where – very much like the Maynards' concealed garments – it lay unexplained and unquestioned for the next few years.

During those years, I wrote and taught several times on the merits and demerits of the Industrial Revolution. It was mostly an exercise in presenting a combination of argument and evidence, all of which is positivistic in nature, in the sense that it builds up to fit the narrative that we call the Industrial Revolution. From time to time, a fellow historian will unearth a new piece of evidence or propose a new

THE AERIAL STEAM CARRIAGE.

Figure 1.6 'The Aerial Steam Carriage', newspaper cutting, *c.*1840–45.

explanation; more rarely we update our technical language or propose new concepts, thus slightly shifting the narrative. At the back of my mind was however an object whose very existence I could explain only by locating it outside the narrative of the Industrial Revolution. This was a print created by someone with a great deal of ingenuity and fantasy, and probably collected by a young lady because it was 'charming'. It had nothing to do with factories, Richard Arkwright, cotton or the Industrial Revolution as a whole; what it represented never existed.

Things: more prints of flying machines

Per se, this print is a trivial object: it does not even have the status of a museum artefact and did not fetch more than 50 pence. But what if someone had really invented a flying machine in early Victorian England? Would this have been the triumph of 'industrialism'? Wasn't it the case that my perceived disconnection between the narrative that I taught and wrote about and this object was about its apparent negative nature (that I thought it represented something that did not happen) rather than its very essence (a flying machine would fit well into a technological and industrial story)?

The reply to my questions was to be found on the internet. Historians are wary of the internet because it can be difficult to assess the accuracy of the information it provides. By contrast historians use footnotes profusely, to make evident the process of scientific validation of each piece of information. In the last few years, however, this state of things has started to change: an increasing amount of material that complies with scientific standards and academic rigour can be found on the internet. In my case, I did not need to find more information on a topic (the Industrial Revolution, for instance), but on an object. Google showed that indeed the web knew about it, and it drove me straight to the website that I use to source images for Industrial Revolution lectures: the Science and Society Picture Library of the Science Museum.[46] The Science Museum online catalogue of images made it clear that my print was not unique, and it provided a rather entertaining story about it.

The Aerial Steam Carriage was the 'invention' of a certain William Samuel Henson (1812–1888). Henson had taken out a patent for a flying machine in 1843, thus confirming that my print was indeed from the mid-nineteenth century. It was easy enough to check his name on *The Times Online* where there is an article on Henson from 1841.[47] The database *The Making of the Modern World* revealed other references to Henson and his Aerial Steam Carriage in the *Mechanics' Magazine* of 1843, the *Scientific American* of 1848 and a plate in John Pennington's *Aerostation* (*c.* 1838) that looked uncannily like Henson's later invention.[48] More information and images were to be found on Wikipedia and a couple of other specialist websites from where the relevance and scale of my finding became apparent.[49]

Henson was an imaginative man and came from a family with substantial technological and industrial expertise as his father owned a lace-making business in Somerset. His technological dream, however, went beyond the textile world as, in his twenties, he put considerable effort and money into developing a patent for what we would now call an aeroplane. The importance accorded Henson by the scientific community suggests that he was more than a failed inventor.[50] He should not be defined as a visionary man, as what he did in the early 1840s was to make people believe that his machine could fly. Although a patent was granted, Parliament denied Henson and his commercial partner John Stringfellow the incorporation of their 'Aerial Transit Company'.[51] What followed was an intense campaign, probably orchestrated by Henson himself, to make his idea more than a figment of his imagination in the hope of raising capital. Several prints were published around 1842–43, picturing the aerial steam carriage in fictitious flights over different parts of the world: the River Thames in London, a European lakeside town, an industrial city, and a capital city like Rome.[52] Henson went as far as to imagine his machine flying over the pyramids (Figure 1.7) on the way to India.[53]

What Henson did was to make an idea real. He was well aware of the fact that the translation of his patent into a prototype was not simply a matter of correct technical application, but depended mostly on a feasible business plan. And this was what he wanted to create. He did so not just by visualizing his machine, but also by explaining it. *The Times* reported that Henson's invention was 'a matter of little less than certainty' and described the aeroplane as 150 feet long by 30 feet wide with a tail 50 feet in length and a propeller 20 feet in diameter.[54] *The Times* hailed Henson a 'first and true inventor' and made his idea even more palpable by indulging in

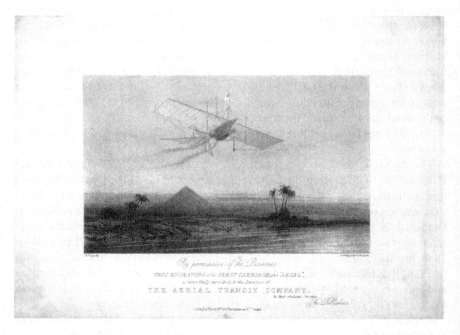

Figure 1.7 'The Aerial Transit Company: By Permission of the Patentees'. Colour print, London, published by Ackerman & Co., the Strand, 28 March 1843. Science Museum, London, inv. 1938–0296.

precise technical descriptions of a condenser producing 20 horse power and the technology for take-off and landing. The article concluded with the cheerful hope 'of what will be the changes, commercial, social and political, which the possession of this new-born power will necessarily bring about'.[55] It is probable that Henson did not disdain even the sarcastic and colourful report made in *Punch*, that 'it is understood that the first line to be established is that to India, the carriages leaving the top of the Monument, Fish Street Hill, every morning, and taking five minutes at the summit of the Great Pyramids for refreshments'.[56] This gave body to his ideas of achievement.

Methodologies: recasting narratives beyond positivism

My fortuitous encounter with a 50 pence cut-image led me to research on a nine-teenth-century inventor. My artefact acquired meaning by contextualizing it within its one small narrative, and by analysing it next to other similar artefacts. The more I discovered about the aerial steam carriage, the more I realized that it was part of a wider 'story' of invention, personal dreams, public imagination and eventual fail-ure. But it was also a story that had several of the ingredients that are commonly present in the narrative of the Industrial Revolution: a machine, a business plan, and the vision of progress so aptly conveyed in the pages of national newspapers.

Two methodological problems seem to me evident in linking this object (and all others belonging to the same story) and the narrative of the Industrial Revolution. First, the print was not necessarily either a source through which to study the Industrial Revolution (*history from things*), nor the subject topic on which to write about (*history of things*). I had tried instead to juxtapose this object to a narrative, putting object and narrative on a par (*history and things*). Object and narrative are both interested in explaining the past, though in different ways. The previously mentioned methodology of 'the social life of things', but also the approach based on the 'biography' of material objects, have attempted to dissociate straightforward connections between artefacts and history and create more methodologically sophisticated relationships between the two.[57]

I would like to confine myself only to one, though major, consequence of this juxtaposition between history and things: the problem of positivism in research. As I stated earlier, the Industrial Revolution is normally explained by providing evi-dence (new sources, new statistics, more qualitative materials, new concepts, etc.). So much so, that a concept is transformed into something that can be pinned down into individual elements. Rarely do historians discuss what was not achieved by the Industrial Revolution: the world of the impossible, what was aspired to, or what was imagined.[58] Material culture would run into the same problem if it was used just as a source or as the subject matter for historical analysis: it would tend to make only positive (though hopefully open) statements. A more flexible relationship between history and objects is needed both to recast narratives (in my case now see-ing the Industrial Revolution as not just what was possible and was achieved, but also as what was impossible and imagined) and rethink methodologies (investing the Industrial Revolution through positive as well as negative evidence).

From object to object

I was content enough by this explanation and by possessing an object that I could now understand and contextualize within a narrative of an 'Industrial Revolution that never happened'. It was by chance that I found a three-dimensional artefact. I had started with an object and concluded my amateur research with another. While writing about design copyright for cotton textiles, I came across a 'Design for a pocket handkerchief' reproduced in an article by David Greysmith and representing Henson's machine.[59] The author reproduced the design for a plate print now at the National Archives at Kew.[60] I therefore checked with curators at the Victoria and Albert Museum, the Airplane Museum of Scotland and the Science Museum. The latter has in its collection what is probably the only surviving example of a pocket handkerchief produced from the plate (Figure 1.8). One can only imagine the pleasure of Mr Henson to see his flying machine going 'to China in Twenty-Four Hours Certain'.

Conclusion

How do we connect artefacts with the universal aspirations of history? This essay has argued against the naïve idea that objects should simply be inserted within

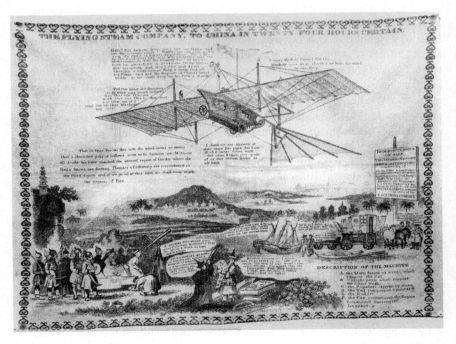

Figure 1.8 'The Flying Steam Company, to China in Twenty-Four Hours Certain'. Cotton handkerchief with sepia brown ink. Science Museum, London, inv. 1938–0295.

historically determined contexts. This would make them redundant, or at best illustrative. I have supported instead the idea that historians should position objects in a dialogue with methodologies and narratives. I have shown that in the same way in which historians mobilize different methodologies and different types of narratives and concepts, so there are highly different ways in which objects relate to history. At first sight the difficulty of connecting objects with narratives could be seen as a problem of size: while objects make small statements, narratives tend to do the opposite. Yet I prefer to see the challenge in another way. At stake is the very nature of the subject of history. Historians tend to present history as a well-woven tablecloth, covering all corners. Objects show how history is instead a rather loosely woven net that sometimes retains – but often is unable to 'catch' – concepts, people, events and explanations. Material artefacts with their multifarious meanings, their innate opaqueness and their difficult heuristic nature remind us that history is always producing but has still a great deal more to do before covering all the corners of human experience.

Notes

1 'Old English bedsteads', *Apollo*, 41 (1945), pp. 150–1; A. Rowand, 'Some early English sea service buttons', *The Connoisseur*, 79 (1927), pp. 90–100.
2 Leora Auslander, 'Beyond Words', *American Historical Review*, 110 (2006), p. 1015.
3 Richard Grassby, 'Material Culture and Cultural History', *Journal of Interdisciplinary History*, 35 (2005), pp. 591–603.
4 This is true to the point of seeing material culture as interchangeable with consumption. See for instance the review article by Dominique Poulot, 'Une nouvelle histoire de la culture materiale?', *Revue d'Histoire Moderne et Contemporaine*, 44 (1997), pp. 344–57. For a broader and more methodologically nuanced analysis of objects, text and representation see Auslander, 'Beyond Words'.
5 Laurel Thatcher Ulrich, *The Age of Homespun: Objects and Stories in the Creation of an American Myth* (New York: Knopf, 2001); Lorna Weatherill, *Consumer Behaviour and Material Culture in Britain, 1660–1760* (London: Routledge, 1988).
6 On this see Jules D. Prown, *Art as Evidence: Writings on Art and Material Culture* (New Haven and London: Yale University Press, 2001). See also W. David Kingery (ed.), *Learning from Things: Method and Theory of Material Culture Studies* (Washington and London: Smithsonian Institution Press, 1996).
7 Interview with Mrs Maynard, finder, Nether Wallop, Hampshire, UK. Interviewed 4 March 2002. http://www.concealedgarments.org/research/oral/maynard.html
8 Dinah Eastop, 'Material Culture in Action: Conserving Garments Deliberately Concealed Within Buildings', *Anais do Museu Paulista*, 15 (2007), p. 195. See also Gabriella Barbieri, 'Memoirs of an 18th Century Stomacher: A Strategy for Documenting the Multiple Object Biographies of a Once-concealed Garment', unpublished MA dissertation, Winchester School of Art, University of Southampton, 2003.
9 Dinah Eastop and Charlotte Dew, 'Context and Meaning Generation: The Conservation of Garments Deliberately Concealed Within Buildings', in David Saunders, Joyce H. Townsend and Sally Woodcock (eds), *The Object in Context: Crossing Conservation Boundaries: Contributions to the Munich Congress, 28 August–1 September 2006* (London: International Institute for Conservation of Historic and Artistic Works, 2006), p. 17.
10 June Swann, 'Shoes Concealed in Buildings', *Costume: The Journal of the Costume Society*, 30 (1996), pp. 59–69.

11 See the Deliberately Concealed Garments Project, Winchester School of Art, University of Southampton, UK: http://www.concealedgarments.org.

12 Dinah Eastop, 'Outside In: Making Sense of the Deliberate Concealment of Garments Within Buildings', *Textile: The Journal of Cloth and Culture*, 4 (2006), pp. 246–7.

13 Arajun Appadurai, *The Social Life of Things: Commodities in Cultural Perspective* (Cambridge: Cambridge University Press, 1986).

14 As done for instance by Hans Medick, 'Une culture de la considération. Les vêtements et leurs couleurs à Laichingen entre 1750 et 1820', *Annales, Histoire, Sciences Sociales*, 50 (1995), pp. 753–74. See also Michel Pastoureau's analyses of the social meaning of colour: *Bleu: histoire d'une couleur* (Paris: Editions du Seuil, 2000).

15 One can cite the relevant literature on the corset as an example. Another area is the investigation of the construction of homosexual identity through apparel, mostly carried out through the means of ethnographic analysis of the use of clothing. Particularly exciting work has been done by integrating dress and literary studies. See Catherine Richardson (ed.), *Clothing Culture, 1350–1650* (Aldershot: Ashgate, 2004), in particular the Introduction, pp. 1–25; and Chloe Wigston Smith, 'Materializing the Eighteenth Century: Dress History, Literature, and Interdisciplinary Study', *Literature Compass*, 3 (2006), pp. 967–72.

16 Judy Attfield, *Wild Things: The Material Culture of Everyday Life* (Oxford: Berg, 2000), p. 132.

17 Ewa Domanska, 'The Material Presence of the Past', *History and Theory*, 45 (2006), p. 338. Historians are now keen to construct narratives that are more careful in balancing the agency of people and things. This does not mean that inanimate objects should be given agency per se, but that historians should unravel the way in which the interaction between person, object and language constructs historical meaning.

18 Gabriella Barbieri, 'The Role of X-radiography in the Documentation and Investigation of an Eighteenth Century Multi-layered Stomacher', in Sonia O'Connor and Mary M. Brook (eds), *X-Radiography of Textiles, Dress and Related Objects* (Oxford: Elsevier, 2007), pp. 203–11.

19 Eastop, 'Material Culture in Action', p. 195.

20 Matthew Johnson, *An Archaeology of Capitalism* (Cambridge, MA: Blackwell, 1996).

21 I have used here some of the questions proposed by Colin Platt in his *The Great Rebuilding of Tudor and Stuart England: Revolutions in Architectural Taste* (London: UCL Press, 1994), especially in the Preface and Chapter 1.

22 Ercoel Sori, *Il rovescio della produzione: i rifiuti in età pre-industriale e paleotecnica* (Bologna: Il Mulino, 1999).

23 See Renata Ago, *Il gusto delle cose: una storia degli oggetti nella Roma del Seicento* (Rome: Donzelli Editore, 2006); Lena Orlin, 'The Textual Life of Things', paper presented at the conference 'Everyday Objects: Medieval and Early Modern Material Culture and its Meanings', the Shakespeare Institute, Stratford-upon-Avon, 27–30 June 2007.

24 The field of history of consumption is not a field with fixed boundaries: in France historians use the label 'history of everyday life' (which includes consumption and more); in the United Kingdom there is also the field of history of retailing and shopping (which could be seen as part of history of consumption). The more recent use of the label 'history of material culture' seems to imply wider definitions beyond the act of purchase and consumption of commodities. For an overview see John Brewer and Roy Porter (eds), *Consumption and the World of Goods* (London: Routledge, 1993). See also the incisive article by Craig Clunas, 'Modernity Global and Local: Consumption and the Rise of the West', *American Historical Review*, 104 (1999), pp. 1497–511.

25 History of consumption, however, is not the only type of history of things. One should also mention other fields, such as history of design, history of architecture or history of fashion, in which material objects play a key role.

26 On the issue of interdisciplinarity and the role of art history in renaissance scholarship see: Curtis Perry, 'Introduction', in Curtis Perry (ed.), *Material Culture and Cultural Materialisms in the Middle Ages and Renaissance* (Turnhout, Belgium: Brepols, 2001), pp. xii–xiii.

27 And, as Ann Smart Martin observes, the study of consumerism is 'a large umbrella under which many areas of scholarship can rest'. Ann Smart Martin, 'Makers, Buyers, and Users: Consumerism as a Material Culture Framework', *Winterthur Portfolio*, 28 (1993), p. 143.

28 Neil McKendrick, John Brewer and J.H. Plumb, *The Birth of a Consumer Society: The Commercialisation of Eighteenth Century England* (London: Europa, 1982). I would like to underline how the excellent book by Joan Thirsk had already shaped the debate, though in a very different way from McKendrick *et al.*: Joan Thirsk, *Economic Policy and Projects: the Development of a Consumer Society in Early Modern England* (Oxford: Clarendon, 1978).

29 Thorstein Veblen, *Theory of the Leisure Class* (orig. edn 1999; New York: Random House, 2001).

30 See in particular Ben Fine and Ellen Leopold, 'Consumerism and the Industrial Revolution', *Social History*, 15 (1990), pp. 151–79.

31 Weatherill, *Consumer Behaviour*.

32 See for instance: Maxine Berg, 'In Pursuit of Luxury: Global History and British Consumer Goods in the Eighteenth Century', *Past and Present*, 182 (2004), pp. 85–142; Jeremy Prestholdt, 'On the Global Repercussions of East African Consumerism', *American Historical Review*, 109 (2004), pp. 755–82. For an overview: Peter N. Stearns, *Consumerism in World History: The Global Transformation of Desire* (London and New York: Routledge, 2001).

33 http://www.apva.org/ngex/c1bart.html.

34 It was once thought that the high-quality Wan Li porcelain was produced only for the Chinese elite. The recovery of the 1613 shipwreck *Witte Leeuw* in 1976 in the Chinese Sea, in which 40 Wan Li wine cups were found, suggested that these items were also traded to Europe. The Jamestown finding confirmed it. See Christine L. van der Pijl-Ketel (ed.), *The Ceramic Load of the 'Witte Leeuw'* (Amsterdam: Rijksmuseum, 1982), and J.B. Curtis, 'Chinese Ceramics and the Dutch Connections in Early Seventeenth Century Virginia', *Vereninging van Vrienden der Aziatische Kunst Amsterdam*, 1 (1985), pp. 6–13.

35 Berg, 'In Pursuit of Luxury', p. 84.

36 Ibid., p. 118; Robert Finlay, 'The Pilgrim Art: The Culture of Porcelain in World History', *Journal of World History*, 9 (1998), p. 168.

37 See for instance Robert Bachelor, 'On the Movement of Porcelain: Rethinking the Birth of Consumer Society as Interactions of Exchange Networks, 1600–1750', in John Brewer and Frank Trentmann (eds), *Consuming Cultures, Global Perspectives: Historical Trajectories, Transnational Exchanges* (Oxford and New York: Berg, 2006), pp. 95–121.

38 Beverly Straube and Nicholas Luccketti, *1995 Interim Report*, APVA Jamestown Rediscovery (1996), 20, Figure 2.

39 Maura Rinaldi, *Kraak Porcelain: A Moment in the History of Trade* (London: Bamboo, 1989). See also Julia B. Curtis, 'Chinese Export Porcelain in Eighteenth-century Tidewater Virginia', *Studies in Eighteenth-Century Culture*, 17 (1987), pp. 119–44; and John Spargo, *Early American Pottery and China* (Rutland, Vermont: Charles E. Turle, 1985).

40 See the Jamestown Rediscovery website: http://www.apva.org/ngex/c1bart.html.

41 For a theoretical perspective see Robert J. Foster, 'Tracking globalization: commodities and value in motion', in Christopher Tilley, Webb Keane, Susanne Küchler, Mike Rowlands and Patricia Spyer (eds) *Handbook of Material Culture*, London: Sage, 2006, pp. 285–301.

42 I think that quantitative analyses in the study of material culture should not be easily dismissed. A single object does not tell us how common or rare it was. The three statements: (i) 'Chinese porcelain were widely available on the Dutch market in 1602–4'; (ii) 'Ten million pieces of Chinese porcelain were available on the Dutch market in 1602–4'; and (iii) 'Five pieces of Chinese porcelain for every Dutch citizen were available in 1602–4' are all correct but vary widely in their precision and implications.

43 Straube and Luccketti, *1995 Interim Report*, pp. 20–1. I would like to thank Ann Smart Martin for pointing out this important fact to me. Ann Smart Martin, 'A Cream-coloured Revolution in Eighteenth-century British America', unpublished paper presented at workshop on 'Ceramic Day', University of Warwick, Waddesdon Manor, 22 June 2007.

44 F.D. Klingender, *Art and the Industrial Revolution* (London: Noel Carrington, 1947).

45 See in particular Michale Fores, 'The Myth of a British Industrial Revolution', *History*, 6 (1981), pp. 181–98. In defence of the Industrial Revolution, see Maxine Berg and Pat Hudson, 'Rehabilitating the Industrial Revolution', *Economic History Review*, 45 (1992), pp. 24–50.

46 http://www.scienceandsociety.co.uk/.

47 *The Times*, 30 March 1841. A further piece is in the *Pictorial Times*, 1 April 1843.

48 *The Mechanics' Magazine, Museum, Register, Journal and Gazette*, 38 (1843), pp. 317–28; John H. Pennington, *Aerostation: or, Steam Aerial Navigation*, s.l. (1838), plate 1.

49 http://www.flyingmachines.org/hens.html; http://www.ctie.monash.edu.au/hargrave/stringfellow.html; http://en.wikipedia.org/wiki/First_flying_machine.

50 The Science Museum in London has a model (in scale 1:7) of Henson's 'aerial steam carriage'. This was produced in 1845–47 by John Stringfellow. Unsuccessful trials were attempted, but in 1847 Henson migrated to the United States. Science Museum, no. 1907–0029.

51 The National Archives, Kew, London: Patent of Invention, no. 9478, 1842.

52 These were commissioned by Henson's publicist Frederick Marriott: Published by Rock & Co. (*c*.1843), Library of Congress, ref. LOT 13416, no. 37 (London); engraving by J. Shury (1843), Science and Society Picture Library, ref. 10219018 (Lakeside); lithograph by W.L. Walton (1843), Science and Society Picture Library, ref. 10304405 (industrial town); the identification of Rome is not certain; lithograph, anonymous, Science and Society Picture Library, ref. 10304402 (Rome).

53 The 'Indian' print shows a plane mid-flight and another taking off from a launching ramp constructed on a tower where passengers should have been given permit to board. The exotic nature of the setting is also conveyed through the presence of an elephant: http://www.flyingmachines.org/hens.html

54 *The Times*, 30 March 1841.

55 Ibid.

56 Ibid. A further print shows the aerial steam carriage flying over the pyramids. The text says 'as proposed to go to India in Four Days'. Published in London by J.T. Wood, Monash University, 2750.

57 See for instance Janet Hoskins, 'Introduction', in Janet Hoskins (ed.) *Biographical Objects: How Things Tell the Stories of People's Lives* (New York and London: Routledge, 1998), pp. 1–24.

58 For a very successful attempt to reconstruct the cultural history of the early railways beyond the narrow confines of evidence-led research see James Taylor, 'Business in Pictures: Representations of Railway Enterprise in the Satirical Press in Britain, 1845–1870', *Past and Present*, 189 (2005), pp. 111–46.

59 David Greysmith, 'Patterns, Piracy and Protection in the Textile Printing Industry 1787–1850', *Textile History*, 14 (1983), p. 171.

60 TNA: BT 43 191, Class 10 (Dress), design 7185, May 1843: design for a pocket handkerchief, registered by Geo. Faulkner, Parker St, Manchester.

2 Ornament as evidence

Andrew Morrall

This chapter will examine some of the ways architectural and domestic ornament intersected with social, political, religious and intellectual life in sixteenth-century Northern Europe. The intention is to use a set of period-specific case studies to establish ornament less as a branch of the 'decorative arts' than as a mode of visual address, which embodied and was often intended to proclaim definable social, political, ideological or cultural values. The ambition is to claim the visual sphere of ornament as a medium of cultural and social experience, and to suggest that its study can offer important evidence for understanding early modern *mentalités* as much as other provinces of culture, which are traditionally apprehended and examined by historians via documents and texts. The underlying assumption is that ornament, like speech or other forms of literary discourse, was a language of some flexibility that contemporaries used to project a social identity, a civil or domestic ideal, or a religious or ethical aspect of themselves, and by which they could proclaim adherence to a social group or a particular set of values, or conversely differentiate themselves from others.

The idea therefore is to take the study of ornament out of a narrowly 'art historical' context and to align it more with the interests of social and cultural history. Some of the methods and approaches to the material used here belong necessarily to art history and may be less familiar to historians used to dealing more exclusively with texts. The starting point of the enquiry is a set of questions about the character, iconographic tradition, production, function and reception of the ornamental imagery applied to a number of varying objects; the primary task throughout, in other words, is to interpret and explain the objects themselves. Yet, in doing so, the argument will move outwards from a close consideration of the structure and meaning of a particular ornamental form, to consider how it operated within society: Who used it? How? To what purpose? And, equally, what resistance, if any, was there towards its adoption, and from whom? If the ambition of the essay is to demonstrate how surviving ornamental programmes showed how people construed the world, by what mental constructs they defined it, how they invested it with meaning, and with what registers of emotion they infused it, then the approach comes close to that of the cultural, social or literary historian, who does the same with ideas or with texts; and the methods of cultural analogy or the application of such concepts as *habitus* that are used here are drawn from their disciplines. A further point to be made is that though the materials under discussion and the issues they raise are specific to the Northern Europe of the sixteenth century and therefore unfamiliar to a general reader, it is hoped that the approach and methods used might be applicable to the ornament and material objects of other periods and cultures.

The study of ornament has for some time not been at the forefront of art history. Its neglect for much of the twentieth century can be linked to the Modernist movement's celebration of purity of form and its explicit rejection of all forms of applied ornament. Most famously, Adolf Loos, in his essay, *Ornament and Crime* of 1908, in making the case for an evolutionary and progressive view of art and society, argued that the progress of a society towards 'civilization' was reflected directly in its art – and its shedding of ornament. According to this evolutionary model, a love of ornament belonged to a culture's most primitive stages. (Loos famously equated the highly ornamental body and face tattoos of Papuan tribesmen with a child's doodles.) The theoretical denigration of ornament was advocated at its most sophisticated by Le Corbusier, in his 1925 essay, 'The Decorative Arts of Today', which led to the further eclipse of decoration and applied ornament as a subject of serious enquiry and theoretical discussion for much of the twentieth century.[1] Now that we stand at the end of the Modernist tradition, it is easier to recognize the interpretive blind spots of Modernism's aesthetic programme and to release the study of ornament from its peculiar teleology. In the case of the arts of sixteenth-century Northern Europe, one can do so with the simple observation that, in this period, the field of applied ornament was central to its aesthetic and constituted an important area of creative artistic activity, craft production and reception. As such, its study raises fundamental questions about the nature of 'art' at this period and the terminologies and distinctions by which we define the various areas of visual imagery of the period.

A definition of terms is required. I shall be using the term *ornament* in a threefold sense. First, in a straightforwardly descriptive way to mean applied decoration, especially of the three-dimensional kind, such as that found in architecture or applied to interior furnishings; and I shall be dealing primarily with figurative ornament. Second, I will argue that 'ornament' in its applications and functions, was understood as an aesthetic principle that one finds invoked routinely and unselfconsciously in commentaries on art as well as in the practical language of the artist's workshop found in pattern books or in the wording of contracts between patrons and artists. That is to say, ornament was understood as an essential building block of a coherent system of ordering visual phenomena from which aesthetic pleasure or significance were derived. Third, I will argue that, in a related manner, 'ornament' was also a broad period concept that was used metaphorically in other domains of culture such as ethics and social values as much as in that of aesthetics. Proceeding from there, I will link the concrete with the metaphorical to show how one operated as the embodiment of the other. As we shall see, the themes of ornament are closely related to the early modern tendency to hypostatize abstract concepts like History or Time, or moral entities like Fortitude or Prudence, qualities that attach to people or things and by which they come to be defined. One of the values of ornament for understanding cultural attitudes and beliefs lies precisely in this function of bodying forth mental constructs and attitudes. The way in which it operated within the culture can be broken down into a number of stages.

Ornament as a structural principle of style

First, I would like to pursue the idea of ornament as a structural principle of *style*. This principle can be vividly seen in the early sixteenth century because this period constituted a point of radical transition between two styles, where an older, native 'gothic' tradition met the 'modern' Italianate manner. One can see how ornament was conceived in the ways Northern artists and craftsmen applied Italianate forms and motifs in their work by copying and adapting prints and pattern books that came from south of the Alps. A revealing example of this process can be found in a printed instructional handbook on art by the artist Heinrich Vogtherr the Elder, first published in Strassburg in 1538. The booklet may indeed be regarded as a conscious exercise in the new Italianate, or 'welsch', manner. The opening words of the title declare Vogtherr's intention of offering German artists and craftsmen the benefits of this 'foreign' and novel style:

> A foreign and wonderful art manual of great use to all painters, sculptors, goldsmiths, stone masons, arms- and sword- makers, the like of which has not been seen or rendered in print before.[2]

The pages that follow offer a series of Italianate designs, of headdresses, armour, weapons, escutcheons, capitals and pilasters. These designs are not direct quotations, but rather, imaginative elaborations upon a series of basic Italianate ornamental types: the capital, the pilaster, the Roman cuirass and so on (Figure 2.1). In the capitals one sees variations of Italianate forms – the mussel shell, the acanthus leaf or the ionic scroll. Vogtherr's approach to the Italian prototypes is one of eclectic adaptation: he does not copy, but invents in the spirit of the new style. His booklet is therefore not merely a pattern book for less gifted artists to follow, it is also a 'how to' manual – it demonstrates process as much as conveying a foreign style. As he explicitly states in the preface, he provides examples of the kind of inventions (his own) he hopes 'intelligent and informed artists' will adapt and develop in their own way.[3]

Above all, Vogtherr's manual represents perfectly the concept of style (here the Italianate, or 'welsch', style) as a language of surface ornament and applied decoration. The fact that he addressed his book not only to painters and sculptors but to goldsmiths, stone masons, metal workers, and so on, reveals the broad acceptance of the decoration of surfaces as a concept.

The Nuremberg artist, Peter Flötner (*c.*1485–1546) – preeminently one of Vogtherr's 'intelligent and informed artists' – was an important pioneer of this idiom. A design for a *Pokal*, or presentation cup, shows how such motifs were adopted and developed into a coherent, unified style (Figure 2.2). One may compare various similar ornamental motifs – note, for instance, the use of the leaf face at the centre of the stem with that in Vogtherr's fragment capital. One might sum-

Figure 2.1 Heinrich Vogtherr the Elder, Capitals, page from *Ein frembdes und wunderbar-liches Kunstbüchlin* … (Strassburg, 1538), woodcut, 18 × 13 cm, Warburg Institute, London University.

marize the elements of the style as an overall covering of form with surface decoration whose characteristic organization depends upon the aggregative and proportionate assemblage of discrete forms. German contemporaries had terms for this process: in the vernacular, 'Bekleidung' ('clothing') or 'Verzierung' ('covering') and, in Latin, 'ornatus', literally a garment of style.

A woodcut of a highly ornamented *Triumphal Arch* normally attributed to Flötner and linked to one of ten documented triumphal arches made for the entry of the Emperor Charles V into Nürnberg in 1544, provides a similar demonstration of this ornamental principle. Significantly, these were described in accompanying verses by the poet, Hans Sachs, as decorated in the Italianate manner ('auff welsch monier') and:

Figure 2.2 Peter Flötner, design for a *Pokal*, pen and ink with yellow wash, 75 × 27.5 cm, Paris, Bibliothèque Nationale de France, Cabinet des dessins, inv. no. RES AA5.

Decoratively clothed here and there,
As though they were marble,
With welsch columns and capitals
With beautiful cornices and fluting.

(my emphasis)[4]

Flötner was chiefly known as a designer of small, carved reliefs, or 'plaquettes', for the use of craftsmen working in many media, including metalwork, woodwork and ceramics. He specialized in serial themes such as the Virtues, the Muses, the Temperaments, the Line of German Kings, and so on, which could fit many different decorative contexts. These were described in a biographical sketch of the artist in 1547 by Johann Neudörffer, the Nuremberg mathematician and writing master, as 'aimed at no other purpose but to furnish "Histories" from which goldsmiths would make casts, *with which to clothe their own works*' (my emphasis).[5] In both these cases, Flötner's art is described in terms of a kind of ornamental clothing with which to cover form. In this latter case, however, we are dealing with the application of figurative art – with 'histories' or 'stories' ('Historien'), with tangible subject matter – which therefore introduces an important additional element into the idea of ornamental covering: that is, a cognitive and ideational component, beyond the abstractly ornamental, to which I will return.

Vogtherr's book and Flötner's works, taken together, indicate the means – and the ease – by which the modern style became tied to what was one of the central aesthetic principles of the age, a principle of applying ornament to form, that ran through many art forms, including music and literature. It is closely related to the classical, rhetorical principle of 'ornatus', which gained renewed stimulus and currency through the efforts of Renaissance philological humanism. For the Roman rhetorician, Quintillian (*Institutio Oratoria*, VIII, 3) the first dictum of good diction (*elocutio*) was that discourse must be 'decorated', and what he termed the '*ornatus*' remained the goal of orators and writers throughout this period. It was guided always by a due sense of decorum as when, for instance, Erasmus of Rotterdam in 1516 gently chided Guillaume Budé for using too many ornamental figures of speech in his writing, where a simpler and more natural style would have been more effective: 'your whole style seems bespangled with gems rather than picked out with them here and there, and might be thought to part company with the simplicity of nature'.[6]

Erasmus was not objecting to the idea of ornamented speech per se, merely to the appropriateness of its application. In this context, the ornaments of speech risked overwhelming the effective communication of the central idea. Yet for others, particularly later in the century, ornament became *the chief means* of conveying ideas through art. As the English poet George Puttenham formulated it for poetry in his *The Arte of English Poesy* (1589):

This ornament we speak of is given to it [the poem] by figures and figurative speeches, which be the flowers and as it were the colours that a Poet setteth upon his language by arte, as the embroderer doth his stone and perle, or passements of gold upon the stuffe of a Princely garment, or as th' excellent painter bestoweth the rich Orient colours upon his table of pourtraite.[7]

The sense here is that the most basic materials of the artist's medium – in poetry, the exempla or sententia, the choice of meter or rhyme – are 'ornaments'; so too are the embroiderer's gold threads and the painter's colours; and that it is by these 'ornaments', superficially applied to an underlying unadorned form, that art is produced (and meaning generated). Form is fundamentally, not superficially, altered by the application of ornament.[8]

In the case of Flötner's *Pokal*, though the traditional *form* of the cup was deeply imbued with connotations of civic and private ceremonial and gift-giving, of the commemoration of family honour and prestige, of monetary value and, not least, of local craft skill, it is primarily through the *ornatus*, the ornament – held in perfect decorous balance with the overall form – that we seek 'meaning', both affective, in its classicizing idiom, with all its associations with the grandeur of ancient Rome, and cognitive, through its figurative scenes (there are tiny representations of Dido, Lucretia and others). One set of 'meanings' is grasped associatively, by a series of analogies via the presentation of style – of 'what it looks like' – the other is acquired via the intellect, by interpreting the figurative elements – 'what they mean'. Here we see the *structural* principle of ornament at work. To repeat: it is chiefly by the application of ornament that the thing ornamented is rendered both cognitively and affectively meaningful.

To sum up so far, therefore: we have identified an aesthetic principle based upon an idea of ornament by examining relevant objects within a context of contemporary documentation – some, though not all, of it writings on art – and paying particular attention to period terminology and its usage. We have also established potentially meaningful parallels in non-visual fields of rhetoric and literary style.

Let us now deal with the implications of the stylistic idiom itself, of the classicism employed in Flötner's *Pokal*, to see what kinds of satisfactions it might have held for its owner or viewer. As noted, an overtly classical surface design has been applied over an older, archetypal Germanic form. We can see in Flötner's *Pokal* therefore a modern and foreign style overtly and self-consciously applied to a traditional and abidingly significant form. The Italianate might therefore stand as a signifier of modernity. A number of historians have associated this taste with a particular social group within the cities of south Germany. Michael Baxandall recognized it as one of a number of novelties coming out of Italy, including Roman law, double-entry accounting, luxury goods, even an affected way of standing ('like a stork', according to Erasmus).[9] He also recognized that contemporaries associated this nexus of interests with the new class of super-rich merchant bankers, represented above all by the Fugger banking family. In an essay on the commercial and cultural links between Venice and Germany, Bernd Roeck took this idea further, sketching out a theory of reception of the Italianate style by applying a notion of *habitus* to the social classes receptive to this style.[10] *Habitus* is a concept with a long pedigree, but which was developed into a systematic theory in the twentieth century by the sociologists Marcel Mauss and Pierre Bourdieu. Simply put, *habitus* may be understood as a set of acquired 'dispositions' or patterns of thought, bodily habits, assumed values, behaviour and tastes, which an individual has unconsciously acquired or 'internalized' in a process of interaction between the subjective self and the set of pre-existing social structures that make up the surrounding social environment. For Mauss, the process of internalization was unconscious and therefore before ideology. For Bourdieu, it extended to conscious beliefs and dispositions.[11] Roeck links the beginnings of interest in Italian art and design among German artists, builders and book publishers and patrons to early commercial crosscurrents between Venice and the northern cities. He identifies Venice as a centre of cultural exchange, as what he calls a 'transformer', where artistic currents are converted and where influences flow into each other and combine to create new forms. As he says,

> Often, but not always, the metamorphosis, which takes place in centers of cultural exchange, reflects economic and social changes. This happens, for instance, when a new, emerging elite chooses, from what is offered by artists and intellectuals, those things which seem appropriate for legitimizing their acquired status, or which are also able to conceal their faults. They, therefore, appear as elements of a *habitus*, as expressions of a mentality of a particular social environment or of strategic options that are more or less well pondered.[12]

Roeck takes up Baxandall's insight of how the newly rich class of international banking and merchant families, who had close commercial and cultural ties with Italy, were distinguished from other social groups, such as the old-established landed nobility, by their adoption of the modern Italianate style in habits of outward display – notably in architecture and interior decoration. Though these elements were part of a broader cultivation of things Italian and the product of a genuine taste for Italian art, learning and culture, they could also, according to Roeck, be employed assertively in the public arena as a demonstration of political prestige and economic influence. The first Italianate building in Germany was the monumental funerary chapel built by the Fugger family in the Carmelite monastery church of St Anna's in Augsburg, completed around 1517. As Michael Baxandall had already demonstrated, criticism of the Fugger chapel's opulent Italianate marbled interior as a kind of *nouveau riche* parading of new wealth was included by the conservative nobleman, Ulrich von Hutten, within a broader attack against the Fugger and what they stood for – their trade monopolies, their economic policies, their political manipulation – as enemies of his own class, the rural nobility, as well as of the craftsmen of the cities.[13] For Roeck,

> The Venetian elements in the artistic projects commissioned by Fugger, immediately became synonymous with good taste and modernity and became an essential attribute of the *habitus* of the new moneyed elite who were still searching for a niche within urban society … . They had … shown how wealth and power could become synonymous with taste. As a result of their activities new artistic forms began to permeate the intellectual environment of Augsburg.[14]

That an Italianate style of ornament could be identified with a specific social group or a set of tastes and values does not in itself explain the reasons for its popularity. How might one determine the kinds of satisfactions such ornament offered? Beyond the fashionable and the modern, the Italianate style was also, on some level, an expression of humanist taste, of an interest in and identification with the values of classical Rome. In the face of the all but complete absence of theoretical writings on art in Germany at this period that might articulate such a connection, we might turn to an approach developed by Baxandall, which he employed under the rubric of 'The Period Eye'. This involves turning to the immediate, surrounding world of significance in order to find analogies in other, related areas of cultural practice that can shed comparative light back onto the object under scrutiny. Thus, for example, Baxandall, looking for ways into a period understanding of the complex formal language of limewood sculpture, found in contemporary instruction books on handwriting styles a set of contemporary terms to describe a range of individual pen strokes. Without suggesting a direct analogy with sculptural practice, his analysis of calligraphy offered, via this vivid taxonomy of pen strokes, a more direct way towards an understanding of the sixteenth-century German perception of line and pattern. It provided 'an insight into a peculiar sensibility, alien to us [and yet] rich in categories of visual interest'.[15] Baxandall's attention to contemporary terminology and the concepts it embodied allowed him to come closer to assessing the sculptures in terms of the kinds of visual categories by which they were originally understood. His ambition was to take the sculptures out of the framework of the acquired visual habits and categories of the late twentieth century and to see them anew in terms of a period understanding.

We might follow a similar method in the attempt to understand what qualities contemporaries found in the abstract language of classicism by turning to the field of script design. In an album of script types, the *Proba centum scriptorum*, by the Augsburg scribe Leonard Wagner, in 1517, the year of the completion of the Fugger chapel, the most favoured script, placed at the beginning, was one known as *gothico-antiqua*, or *Rotonda* (as Wagner himself called it). He described it thus:

> Of all the scripts it is the most noble. It is called the mother and queen of the others, and excels over all other scripts in its style [racione], its authority and its excellence. Style, because it is more legible, authority because it is more noble, excellence because it is more distinguished [praestancior] and more ancient [antiquior].[16]

Here, in the field of script design, are to be found ethical qualities attached to a particular style: authority through nobility of style, excellence through historical precedent and its antiquity. As its name implies, the *gothico-antiqua* conjoined gothic forms with simpler, clearer, 'antique' elements, derived in fact from a form of *romanesque minuscule*. Similar values were conferred upon the standard italic, *antiqua* script by humanists and artists like Erasmus and Albrecht Dürer. From Basel to Antwerp it became the favoured type for classical and humanist texts, while the old-fashioned gothic *Fraktur* was reserved for books that served the liturgy.[17] By this kind of examination we can come closer to discovering not merely how a particular style embodied particular values; it allows us to sense more directly the emotional registers they originally expressed. We can then apply this argument back to Flötner's *Pokal*.

Ornament as metaphor

We have thus far found in the concept of *habitus* a flexible tool to tie ornament to a broader context of taste and, further, to a form of social differentiation. We have also gathered a cluster of semantic meanings around Flötner's *Pokal*, expressed through its classicizing surface decoration. Using a similar method of analogy, let us now examine decoration on the level of *cognitive* meaning – that is to say, in terms of intelligible concepts. This is possible where the ornament contains a figurative element. The aesthetic principle of *ornatus*, of a covering of form with ornament, in the *visual sphere* of decoration was conceptually very closely linked to an idea of ornament within other domains of contemporary culture, in particular the social ideals and ethical values to which contemporaries aspired and by which they defined themselves. The link, moreover, was made explicit, I would argue, in that the aesthetic concept, outlined above, was fundamental to their expression. That is to say, contemporaries used exactly the same concept of ornament as a metaphor in text and speech to articulate these social and ethical ideals with respect to persons and institutions; and they surrounded – literally ornamented – themselves with objects and images to body forth these aspects of themselves.[18]

We may look, for example, to the realm of moral philosophy and civil ethics, which assumed great importance as a locus for the construction of individual and collective identity. It was a commonplace of the stream of didactic publications – conduct books, moral compendia, educational handbooks and panegyrical literature – 'to shewe how a man or a woman ought to be adorned with virtues'.[19] The late fifteenth-century Bishop Wilhelm von Reichenau and Eichstaett was described quite conventionally by his early biographer and encomiast as 'viro omnium virtutum ornatissimo' ('a man most completely ornamented in all the virtues').[20] The entire form of a 'Mirror of Virtue', the *Tugentspiel, oder Kleinodtschatz*, a panegyric written by the Jesuit, Jeremias Drexel (1581–1638), confessor to Archduchess, Elizabeth of Bavaria, and dedicated to her memory, is structured around the image of a mirror, ornamented with jewels, each one of which represented one of the archduchess's virtues and which in their totality form her portrait.[21]

The close connection between literary, visual and *material* forms of exposition of moral lesson and of moral identity is made explicit in Erasmus's instructions on the education of the young Prince, in which he urged the judicious use of images and material objects as well as texts to inculcate awareness of the virtues:

> [T]hey [the virtues] must be fixed in his mind, pressed in, and rammed home. And they must be kept fresh in the memory in all sorts of ways: sometimes in a moral maxim, sometimes in a parable, sometimes by an analogy, sometimes

by a live example, an epigram, or a proverb; they must be carved on rings, painted in pictures, inscribed on prizes, and presented in any other way that a child of his age enjoys, so that they are always before his mind even when he is doing something else.[22]

In his treatises *Upon Christian Marriage* (*Institutio Christiani Matrimonii,* 1526), and *De Pueris Instituendis* (1529), it is in the home where the foundations of belief and of social duty were to be laid.[23] Scripture, read aloud, but also hung on the walls as a gallery of images, would provide the pattern of good conduct that would be impressed upon the soul of the child. The reformist Lyons book publisher, Jean de Tournes, summed up his own convictions about the workings of the image upon the sensibilities of his contemporaries at the beginning of his hugely influential Picture-Bible, the *Quadrins Historiques de la Bible* (1560 edition) where he advised his readers, that:

> ... should you not have the leisure to read and to enjoy the Word as you might wish, you may at least adorn the chambers of your memory with these said images, and more worthily, as we think, than if you covered those same rooms and halls with genre histories ('histoires éthniques'), which are less appropriate to the faithful.[24]

These various didactic materials, whether textual, visual or material, are consistently conceived of as a form of adornment, a moral habitus assumed by the person, or applied to the home, to embellish – and thus to transform – the ordinary, unformed chambers of the heart. For the humanist reformers, ornament – whether actual, as in Erasmus's carved rings and prizes, or metaphorical as in de Tournes' figure of speech – was an active, dynamic principle. It was literally transformative, its aim nothing less than the transformation of human nature.

The concept of the ornamented moral personality is vividly borne out in a didactic woodcut of the early 1540s by the Amsterdam artist, Cornelis Anthonisz, entitled *The Wise Woman and Wise Man* (Figure 2.3). It presents us with a very literal visual exposition of the idea of *ornatus* in order to illustrate the ideal moral economy of the home. Both man and wife are literally hung about with attributes symbolizing a particular virtue appropriate to his or her married state and sex.[25] The attributes of both man and woman, explained in the text, form a compound of both classical and biblical morality that is typical of the humanist literary moral compendia. To each is given the virtues appropriate to his or her gender: to the Wise Woman – chastity, piety, discretion and obedience to her husband (key, mirror, padlocked lips, horse's hooves) – virtues exclusively to do with the *oeconomia* of the home. By contrast, the Wise Man's virtues – temperance, courage, fortitude, faith (set square, helmet, lion's heart, cross) – straddle both spheres of home and the public realm of *politica*. The image reflects quite literally the division of social duties, commonly laid out in the prescriptive literature. Juan Luis Vives, in his widely influential *Institutio Foeminae Christianae* (*The Education of a Christian Woman*) (Antwerp, 1525) expresses it thus:

Figure 2.3 Cornelis Anthonisz, *The Wise Man and the Wise Woman*, *c.*1540, hand-coloured woodcut, 28 × 40 cm, Amsterdam, Rijksprentenkabinet, P-RP-P-1932–127.

[While] the rules of conduct for men are numerous, the moral formation of women can be imparted with very few precepts, since men are occupied both within the home and outside it, in public and in private, and for that reason lengthy volumes are required to explain the norms to be observed in their varied duties. A woman's only care is chastity …[26]

The insistent presence of the Virtues and of Old Testament and Roman exemplars of moral worth, such as Susanna or Lucretia, as the theme of domestic ornament, on the surfaces of utilitarian household ceramic vessels, embossed onto metalwork, as carved decoration upon wooden furniture or painted upon glass, or as part of the entire programme of interior decoration in carving, plasterwork or textiles, demonstrates the centrality of these ethical ideals in framing the way domestic life was lived.[27] They acted as material signifiers of an entire ethical system, embodying the set of moral principles that bound familial relationships by ties of reciprocal duties and expectations. Second, they could act as a visual/material *habitus*, which bodied forth their idea of themselves.

A striking example of this latter usage is a monumental tiled stove, made in *c.*1609 by Ludwig II Pfau of Winterthur for the prominent catholic citizen of Lucerne, Heinrich Pfyffer of Altishofen, and his wife, and still in its original position.[28] Such stoves, monumentally conceived and encyclopaedic in their decorative programmes, became prestige items for patrician families of the alpine regions in the latter part of the sixteenth century. In this case, the dense programme of images includes Old Testament stories, the Evangelists, the Liberal Arts and the Seasons, as well as portraits of the husband and wife, and family coats of arms. Yet the most prominent scenes, placed around the main body of the stove, are images of ancient Roman heroes, notably Manlius Curtius and Marcus Manlius, acting here as exemplary figures of personal bravery, sacrifice and unconditional patriotism. Representations of the Virtues – Justice, Temperance, Charity, Faith and Patience – are interspersed between them and are thus intimately linked with these exemplars of public duty. Pfyffer was a prominent public servant, whose family also held a succession of important political positions within the canton as well as abroad. In the context of these great Roman forebears, with whose example he clearly wished to identify, Pfyffer's choice of these virtues may be understood as political virtues, underlining his own devotion and obedience to the state.

A related political ethos – of good rulership – is to be seen similarly concretized in the dense iconographic programmes of the highly decorated writing cabinets and *Kunstschränke*, which found their place in the *Kunstkammer* and *studioli* of the high nobility in the later sixteenth and early seventeenth centuries. The magnificent 'Hercules' cabinet, today in Kunsthistorisches Museum, Vienna, once almost certainly in the collection of Archduke Ferdinand of Tyrol, is a characteristic example.[29] The manner by which such complex iconographic programmes were intended to be read is conveyed in a surviving description of just such an elaborate writing cabinet in a letter of 5 December 1587, from the Augsburg merchant, Hans Fugger, to Archduke Ferdinand of Tyrol, in which he tried to persuade the Archduke to acquire it.[30] This piece is not known to have survived and it is unclear whether Ferdinand accepted the offer. Fugger describes the surface ornament thus:

> The outer and inner parts are decorated beautifully with great skill, with silver and gilded pictures and histories, in which a *summa* is shown, how, and in what ways princes and lords and all those who almighty God in his divine Wisdom has placed on the highest seats of worldly government shall account piously and worthily both to God and to their subjects here below on earth; or what spiritual and worldly virtues should ornament a regent. And such things are demonstrated not only through the representation of most beautiful and most worthy portraits ['bildern'] and virtues themselves; they are also brought before the eyes through biblical and pagan Roman Histories and exempla, that such things may be experienced in a much livelier and splendid way than can be described in words ...[31]

The broad didactic intent having been established, there follows a description of the iconographic programme that establishes the position of the ruler within the Divine Order. The central door of the inner register was mounted with a gilded plaquette of the Judgement of Solomon, framed by two statues of David and Isaiah and 24 drawers, decorated with reliefs of the Cardinal and Theological Virtues, together with portraits of eight of 'the most praiseworthy Roman emperors from the house of Austria', from Rudolph I to Rudolf II. Placed thus, the Virtues made numinous by their aura of moral authority the line of German emperors they surrounded and formed the link between them and the grand Old Testament figures.[32] Further reliefs of scenes from the Old and New Testaments, the Four World Monarchies and the

Four Seasons, surrounded in turn by the first 12 German Kings, from Tuiscon to Charlemagne and by the 12 months of the year, thus enshrine the Virtues and the Ancient Wisdom they embody as a constant within the various orders of time: eschatological, natural and the march of human history. Finally, the upper register of Fugger's cabinet was ornamented with reliefs depicting Labour overcoming Sloth and Fame and Eternal Glory, 'in order to show', as Fugger insisted, 'that in all affairs, effort, labour and industry must be expended, to ensure eternal praise, honour and fame'.[33] Crowning the piece was a recumbent figure of Geometry, holding up a globe and a pair of compasses, set above the Seven Liberal Arts.

Such a programme would have assumed particular significance within the context of the *Kunstkammer*, set amid the physical attributes of the cosmos, of the natural world, of human history and of human achievement. Such programmatic imagery was conceived of in terms that were as much epideictic as they were didactic. That is to say, while the decorative programme reinforced an Erasmian sense of moral duty and bodied forth a set of ethical ideals by which the princely owner should conduct his affairs, the glittering magnificence of its materials, the virtuosity of its manufacture as well as the metaphysical grandeur of its theme produced an artwork that was celebratory in mode and rhetorical intent, dedicated to praising the owner by reinforcing his divinely ordained place within the cosmic order and ornamenting him, quite literally, with the virtues appropriate to his rule.

Figure 2.4 Anon., *Family of Hans Conrad Bodmer*, Landvogt von Greifensee, 1643, oil on canvas, Zürich, Schweizerisches Landesmuseum, Dep. 3721, on loan from a private collection.

To return finally to the moral *habitus* of the household: in a family portrait of a Bürgermeister of Zürich, Hans Conrad Bodmer, Landvogt von Greifensee, of 1643, attributed to Heinrich Sulzer (Figure 2.4), one sees a conscious representation of a specifically Protestant ideal of the well-tempered home, and in particular how the surrounding furnishings project a particular ethical attitude: the display of wealth in the plate on the buffet to the left signifies the family's social position, but is tempered by a sobriety of setting, dress and mien; the painted glass roundels in the window casings are decorated with biblical scenes; a tablet with written – almost certainly biblical – injunctions hangs on the wall. Above all, in the tiled stove decorations, the family proclaims the ethical mores by which it lives – visible in a scheme that extends beyond the spectator's viewpoint are four of the Cardinal and Theological Virtues: Justice and Prudence topped by Faith and Hope. Yet in choosing specifically to be portrayed during the saying of Grace, in a manner that recalls the prototypical meal of the Last Supper, the family members demonstrate – and memorialize – their collective piety. Their faith in God, the chief virtue of Luther's theology and the foundation of Protestant ethics, is here brought to the fore as the fount and source of the holy household. The painting thus neatly demonstrates the extent to which the vocabulary of ornament was deeply bound up with the aims of a reformist cultural ideal: with the ordination of civility, the control of appetite, the transformation of nature by breeding and piety; even, in a sense, a means of Grace. We see here, too, how figurative ornament formed not just a visual equivalent but a concretization, a physical *habitus* of those ideals and beliefs.

To sum up this section, we have examined how the metaphor of ornament was central to contemporary definitions of human personality; and we have demonstrated how this concept was concretized in the adornment of material objects, mainly domestic, how this process was encouraged by leading reformers, and how, by an examination of a number of decorative programmes, such ornament could be used as an ideal to be followed as well as a projection of values, social, ethical and political, already possessed.

The contrast between the sense of restraint in decoration and behaviour evident in the Bodmer family group and the extravagant opulence of the princely writing cabinets demonstrates the opposite poles of the two decorative traditions that emerged during this period. The former are qualities conventionally identified with Protestantism, and indeed, in its severer manifestations, an absence of ornament came to be a marker of reformed, even dissenting belief. A sophisticated application of the concept of *habitus* to this dimension of English Reformation design is to be found in David Brett's *The Plain Style* (2004).[34] This highly original and wide-ranging study deals with the development of a Protestant and, more specifically, a radical Puritan aesthetic, which had at its heart simplicity, plainness and clarity – a concept of design characterized by its very *lack* of ornamentation. Brett shows how such visual constituents of style were the outward expression of a Puritan ideology, which, he argues, effected profound inner changes to the psychic landscape of British culture. The aesthetic impulse to plainness sprang from theological motives: from the Reformation desire to remove all mediating factors between the individual and God, primarily in the form of the distracting visual richness of church furnishings, regalia and ritual. In its most radical form, this was extended to *all* visual imagery. For John Calvin, even the imagination was 'a factory of idols' that had to be purged of mental images. Brett demonstrates how the Plain Style began with the removal of church decoration and led in time to the development of a distinctive Protestant church architecture, which emphasized clarity and openness of space and lighting to reflect the new inclusiveness of the congregation in the act of worship and the new emphasis on preaching. He goes on to demonstrate how the same principles entered the sphere of Protestant lay domestic design and architecture. Expressed in extreme form in the works of Quakers and other non-conformists, the chief qualities of this Plain Style can be summed up as: a minimal use of ornament, a restrained use of colour, a pleasure taken in fine workmanship, in finely calculated proportions, and in the innate qualities of materials such as brass or wood. The same qualities of plainness and restraint extended as well to dress and to comportment. As Brett put it, Protestant behaviour was designed 'as one designs a house, around an inward principle of proportion which regulates the rest'.[35] Reformed aesthetics were therefore closely bound up with a sense of self.

Brett's thesis is founded on the argument that aesthetic change came about through a relocation of authority, both theological and secular. This, he argues, was the central issue of the Reformation. 'Did [authority] reside in the accumulated teachings of the Church, or in Scripture only? And if in Scripture, by whom was it to be interpreted? By a learned clergy, by the congregation, or by the individual?'[36] Just as a stripped and whitewashed church signified a rejection of the authority of the Catholic hierarchy, so the characteristic sobriety of design, dress and behaviour of communities like the Quakers connoted both separateness from conventional society and a form of common association among themselves. Brett invokes both Pierre Bourdieu's concept of *habitus* and a distinction 'between Gemeinschaft ['community'], that form of community established on the basis of traditions, social customs and beliefs, and its modernising successor, *Gesellschaft* ['society'], which replaces custom by contract, rationality and codified law'.[37] The plainness of garb and the stiffness of address, the refusal to bow or remove one's hat, which characterized the social behaviour of the Quakers, constituted a deliberate refutation of the normal conventions of deference, which in turn implied a rejection of existing social hierarchies and therefore challenged the central principles of political and social authority. The Plain Style, Brett argues, thus became the aesthetic *habitus* of religious dissent, an assertion of *Gemeinschaft* over *Gesellschaft*.[38]

Brett succeeds in giving the visual field a place of central significance within the historical development of Protestantism by relating it to other areas of the same culture and tracing their common intellectual roots. First, the injunction to plainness in design was the result of the same convention of decorum inherited from the classical rhetorical tradition that we have already discussed above. It was an argument that had been invoked by reform-minded churchmen at regular points throughout the Christian Middle Ages to argue against excess of ornament and richness of church architecture and furnishings, but which was argued with particular intensity during the Reformation. The injunction to plainness in manners and matters of design Brett shows to be intimately linked to the injunction by Protestant preachers for plain speaking. He quotes Bishop John Jewel's requirements for the preaching style necessary in the 'reformed minister' of 1548: 'Truth is indeed clear and simple; it has small need of the argument of the tongue or of eloquence. If it is perspicuous and plain, it has enough support in itself. It does not require flowers of artful speech.'[39] Plainness is equated with Truth. Brett follows this trajectory of plain speech from the pulpit on into a long tradition of English intellectual and literary life: to the language of intellectual discourse, noting how the founders of the Royal Society in the mid-seventeenth century elected for the language of artisans over the wits and scholars – that is, for plain speech over the rhetorical conventions of courtly and polite society – and from thence down to Wordsworth and Coleridge in the preface to *Lyrical Ballads* (1798), and on into the present where it 'remains a standard of good usage'.[40] Protestant taste thus in time became an orthodoxy.

Brett's second argument is theological. As he says, 'theological arguments against decoration and visual pleasure are not arguments of taste, but of ontology. They are founded not upon the question "what is fitting?", but upon the prior demand to know "what is real?"'[41] He argues that though the objections to ornament are founded upon the injunctions against imagery found in Mosaic Law, they were developed especially in the platonic tradition of Augustinian theology. 'When Jewel or so many other Puritan divines called for "*plainness and perspicuitie*", by the first term they meant the Attic Virtues [of classical decorum], and by the second they meant that the words of a sermon (and the forms of objects) were to be transparent; thus through the screen of sense we might descry what Wycliff called the *esse intelligibile* of a word or a thing – its prior Intellectual Form of Existence in the Eternal Mind.'[42] The development towards extreme plainness of the English table as a furniture type over the course of the seventeenth and eighteenth centuries, he argues, was not just a matter of a taste for utility and practicality; for a minority of religious Dissenters, such as the Quakers and Mennonites or Shakers in the nineteenth century, the pared-down simplicity of their tables carried a spiritual, platonic significance, which Brett explains in terms of a 'spiral of interaction continuously raising domestic design toward heavenly design ... We rise from the actual table, to its potency in liturgy and thence to its intellectual essence as the eternal and necessary locus of God's encounter with Man.'[43] Brett's achievement is therefore to reveal, through a study of design, the spiritual, theological foundation beneath common ideas about plainness, utility and 'good sense' that run through the fabric of secular English society.

To conclude: the foregoing investigation of ornament has moved from a consideration of the mechanics of style, to ways of investigating its semantic meanings, to its ability as a function of taste to operate as a *habitus* of certain social groups; to its operation as the reification of a system of ethical values; and finally as the *habitus* of Dissent and the wider participation of the visual in the formation of culture. In the process, ornament has been taken from its traditional place within art history (and its unsatisfactory antithetical position vis-à-vis the 'fine arts'), to be understood rather as a potentially important branch of social experience. Yet though this approach to the study of ornament can contribute substantially to cultural, social, intellectual and religious history, it should be stressed that its purpose and methods remain thoroughly art historical – that is to say, its main task is the elucidation of the production, meaning and reception of works of art and craft by a process of careful, inductive examination within a context of contemporary documentation.

Notes

1 For a full discussion of this debate and its consequences for decoration, see David Brett, *Rethinking Decoration. Pleasure and Ideology in the Visual Arts* (Cambridge: Cambridge University Press, 2005), esp. pp. 194–204. Other recent studies that have done much to rehabilitate study of decoration and have addressed its social and ideological dimensions include: E.H. Gombrich, *The Sense of Order: A Study in the Psychology of Decorative Art* (London: Phaidon Press, 1979); Adrian Forty, *Objects of Desire: Design and Society 1750–1980* (London: Thames & Hudson, 1986); Jules Lubbock, *The Tyranny of Taste: The Politics of Architecture and Design in Britain 1550–1960* (New Haven and London: Yale University Press, 1995); and Debra Schafter, *The Order of Ornament, The Structure of Style* (Cambridge: Cambridge University Press, 2003).

2 Heinrich Vogtherr, *Ein Frembdes und wunderbarliches Kunstbuechlin/allen Molern Bildtschnitzern/Goldschmiden/Steynmetzen/waffen/und Messerschmiden hoch nuetzlich zuegebrauchen/Dergleichen vor nie keines gesehen/oder in er Trueck kommen ist* (Strassburg, 1538).

3 '… die hochverstendigen visierlichen Künstler dardurch ermundert unnd ermanet werden/ noch vil hoher und subtiler kunsten,,,an tag zu bringen …', Vogtherr, *Kunstbuchlin*, iir.

4 'Zierlich bekleydet hin und her,
  Als ob sie merbelstaynen wer,
  Mit welsch columnen und capiteln,
  Mit schoen gesimsen und hol-keln.'

Illustrated in Max Geisberg, *The German Single-Leaf Woodcut, 1500–1550*, revised and edited by Walter L. Straus (New York: Hacker Art Books Inc, 1974), vol. 3, p. 787.

5 'Seine Lust aber in taeglicher Arbeit war in weissen Stein zu schneiden das waren aber nichts anders dann Historien den Goldschmidern zum Treiben und Giessen *damit sie ihre Arbeit bekleideten,* geordnet.' *Nachrichten von Kuenstlern und Werckleuten aus dem Jahre 1547, Des Johann Neudörffer Schreib- und Rechenmeisters zu Nuernberg Nachrichten von Kuenstlern und Werkleuten daselbst aus dem Jahre 1547*: nebst der Fortsetzung des Andreas Gulden: nach den Handschriften und mit Anmerkungen; hrg. von G.W.K. Lochner (Quellenschriften fur Kunstgeschichte und Kunsttecknik des Mittelalters und der Renaissance) (Wien: Baumueller, 1875), 10, p. 115.

6 Erasmus of Rotterdam, *The Correspondence of Erasmus: Letters 446 to 593, 1516 to 1517*, edited by R.A.B. Mynors, D.F.S. Thomson and James K. McConica, *Collected Works of Erasmus* (Toronto: Toronto University Press, 1977), vol. 4, 110, no. 480; first published in Erasmus's *Epistolae elegantes*, 1517.

7 George Puttenham, *The Arte of English Poesy. A Critical Edition*, edited by Frank Whigham and Wayne A. Rebhorn (Ithaca and London: Cornell University Press, 2007), p. 222.

8 See David Evett, *Literature and the Visual Arts in Tudor England* (Athens and London: University of Georgia Press, 1990), p. 24.

9 Michael Baxandall, *The Limewood Sculptors of Renaissance Germany* (New Haven and London: Yale University Press, 1980), p. 136.

10 Bernd Roeck, 'Venice and Germany: Commercial Contacts and Intellectual Inspirations', in Bernard Aikema and Beverley Louise Brown (eds), *Renaissance Venice and the North. Crosscurrents in the Time of Bellini, Dürer and Titian* (Rizzoli: New York, 2000), pp. 44–55.

11 The *loci classici* for these views are: Marcel Mauss, 'Les Techniques du corps', *Journal de Psychologie*, 32, 3–4 (1934). Reprinted in Mauss, *Sociologie et anthropologie* (Paris: PUF, 1936); and Pierre Bourdieu, *Outline of a Theory of Practice* (Cambridge: Cambridge University Press, 1977). See also Pierre Bourdieu, *The Field of Cultural Production: Essays on Art and Literature*, edited and introduced by Randal Johnson (Cambridge: Polity Press, 1993), 'Introduction', pp. 1–28, 'The Field of Cultural Production', pp. 29–73.

12 Roeck, 'Venice and Germany', p. 45.

13 Baxandall, *Limewood Sculptors*, pp. 135–42, esp. 136–7.

14 Roeck, 'Venice and Germany', p. 51.

15 Baxandall, *Limewood Sculptures*, p. 150.

16 For references and discussion of this see: Andrew Morrall, *Jörg Breu the Elder. Art, Culture and Belief in Reformation Augsburg* (Aldershot: Ashgate Publishing Ltd, 2002) pp. 234–5.

17 Ibid.

18 The following arguments are taken from my article 'The Reformation of the Virtues in German Art and Decoration', in Tara Hamling and Richard Williams (eds), *Art Reformed? Reassessing the Impact of the Reformation upon the Visual Arts* (Cambridge: Cambridge Scholar Press, 2007), pp. 105–26.

19 *The Booke of wysdome, otherwyse called, the Flower of Vertue: following the authority of ancient doctoures and Philosophers, decyding and speaking of vices and virtues with many goodly examples ... Translated out of Italyon into French and out of French into English by John Larke* (London: Hugh Jackson, 1580), Preface.

20 Jeffrey Chipps Smith, *The Art of the Goldsmith in Late Fifteenth-Century Germany. The Kimbell Virgin and her Bishop*, New Haven: Yale University Press, 2006, p. 49.

21 'Solche seynnd wol als Edelgstain in grossen werh zuhalten/und hoch zuachten.' Preface, Jeremias Drexel, Tugentspiel, oder Keinodtschatz, welchen der welt nach ihrem ableihen hinderlassung ... von Hieremia Drexel der Societes IESU Priester teutsch beschriben 1636 (Munich, 1636).

22 Erasmus of Rotterdam, *The Education of A Christian Prince*, transl. Neil M. Cheshire and Michael J. Heath, ed. Lisa Jardine (Cambridge: Cambridge University Press, 2003), p. 10.

23 William Harrison Woodward, *Desiderius Erasmus concerning the Aim and Method of Education* (New York: Teachers College Columbia University, 1904, reprinted 1964), pp. 154–60, and 180–222 for translation of *De Pueris Instituendi*.

24 *Quadrins Historiques de la Bible* (Lyons: Jean de Tournes, 1560), Preface.

25 F.W.H. Hollstein, *Dutch and Flemish Etchings, Engravings, and Woodcuts ca. 1450–1700* (Amsterdam, 1949–), p. 38; woodcut, 28 x 40 cm. Amsterdam, Rijksprentenkabinet. See Christine Megan Armstrong, *The Moralising Prints of Cornelis Anthonisz* (Princeton: Princeton University Press, 1990), pp. 78–9 and Figure 89 for an exposition and translation of the accompanying text.

26 Juan Luis Vives, *The Education of a Christian Woman, A Sixteenth-century Manual*, ed. and transl. by Charles Fantazzi (Chicago: University of Chicago Press, 2000), p. 47.

27 For ceramic decoration see, for instance, David Gaimster, *German Stoneware 1200–1900* (London: British Museum Publications, 1997), p. 174, cat. no. 10: Siegburg drinking jug with figure of Justice in relief; 183, cat. no. 23: Siegburg stoneware tankard with figure of Charity in relief. Sometimes Virtues could also refer directly to current political events. In the case of the stoneware jug (256, cat. no. 110) by the workshop of Jan Emens, c. 1600, the Virtues are associated with the Revolt of the Netherlands and the advantages of union of all the Netherlandish states under the Habsburgs. The frieze showing Faith, Charity and Justice, flanked by inscriptions 'Salich Yst Landt Dear/Gewelt En Wr-et Lycht Ynden/Bant Yan Emens' ('Happy is the land whose strength and virtue lies in union. Jan Emens') and 'Dis wel gefondert/daer Geloef endey/Lyfden Endey ger/Echeit regeyrt 1586' ('This [land] is well established where

Faith, Charity and Justice rule 1586.'). For plasterwork in England, see Anthony Wells-Cole, *Art and Decoration in Elizabethan and Jacobean England* (New Haven and London: Yale University Press, 1997), pp. 159–68, esp. 166–7; also his account of the decorative programme of Hardwick Hall including the Virtues Hangings, pp. 237–96. For the frequency of the appearance of the Virtues in furniture and carved panelling, see the many examples of German carved furnishings in Heinrich Kreisel, *Die Kunst des deutschen Möbels, erster Band: Von den Anfängen bis zum Hochbarock* (Munich: Verlag C.H. Beck, 1981), Figs 314, 317, 318, 319, 459, 435 and passim.

28 Ludwig II Pfau, *c.*1609 after designs by the glass painter Hans Jegli. Today in the Friedkommisshaus Göldlin von Tiefenau, Lucerne. See Ueli Bellwald, *Winterthurer Kachelofen. Von dem Angang des Handwerks bis zum Niedergang im 18. Jahrhundert* (Bern: Stämpfli & Cie Verlag, 1980), p. 230, no. 5, Figure 12, p. 33, and Figure 29, p. 69.

29 Vienna, Kunsthistorisches Museum, Sig. für Plastik und Kunstgewerbe, inv. no. 883. Illustrated in Dieter Alfter, *Die Geschichte des Augsburger Kabinettschranks*, Schwäbische Geschichtesquellen und Forschungen. Schriftenreihe des historischen Vereins für Schwaben, 15 (Augsburg, 1986), p. 96, cat. No. 9, plates 27 and 28.

30 The letter and description (provided by the goldsmith who made it) is published in the *Jahrbuch der Kunsthistorischen Sammlungen des Allerhöchsten Kaiserhauses*, 14 (1893), p. 212, no. 11205. The description Fugger supplied is entitled thus: 'Beschreibung ains schönen kunstlichen werkh und schreibtisch, so dises ablaufenden 1587 sten jar durch Jonasen Ostertag, burgern und goldschmid zu Augspurg, glücklich absolviert und vollendt worden.' The text is also reproduced in Alfter, *Augsburger Kabinettschrank*, pp. 32–3.

31 Alfter, *Augsburger Kabinettschrank*, p. 33: 'Gemelter schreibtisch steet ob vier schönen silbern und vwergulten bildern, die ine gleichsam tragen darzue inwendig und auswendig mit silberin und vergulden bildern und istorien von tribner arbait schön geziert, in welchem in einer summa angezeigt würdet, wie sich fürnemlich fürsten und herren und alle diejenige, so der allmechtig Gott aus seinem sondern göttlichen rhat zu dem hochen weltlichen regierstand oder oberkeit gesetzt und geordnet hat, baides gegen Gott dem herrn als irm obersten lehenherrn im himmel und dann gegen iren underthonen hieunden uf erden christlich und loblich verhalten sollen oder mit was gaistlichen und weltlichen tugenden ein regent geziert sein soll. Und solches ist nit allein mit den schönsten herrlichsten bildern und tugenten selbst abcontrafeiert sondern auch mit biblischen und haidnischen Römischen historien und exempeln dermassen ad oculum demonstriert, das solches weit lustiger und herrlicher zu sehen ist, als hiervon geschriben werden mag.'

32 Ibid., p. 33: 'als mit welchen obgemelten tugenten höchstgemelte, löbliche Kaiser fuernemlich geziert gewesen'.

33 Ibid., p. 33: 'damit anzuzeigen, das in allen sache[n] mühe, arbeit und fleiss ervordet werde, darauf dann ein ewiges lob, her und rhum erfolge'.

34 See also a summary of the argument of his book in his subsequent book: David Brett, *Rethinking Decoration*, Chapter 5: The Refusal, pp. 184–214.

35 David Brett, *The Plain Style*, embargoed 2nd edn (Lutterworth Press, Cambridge, 2004), p. 105.

36 Ibid., p. 13.

37 Ibid., p. 17.

38 Ibid., Chapter 3.

39 Ibid., p. 53.

40 Ibid., p. 53.

41 Brett, *Rethinking Decoration*, p. 188.

42 Ibid., p. 193.

43 Brett, *Plain Style*, p. 98.

3   Back yards and beyond

Landscapes and history[1]

Marina Moskowitz

Lucy Maynard Salmon (1853–1927) was a professor of history, economics and political science at Vassar College in Poughkeepsie, New York. As the first instructor in these subjects at the women's college, Salmon had considerable latitude to develop her own pioneering ideas about how these disciplines should be undertaken and taught. By the turn of the twentieth century, she was committed to the study of history and politics through the stuff of everyday life – newspapers, laundry lists, household goods, even the view right outside her door. Although Salmon has been 'rediscovered' as an intellectual influence only recently, her writings from the late nineteenth and early twentieth centuries anticipate later trends in social history, the history of domestic life, material culture and cultural landscape studies.[2]

Starting in the late nineteenth century, Salmon found opportunities to travel to Europe, to pursue her own research and to keep abreast of developments in education, and in light of these stimulating adventures, the prospect of summers in Poughkeepsie paled in comparison. But as Salmon became increasingly interested in pursuing historical evidence in new places and in new ways, she realized that overlooked sites close to home could be as fertile ground for research as the great capitals of Europe. Salmon's essay 'History in a Back Yard' shares this revelation:

> … the chance question of a friend put Aladdin's lamp in our hands and opened up before our eyes as large an undiscovered world as could be found in seven kingdoms. She had asked how she could study history in a back yard, and lo, the whole past opened up at our door! Why search for hidden treasure abroad when the history of the world was spread out in the back yard? Perish the thought that we had ever sought knowledge elsewhere – we could study historical records in a garden seat, and search for archaeological remains in the summer house. If Mahomet could not go to the mountain, the mountain could summer in the back yard. The world was still ours to explore![3]

Salmon then takes in turn the different elements of her back yard and those of the neighbours she can see: the size and shape of the yards, the fencing that divides them, the plantings in evidence, garden furniture, electric wires running to the houses, outbuildings, laundry lines, garbage cans, as well as traces of elements no longer in use. In each of these, she sees reflections of past traditions of land use and

Figure 3.1 Lucy Salmon back yard. The back yard of Lucy Maynard Salmon's home in Poughkeepsie, New York, early twentieth century (Lucy Maynard Salmon Collection, Archives and Special Collections, Vassar College, Poughkeepsie, NY).

the layering of this history that has created the present-day view from her back door. Salmon summarizes her more detailed discussion in the following way:

Sanitation is recorded in our garbage can, municipal improvement in our disused cistern, higher standards of living in the garage, education in the sand box, wholesome recreation in the tennis court, love of fresh air in the garden seat, summer migration in the abandoned garden, housing problems in laundry line and pulley, and progress in invention in electric wires. Genealogy is concealed in our flowers and biography in our vines; democracy lifts up its head in the single tax on land and economic research delves into enclosures, while over all broods the spirit of historical investigation.[4]

This essay covers primarily residential or domestic landscapes (with nods to the history of trade relations and industrial circumstances) while a companion piece on Main Street in Poughkeepsie (thinly veiled as 'Apokeepsing') comments on landscapes that reflect the economy and industry of a place.

Salmon's close consideration of her neighbourhood and city centre provides a template for historians seeking to expand their base of sources about particular places, or indeed for anyone who is curious about the environs in which they find themselves, whether at home or while travelling. Salmon encourages her readers to consider the landscape around them in the same ways in which they might consider an artefact, or other historical document, and ask the same questions of it in order to discover its historical import. In essence, the historian is asked to observe as many details as possible, try to gauge the historical sequencing of those details, and interrogate the choices that were made, and who made them, that resulted in the inclusion of anything observed or the exclusion of anything that one might expect to find. In this way, landscape becomes one more form of material culture, albeit one that encompasses other forms, such as architecture, or large-scale technology, or memorial statuary. Although landscape is material culture writ large, a particular place or view can still be considered an artefact of human society, politics, economics and culture.

Many artefacts serve as historical evidence of a lengthy period of time, as their production, acquisition, use and even decay all offer a record of the past. This long-range historical view is a particular facet of landscape study, as any landscape that can be observed today is a composite of myriad decisions and uses of the past. One can take an almost archaeological approach to the phases of development, but in the landscape, different historical traces may be haphazardly combined rather than layered physically on top of one another. The landscape historian Michael Conzen writes,

> Landscape history gives precedence to time as the key element in landscape formation. Each generation has inherited a landscape shaped in certain ways, and has added its own distinguishing traits while modifying or removing others as it is succeeded by the next generation. The aim of the landscape historian, then, is to distinguish the threads woven into this complex, changing fabric and account for their respective appearance, arrangement, and disappearance.[5]

Many historians are most familiar with the study of landscape at designated 'historic sites' – a building, or battlefield, or plantation – that have been preserved from later development by design or chance and are often interpreted as reflective of a particular era or event.[6] But following the words of Salmon and Conzen, all landscapes are historic. Landscapes are dynamic, recording historical change over time, which is why they are so useful to study, but also why it is important to balance the observation and interpretation of an environment with other forms of historical evidence in order to help 'distinguish the threads'.

The spirit of Salmon's writings on the American landscape was renewed by John Brinckerhoff (J.B.) Jackson (1909–1996), the pioneer of what is now called cultural landscape studies, an interdisciplinary pursuit forged by geographers, historians, architects and landscape designers, among others. The founding editor of the journal *Landscape*, started in 1951, Jackson was also a professor of landscape history and environmental design at Harvard University and the University of California at Berkeley. Through his writings and in the classroom, Jackson inspired subsequent generations of landscape historians, geographers, designers and journalists (such as Grady Clay, Paul Groth, John Jakle, Hildegard Binder Johnson, Pierce Lewis, D.W. Meinig, John R. Stilgoe, Yi-Fu Tuan and Wilbur Zelinsky, to name but a few) to observe and interpret the world around them. Although Jackson, his contemporaries and his students drew on a variety of influences, and had a particular affinity for the rich vein of study promoted by British geographers, their academic interest stemmed at least in part from their fascination with the world around them. The modern American landscape, in its sheer scale, variety and the perceived democracy of those who could make a mark upon it, provided endless subjects for observation, speculation and research, and provides the basis for this essay as well. However, as the vastness of the American terrain shows, the approaches and methods employed in cultural landscape study are portable; all of these authors gave primacy to the simple act of looking at, or paying attention to, the landscape, without need for the tools of the archaeologist or surveyor.

Although these authors sought to promote landscape as worthy of study and rich in meaning, they did acknowledge the difficulty of firming up the definition of a term that can be used in a variety of ways with a variety of connotations. Both Meinig and Conzen concede the 'ambiguity' of the term, while Stilgoe calls it 'slippery'.[7] Perhaps some of this ambiguity stems from the very derivation of the word as it is used today, an amalgam of the Dutch *landschap*, the German *landschaft* and the Old English *landskipe*: the first connoted a scene, often in a painting or other framed image; the second referred to a bounded area and the visible physical elements of which it was composed; and the third had a more social meaning, encompassing the community associated with a given place.[8] All three of these meanings inform the way we think about landscape today, and the ways in which we might interpret it. Despite his acknowledgment of its 'slippery' nature, Stilgoe offers perhaps the clearest definition of landscape as it is used by those who study it, writing, 'It means shaped land, land modified for permanent human occupation, for dwelling, agriculture, manufacturing, government, worship, and for pleasure.'[9] Stilgoe defines landscape in terms of the uses to which it is put, but each of these uses corresponds to physical manifestations that were readily observed at some point in history, if not still extant today. Meinig writes of landscape, 'It is important because it is a common word which is increasingly used to encompass an ensemble of ordinary features which constitute an extraordinarily rich exhibit of the course and character of any society.'[10]

Both Stilgoe and Meinig suggest the core belief shared by those seeking to trace a historical record in their surroundings: landscape is a product (or a by-product) of human endeavour. The landscape historian Paul Groth writes, 'Landscape denotes the interaction of people and place: a social group and its spaces, particularly the spaces to which the group belongs and from which its members derive some part of their shared identity and meaning.'[11] It is this incorporation of human influence into the understanding of landscape that distinguishes it and in particular sets it apart from other terms that denote humans' surroundings. In Meinig's terms, landscape 'is related to, but not identical with' a number of other terms such as environment, or region, or area, but in particular it is not synonymous with nature.[12] Conzen writes of the distinction between nature and landscape, 'This is not to say that nature has lost power in shaping the visible pattern of the landscape, even in the modern age; rather, that the human imprint is by this stage so deep that even natural elements, such as forests and rivers, have not remained untouched in their extent and composition by human occupance.'[13] Landscape serves as a historical source because it reveals a record of human contact with the land and because the traces of that contact are often still visible.

Like other forms of material culture, landscape has the potential to broaden the scope of historical enquiry beyond those persons who had the skill and power to leave a written record. Although some landscapes may reveal a singular vision, of a designer or patron, for example, most are touched in some way by a wide variety of human endeavour, encompassing the difference as well as commonality of a particular society over time. Landscape is frequently used as a tool to study ordinary or everyday life; the term *vernacular* is frequently applied to landscape (as well as architecture and other artefacts) to suggest the breadth and commonality of human experience that it reflects. Meinig writes of vernacular landscapes, 'In this sense, landscape study is a companion of that form of social history which seeks to understand the routine lives of ordinary people.'[14]

Part of the 'ambiguous' nature of landscape, and the study of it, is the variety of scales at which it can be considered. Lucy Maynard Salmon suggests a yard, or single house lot, as an object of study, though in fact she also considers the contiguous properties that are encompassed in the view from her back door. These two ideas of landscape, as an entity unto itself and as something essentially created by the human viewpoint, are described by Conzen as the 'dual nature of landscape: as object and subject'.[15] Thus, humans shape landscape not only by leaving traces upon it but by choosing how and by what means it is framed. Salmon's companion essay, 'Main Street', shows another configuration of landscape: a dense, ribbon-like development. Still, as a single house lot might exemplify the landscape of a residential neighbourhood, and Main Street might encompass an urban landscape in its single linear stretch, other authors have addressed these larger contexts, studying particular residential subdivisions or suburbs, villages or cities. Other projects might seek to typify the landscape development of a particular region, and many authors suggest commonalities even at the scale of the nation: the cultural geographer Peirce Lewis writes, 'the culture of any nation is unintentionally reflected in its ordinary vernacular landscape'.[16] Though, of necessity, different scales of landscape can be studied at different degrees of detail, all yield profit for the historian. The choice of the scale of landscape to be studied, and the ways in which that landscape is defined, is linked to the history that it might reveal. Salmon's cluster of back yards instructs its viewer about the history of property law and social relations, while her hometown's Main Street uncovers economic and environmental history.

Salmon set the agenda for a rich vein of literature on American Main Streets. Meinig considers Main Street as one of three symbolic American landscapes (along with the New England village and the California suburb), each encapsulating in physical form a particular cultural ethos of the United States.[17] Meinig discusses these landscapes as typologies, rooted in the American imagination as much as they are rooted on the soil. In this way, the landscape of specific places contributes to a generalized impression of a landscape type, which can in turn influence the development or re-development of other places. For example, the geographer Joseph Woods has drawn on one of Meinig's other examples, the New England village, to show how subsequent generations can idealize and revise the perception of a particular landscape, in this case how the 'typical' New England colonial village – with a group of houses tightly centred around a white clapboard church and town green – was more of a nineteenth-century invention than an eighteenth-century legacy.[18] The link between specific places and the more generalized types of landscapes they seem to exemplify also provides a link between the history of a specific place and a broader regional, cultural, or even national history. If we think about Meinig's examples of three quintessentially American landscapes – the Main Street, the New England village and the California suburb – we can consider how the specific and the type are related. In the first instance, a study of a specific Main Street (whether in Poughkeepsie or Disneyland), or a particular New England town such as Dedham, Massachusetts, or an identifiable suburb such as Glendale, California, would offer clues to local history. But in recognizing the shared elements and organizing principles between these sites and others like them, a broader national history might come to light, perhaps in relation to a specific era, or socioeconomic class, or racial and ethnic group. Looking at, and comparing, landscapes as historic sources allows for elements of both microhistory and broader historical trends.

To call these landscapes 'quintessentially American' is not, however, to call them exceptional – obviously, other countries and cultures maintain central shopping districts, compact villages or disaggregated suburbs. Indeed, the description of a landscape as representative of a unit broader than the actual boundaries of that landscape (e.g. a particular plantation representing the 'Southern landscape' or a particular Midwestern town as 'small town America') requires precision of observation and description, understanding of the historical sequencing of the features observed, and research into the broader political, economic and cultural connotations of those features.

The cultural geographer Mae Theilgaard Watts coined the phrase 'reading the landscape', which is used as metaphorical shorthand for the process of observing and analysing landscape for its historical and cultural import.[19] Geographer Peirce Lewis plays on Watts' phrase in his landmark 1976 essay 'Axioms for Reading the Landscape':

> ordinary landscape seems messy and disorganized, like a book with pages missing, torn, and smudged; a book whose copy has been edited and re-edited by people with illegible handwriting. Like books, landscapes can be read, but unlike books, they were not meant to be read.

Lewis offers advice for interpreting these 'messy' sources, telling his reader to trust that landscape is revealing of a local, regional, and even national culture; that all recognizable parts of a landscape are important to the whole and equally important of study, but need to be considered in context; and that vernacular landscapes are as revealing as formally designed spaces. He suggests a set of questions about landscapes: 'What does it look like? How does it work? Who designed it? Why? When?' Though Lewis is as interested in learning about contemporary society through these questions as he is in investigating the past, he recognizes the inevitable link between past and present in this particular form of material culture. He writes, 'In trying to unravel the meaning of contemporary landscapes and what they have to "say" about us as Americans, history matters.'[20]

One way to approach the study of landscape is to consider it as the sum of a set of parts. Although individual elements of landscape are interrelated, and need to be studied in conversation with one another, they are helpful as a means of observation and analysis; if one can temporarily disaggregate the whole of the landscape, the historical sequence of its features and influences might become more readily apparent. Consider any given landscape in terms of seven attributes: edges, pathways, structures, reserves, geography, economy and community. The first four of these attributes are components, the building blocks that comprise any given landscape; these components often take physical form that is easily observed, or they may be more apparent in certain representations of landscape, as discussed below. The other three attributes are broad influences on landscape development, and are often visible in the overarching patterns and organizing principles of the first four components. When separated into discrete elements, these facets of the landscape may be more or less apparent or significant in different settings, but all are present and give clues about the historical development of a place, scene or view.

Because of the issues of scale discussed above, and the variety of what can be considered the unit under study, perhaps the most important components of a landscape to determine are its edges, whatever boundaries define or describe the area you wish to study. These boundaries can take a variety of forms. A geographical feature – a river or mountain range – may provide the edge of a particular landscape; others may be defined by economic activity – the urban landscape of a central business district is defined by commercial streets; boundaries may be political designations of a place, sometimes contested and negotiated with difficulty. While some, such as the geographical features, may be visible, others, such as property lines, may be fixed in other ways – such as survey lines recorded on paper. People may choose to represent edges of a landscape, whether their own property, or a residential subdivision, or a town, by constructing markers: boundary stones, fences, walls and hedges, for example.

Lucy Maynard Salmon devotes the longest discussion of any element of her back yard to the issue of fencing: the social and cultural meanings of the different types of barriers people construct (or their decisions not to have such barriers), and the political and economic meanings of the divisions represented by these physical markers. 'But after all, wall and fence and hedge are but outward symbols of a crude method of marking private ownership,' Salmon writes, continuing, 'The real boundary lines have been long ago established by the theodolite of the surveyor and they have been recorded in the office of the county clerk in the county court-house.'[21] Thus, though boundaries can often be 'read' on the landscape, in order to make sense of their meaning, it is important to corroborate the observation of the landscape with other forms of research, such as property records.

Jackson also considers boundaries as a defining element of a community's history on a particular landscape, but looks as much at the positive aspect of inclusion *within* boundaries: 'The boundary creates neighbours; it is the symbol of law and order and permanence. The network of boundaries, private as well as public, transforms an amorphous environment into a human landscape, and nothing more clearly shows some of the cherished values of a group ...'.[22] Jackson's words show the ways in which boundaries are used to derive identity from shared landscapes. This sense of identity may be local, but it can be felt at a regional or national level as well, as boundaries between broader areas are traversed. These divisions may be geographical markers, as for example the Appalachian Mountains provided a clear edge to the Eastern seaboard during the early nineteenth century or the Mississippi River loosely divides the United States today. Or they may be symbolic lines negotiated on a map, such as the Mason-Dixon line, which was originally surveyed in the 1760s in an attempt to settle colonial border disputes. The line fixed the boundaries of Pennsylvania, Delaware, Maryland and Virginia (now West Virginia) but over time became just as significant as a symbolic boundary between the North and South.

The idea of crossing boundaries into other properties, or other regions, raises the question of how people navigate through landscapes. The pathways that develop or are constructed show the patterns of circulation deemed important to those who establish or use any given landscape. In their most recent form, these pathways may be forged by transportation technology as physical markers upon the landscape – railroad tracks, canals or streets are obvious examples. Pathways may also be routes that are well known within a community: combinations of these more visible elements. (These routes also may be purposely obscured, such as the symbolic Underground Railroad, a route between safe houses through which Southern slaves could be led by abolitionists from plantations to free states or to Canada.) Recent historical manifestations of pathways may replicate earlier forms – a Native American path might have spawned an early road, which was then paved, and later widened, to become a major thoroughfare.

Pathways have a particular relationship to edges in showing how different scales of landscape interrelate – the edges of one landscape might be a pathway through a larger one, and vice versa. Railroad tracks might be a pathway through a larger metropolitan region – linking city and suburb, or an even larger region, such as the Eastern seaboard. But a phrase such as 'the wrong side of the tracks' suggests that railroad tracks going through a city might become an 'edge' or boundary between two neighbourhoods – in this case a value judgement is attached to the different sides of that edge.[23] In urban areas, regional ring roads might act as the boundary between urban and suburban areas, dividing not just space but culture. In and around Washington, DC, the physical manifestation of the Capital Beltway creates a border around the inner city that is translated into a parlance of political and cultural status as 'inside the Beltway' or 'outside the Beltway'. (While the first suggests ties to the current status quo in the federal government and its attendant media and the latter an outsider or even maverick status, the connotation of the two phrases depends on who is using them.)

Even when considering a fixed scale of landscape, pathways can take on other meanings beyond a way to traverse space. Pathways carry not just people and goods, but other services; in the industrial era, many pathways gained stability as defining features of landscapes rather than simply means of traversing them. J.B. Jackson writes:

> the street itself began to assume a new role: the practices of placing utilities under the street pavement – water, gas, sewerage, light, and eventually telephone lines – gave the street a permanence which it had never previously had, so that it became more important than the property on both sides ... the road, or street or highway became the armature, the framework of the landscape.[24]

The endurance of the American Main Street as a part of not only the national landscape, but also the historiography of the national landscape, shows the way in which the pathways may become important landmarks in their own right.

Perhaps the most apparent elements of landscape are the structures that are built upon it, showing the ways that people inhabit a space. Architecture and engineering are the backbone of these constructions, resulting in all manner of buildings – houses, churches, schools, libraries, barracks, barns, factories, courthouses – but they can also be other markers on the land, such as monuments, gravestones, bridges or utilities. Structures are important in their very visibility – they are seen by many more people than those who might use them. A family of four might live in one dwelling house, but depending on the location of that house, hundreds, or even thousands, of people a day might see it. Structures are often useful, providing shelter, livelihood or amusement, but the style and symbolism of their construction might be as important to a landscape on which they are placed as that intended use. For example, citizens of the Federal-era United States wanting to assert the importance of their young republic drew on the neoclassical style of architecture for institutions and monuments, referencing democratic ideals and republican structures in built form.

Structures can provide focal points and order but they can also be thought to mar a landscape, when they are considered out of character in comparison with surrounding components. Landscapes might grow up around particular structures, or vice versa, so the historical fixing of this component in relation to others around it can be helpful in tracing development. The sequence of types of structures may also show changing community priorities over time, or shifting economic development. The diffusion of a structure type or style may also be traced in spatial, as well as historical, terms, using this element of the landscape as a key to migration patterns. Local traditions of building and ornament might fuse into national styles. The development of balloon-frame housing in the 1830s, with a strong but lightweight wooden frame usually constructed of pre-cut two-by-four-inch lumber, developed to address the housing needs of a population moving westwards across the expanding United States; though this form of construction was adaptable to any type of ornament, in practice, pattern books and common practice encouraged replication. The landscape historian John Stilgoe writes, 'Common builders replicated squares, arches, and diamond-shaped trusses until they spanned chasms and rivers, accepting a standardization of building unknown to earlier generations of Americans.'[25]

As with other elements of the landscape, Lewis' 'axiom' of the importance of 'common' or vernacular elements of the landscape pertains to structures. Writing in 1976, Lewis wrote of the difficulty of finding 'intelligent writing which is neither polemical nor self-consciously cute on such subjects as mobile homes, motels, gas stations, shopping centers, billboards, suburban tract housing', and other forms. However, a subsequent generation of landscape historians has taken up Lewis' challenge, addressing exactly these topics, such as John Jakle and Keith Sculle on gas stations, Catherine Gudis on billboards, and Pamela Simpson on mass-produced architectural materials, to name but a few.[26] When considering architecture as a component of landscape, as opposed to a discrete form of material culture (as other essays in this volume do) it is important to retain a sense of context: the placement of the structure in relation to others, the patterns of similar and different structures within a landscape, and the relationship of structures to other landscape attributes.

While pathways and structures 'fill' the landscape, it is also important to consider the spaces in between, the reserves of land that are not built upon. These reserves, or open spaces, may in fact be 'constructed' – a public park, for example. Central Park in New York City, planned in the 1850s by Frederick Law Olmsted and Calvert Vaux, is well known as the first landscaped public park in the United States, providing a much-loved reserve in the centre of the most populous city in the country. But this 'reserve' of over 800 acres in the landscape of New York City is also a landscape unto itself, with carefully constructed pathways, regulating the passage of pedestrians and other forms of traffic, and a variety of structures. Central Park could also be said to form a boundary between the east and west sides of Manhattan, again showing the ways in which features of the landscape intertwine.[27]

The placement of reserves on any given landscape might be haphazard, such as building lots that have not (yet) been sold; or regulated, such as the space between houses as mandated by building codes that state what percentage of a building plot the footprint of a building may occupy; or it might be intentional, such as a wildlife preserve. The scale of these interstitial spaces as a proportion of a given landscape may be revealing of a community's values or priorities, and may change over time. In the wake of the building of Central Park, landscape design and comprehensive urban and regional planning grew in professional stature in the United States at the turn of the twentieth century, corresponding with other reforms of the Progressive Era. Planners incorporated parks, playgrounds, and leafy parkways and boulevards into their plans, as they sought literally to 're-form' the urban landscapes that had been industrialized in the nineteenth century. Although not all reserves are consciously constructed or even placed, they are still an important consideration to the overall impression of a landscape as it is inhabited, and as it is studied.

Taken together, these four components of edges, pathways, structures and reserves reveal how landscape is developed and ordered. These markers correspond to what J.B. Jackson considers to be the distinction between landscape history and 'conventional' history, which he suggests is largely about the establishment of institutions. He writes:

> But the student of landscape has another interest: how space is organized by the community. This means the drawing of a boundary, the efficient dividing up of the land among the several families, the providing of roads and a place of public assembly, and the setting aside of land for communal use.[28]

The physical and sometimes symbolic components of edges, pathways, structures and reserves are perhaps most easily 'read' in the landscape; their placement, patterns and interrelations begin to reveal the broader influences of geography, economy and community.

Even with a shared understanding of landscape as a human construction, one must consider the 'blank slate' on which that development occurs. When studying modern history, that blank slate will rarely have been untouched before but the traces of previous human activity may be erased, obscured or sometimes consciously ignored (as indeed were many traces of Native American use of the North American landscape at the time of European settlement). This first influence on a landscape – the pre-existing condition of the land on which it is shaped – can be termed its geography. This term encompasses a number of features such as topography, soil condition, water sources and climate, any of the starting points that humans must consider and negotiate. As Conzen suggests above, these conditions cannot be considered strictly as 'nature' because, over time, these elements may reveal manipulation by historical actors: rivers can be filled in, water can be diverted, soil can be moved, and climate, as the twenty-first-century historian knows well, can change as a result of human activity. Nonetheless, the way one historical era chooses to use, alter, manipulate, preserve or indeed ignore the geographical features of the land is revealing of its values and priorities.

The economic system that underpins a particular community is often reflected in the landscape that community inhabits. At its most obvious, the economy may be 'found' in visible agricultural fields, or the structures of a factory or oilrig, or trucks on a regional highway. The geography of a landscape may determine its economic history, at least at the point of settlement of a particular community: a good harbour might spawn shipping and trade; the topography might reveal natural resources such as oil or mineral ores; a river valley with productive soil might lead to farming. Still, economic markers on the landscape do not need to be sites of production: a giant supermarket on an ex-urban highway suggests a community buying in its food supply and earning the money to do so elsewhere. The landscape may also reveal patterns of economic status, for example through housing types. Landscape may indicate not only what the economic system is, or was, but to what degree it is thriving.

Landscapes also reflect the communities that established and continue to inhabit them. While the core assumption of landscape studies is that human influence is present in the landscape and therefore landscapes may be used as historical evidence, the idea of community as an attribute of landscape refers to specific social, cultural or political circumstances or beliefs that may result in specific patterns of land use or arrangement of other features of the landscape. For example, in the early twentieth century, starting with New York City in 1916, numerous cities and towns across the United States implemented zoning codes, which allowed for different uses of the land to be confined to different zones, creating a distinctive American urban landscape that, generally speaking, separates residential, commercial and industrial regions of any given place. These zoning codes exemplified in built form a core industrial-era impulse towards the separation of functions, applying industrial management concepts to the space of the city. Zoning codes also betrayed a new emphasis on the nuclear family as the core unit of society, enshrined in zones of single-family houses deemed the 'highest and best' use of land, with no other building type allowed in the zone beyond schools, churches, libraries and other institutions classified as supportive of family life.[29]

One of the most enduring examples of the impact of the influences of economy and community on the American landscape is the rectangular grid of agricultural fields that one sees particularly well in the Midwest, and differs from traditional agricultural land use in many other countries. These seemingly endless array of rectilinear fields, particularly apparent from the air, but also experienced from the many straight roads that run between them, are the vestiges of the United States National Survey, first established in the Land Ordinance of 1785, and maintained and refined in a series of land policies stretching to the American Civil War (1861–1865). The Ordinance stipulated that the United States should be surveyed on a regular rectangular grid; the land would be divided into square townships six miles long per side, each further divided into 36 sections of one square mile. These sections were to be sold off in an alternating pattern of whole and subdivided sections, providing different-sized properties for different needs and purses; in each township, the proceeds from the sale of Section 16 would be used to fund public education, encouraging civic responsibility in new communities. Although by the time the Survey was implemented, the Eastern seaboard of the United States was already considerably settled, the landmass of the United States more than doubled after the Louisiana Purchase of 1803, in which the United States acquired vast

Figure 3.2 Photographic postcard showing aerial view of Winona, Kansas, *c*.1930. The left
side of the image demonstrates how the town developed within the grid of the
United States National Survey, and the right shows how the railroad line and
Highway US-40 serve as boundaries for the town. © SS. Collection of the author.

tracts of the North American terrain from France. Over time almost 80 per cent of
the land in the 48 continental states was charted by the US Survey Grid. Later land
policies refined the ways in which land was distributed, over time allowing for
smaller land parcels to be sold at lower prices; in 1832, a provision to sell 40-acre
plots (representing one-sixteenth of an original section) resulted in the common
size of family farms in the United States, and finally the Homestead Act of 1862
allowed these farms to be basically given away, with a small administrative fee and
a promise to improve the land.[30]

The gridded landscape of family farms was of course an idealized vision; though
in some places this vision was achieved, in others the squares struggled for a
foothold on mountainous terrain, while in still other places large portions of townships were bought by the railroads or other corporations. Still, the land use pattern
is common enough to suggest the influences of geography, economy and community on the American landscape. If the US National Survey appeared to turn a
blind eye to geography, relentlessly setting down squares on land regardless of
topography or terrain as if to master them, it did at least address the vastness of the
North American continent, a sheer expanse of land that required organization in
order to manage. The Grid also speaks to at least one form of the American economy, encapsulating an agrarian vision of individual farms organized into small

communities, even as parallel developments in mechanization and industrialization suggested other forms of more concentrated landscape development. Finally, the gridded landscape reveals the culture and politics of the community that developed it, showing even in the contemporary landscape the spirit of the age in which the survey lines were drawn. The cultural geographer Hildegard Binder Johnson, who has produced some of the most cogent work about the cultural importance of the US Survey, sees it as reflective of the 'Cartesian *esprit geometrique* during the century of the Enlightenment'.[31] Just as Enlightenment thought was incorporated into early American political culture, what J.B. Jackson called its 'rationalist' spirit was also applied to the landscape. At the same time, Jackson sees the small-scale community structure imposed by the Grid as also reflective of the religious revivals of the Second Great Awakening, the evangelical impulse that swept the United States in the late eighteenth and early nineteenth centuries.[32] Thus, these varied influences, from the scale of landmass to the attempt to instil a dominant economic system to intellectual and religious beliefs, worked together to create one of the most enduring landscapes in the United States.

The example of the United States National Survey Grid and its permanent influence on the American landscape raises an issue about the ways in which landscape serves as a historical source. As Jackson noted, one of the oldest influences on the American landscape (in the most official sense of stemming from federal policy of the United States government) became readily apparent to many citizens only after the introduction of commercial air travel in the mid-twentieth century.[33] At its most accessible, as Lucy Maynard Salmon discovered, landscape may be viewed from the privacy of one's own home, revealing historical evidence of an area bounded by the historian's view. In order to study broader patterns or larger areas, one needs more complex vantage points, such as Jackson's aerial view.

But what if a given landscape – a specific place or typology – is not easily accessible for the individual who wishes to study it, whether because they are geographically removed from it, or because it is no longer extant in the form they wish to study? Even if a landscape is physically accessible, how does a historian 'take notes' about this form of historical source? Landscape may present a particular challenge in the realm of material culture studies in that it is often difficult to study 'first hand' and yet it is necessary to study in its totality – the sum of the seven attributes discussed above – and in context. While landscape itself is a historical source, there are also numerous sources that represent landscape and make it more accessible to the historian who is otherwise at a distance: maps, atlases, landscape paintings, aerial photographs and written travel guides are among the most obvious sources that record the cultural landscape, and these sources, both historical and contemporary, are increasingly accessible in the era of digital communication. (One can only imagine what J.B. Jackson would have thought about software programs and websites such as Google Earth or Live Maps, which offer the experience of 'flying over' the American Midwest to chart the endurance of the US Survey Grid while sitting in front of a computer half a world away.) These representations broaden the horizon of possible landscapes to interpret, but they also offer the opportunity for greater depth of analysis. Even if one is able to view a place with one's own eyes at close range, comparing the present-day view to historical images, especially a series of historical images, allows the historian to learn the sequence of particular components of that landscape, and make sense of its historical development. As Meinig writes, 'By classifying features according to age, the landscape can be visualized in terms of layers of history, which are sometimes rather distinctly separated in area ... but more often complexly interwoven.'[34]

Just as landscapes range on a spectrum from vernacular and organically developed to formal and planned, the images that represent them vary broadly in their style, substance and purpose. Maps can be anything from hand-drawn sketches showing someone how to get from one place to another; to printed road atlases privileging pathways as the most important features of the landscape; to the wonderful panoramic maps, or bird's eye views, of late nineteenth- and early twentieth-century American towns, which proudly highlight the structures and natural resources deemed most important to a given place; to the colour-coded maps of urban properties produced for the Sanborn fire insurance company, also in the late nineteenth and twentieth centuries, which have proven invaluable to American urban historians; to an interactive electronic map that allows viewers all over the world to add designations for their homes, schools, favourite restaurants and shops, and other increasingly quirky information.

All these are rich sources, as long as the historian considers the circumstances of their production, just as one would evaluate any historical evidence. Who produced the map and for what purpose? What technology was used and to what purpose? Who was the intended audience? How was it disseminated?[35] Some forms of representation may 'seem' more accurate than others – for example, the rigid structure of a printed map may have a more authoritative aura than a painting in which one might more readily imagine the 'artistic licence' involved. However, all representations should be mined for their historical importance and cultural bias. The simple exercise of asking a number of people to each draw quick maps of a shared environment – their neighbourhood or a university campus, for example – will yield a variety of orientations, scales, precedence of some landscape attributes over others, and show how representations of even highly familiar places are subjective. They are nonetheless valuable, as long as one takes the time to analyse the source, as well as the landscape that it represents. Although landscape development is an inherently visual endeavour, the representations that capture it do not need to be graphic ones. Textual evidence, ranging from tourist guide descriptions to property records to novels (Sinclair Lewis' 1920 novel *Main Street* would be excellent company for Salmon's essay of the same title) works in concert with visual sources; the geographer Deryck Holdsworth cautions that landscape historians should always balance the landscape and the archive as sources of their enquiry, and never rely solely on observation of a present-day landscape, as much as it may show numerous traces of the past.[36] Gathering a portfolio of different types of representations of a given landscape, especially over a period of time, should yield answers to the historical questions we may hold about a particular site or landscape typology, and will amplify whatever detail can be observed first hand.

As noted above, there are a host of obvious sources to which one might turn as evidence for the historical development of landscapes; atlases or landscape paintings foreground the subject of particular or idealized scenes, views or places. However, as the activities of daily life are set into a landscape, landscape might also appear as the 'background' of other types of representation. An eighteenth-century portrait with the sitter's plantation or mercantile interests spied through a window in the background might offer as many historical clues as an image more squarely focused on those same properties. A film shot on location in a particular city, using the streets and buildings as backdrop to a complex plot, might reveal as much to the landscape historian as a documentary about the same place. These less self-conscious portrayals of places or views are helpful additions to a set of representations because they may show the landscape in its dynamic form, in use by humans, rather than as a static object. The background of a historical document might become the foreground of a study of landscape history.

The dynamic nature of landscape development means that new features, patterns and uses are constantly being added to or replacing those that have come before; each generation, and even many individuals within each generation, leaves a trace of some sort, and so the historian's task in learning history from the landscape is complex. At the same time, it is an exceptionally fertile ground for study. As D.W. Meinig writes:

> Every landscape is an accumulation. The past endures; the imprint of distant forebears in survey lines, land parcels, political jurisdictions, and routeways may form a relatively rigid matrix even in areas of rapid change. The landscape is an enormously rich store of data about the peoples and societies which have created it ...[37]

In order to uncover this 'rich store of data' any given landscape chosen as the subject of study may be disaggregated into its component features and dominant influences in order to observe their historical sequences; in this way landscapes reveal historical narratives. Just as with other forms of material culture, the use of landscape as historical evidence takes practice, and needs to be balanced with other types of sources in order to garner its rewards. Though the study of landscape is often linked to the field of geography as a spatial discipline, landscape is also invaluable as a dynamic example of change over time, the core subject of any historical enquiry.

Notes

1 I would like to acknowledge the immeasurable influence of my friend and colleague Amy Hufnagel. The consideration of landscape as the sum of the seven attributes, discussed in the latter half of this essay, was originally developed in a wonderful collaboration with Amy that resulted in an exhibition on the cultural landscape of southern Maine at the Old York Historical Society, York, Maine, in 1991; I have continued to work with these ideas in my subsequent research and teaching in American landscape history. While I wish to share any credit for the intellectual underpinnings of this essay with her,

any flaws or mysteries in its expression remain my own.

2　Lucy Maynard Salmon, *History and the Texture of Modern Life: Selected Essays*, Nicholas Adams and Bonnie G. Smith (eds) (Philadelphia: University of Pennsylvania Press, 2001). This recent reprinting of some of Salmon's essays and curricular plans is a great boon to historians of material culture and landscape, as well as other topics; for additional details of Salmon's biography and a helpful overview of her career, see Adams and Smith, 'Introduction: Lucy Maynard Salmon and the Texture of Modern Life', in *idem, History and the Texture of Modern Life*, pp. 1–26.

3　Lucy Maynard Salmon, 'History in a Back Yard', in *History and the Texture of Modern Life*, pp. 76–84; quotation, p. 76.

4　Salmon, 'Back Yard', p. 83.

5　Michael P. Conzen (ed.), *The Making of the American Landscape* (Boston: Unwin Hyman, 1990), p. 5.

6　The geographer David Lowenthal is particularly helpful on the meanings of preserved or 'heritage' sites; see, for example, David Lowenthal, *The Past is a Foreign Country* (Cambridge: Cambridge University Press, 1985).

7　D.W. Meinig, 'Introduction', in Meinig (ed.), *The Interpretation of Ordinary Landscapes: Geographical Essays* (New York: Oxford University Press, 1979), p. 1; Conzen, *Making of the American Landscape*, p. 1; John R. Stilgoe, *The Common Landscape of America, 1580–1845* (New Haven: Yale University Press, 1982), p. 3.

8　Paul Groth and Chris Wilson, 'The Polyphony of Cultural Landscape Study: An Introduction', in Wilson and Groth (eds), *Everyday America: Cultural Landscape Studies after J.B. Jackson* (Berkeley: University of California Press, 2003), pp. 2–3. John Stilgoe also considers past meanings of the word *landscape*, with particular emphasis on the German *landschaft* in *Common Landscape of America*.

9　Stilgoe, *Common Landscape of America*, p. 3.

10　Meinig, 'Introduction', p. 2.

11　Paul Groth, 'Frameworks for Cultural Landscape Study', in Paul Groth and Todd W. Bressi (eds), *Understanding Ordinary Landscapes* (New Haven: Yale University Press, 1997), pp. 1–21, quotation, p. 1. It is also worth noting that Groth and Bressi have compiled an extraordinarily useful bibliography for cultural landscape studies as part of their editing of *Understanding Ordinary Landscapes*.

12　Meinig, 'Introduction', pp. 2–3.

13　Conzen (ed.), *Making of American Landscape*, p. 2. Some theorists argue that in fact nature itself is a human construction, in that it exists only as it is defined by humans, in contrast to other forms of development; for a helpful overview of this argument, see Alexander Wilson, *The Culture of Nature: North American Landscape from Disney to the Exxon Valdez* (Toronto: Between the Lines, 1991).

14　Meinig, 'Introduction', p. 6.

15　Conzen (ed.), *Making of American Landscape*, p. 2.

16　Peirce F. Lewis, 'Axioms for Reading the Landscape: Some Guides to the American Scene', in Meinig (ed.), *The Interpretation of Ordinary Landscapes*, p. 15.

17　D.W. Meinig, 'Symbolic Landscapes: Some Idealizations of American Communities', in Meinig (ed.), *The Interpretation of Ordinary Landscapes*, pp. 164–92. For further literature on the American Main Street, see Alison Isenberg, *Downtown America: A History of the Place and the People Who Made It* (Chicago: University of Chicago Press, 2004); Chester H. Liebs, *Main Street to Miracle Mile: American Roadside Architecture* (Baltimore: Johns Hopkins University Press, 1995); Richard Longstreth, *The Buildings of Main Street: A Guide to American Commercial Architecture* (Washington: Preservation Press, 1987).

18　Joseph Wood, *The New England Village* (Baltimore: Johns Hopkins University Press, 1997).

19　Mae Theilgaard Watts, *Reading the Landscape: An Adventure in Ecology* (New York: Macmillan, 1957).

20   Lewis, 'Axioms', pp. 11–32; quotations, p. 12, 26, 22.
21   Salmon, 'Back Yard', p. 78.
22   Jackson, 'Conclusion', p. 116.
23   John R. Stilgoe, *Metropolitan Corridor: Railroads and the American Scene* (New Haven: Yale University Press, 1985).
24   J.B. Jackson, 'By Way of Conclusion: How to Study a Landscape', in *The Necessity for Ruins, and Other Topics* (Amherst: University of Massachusetts Press, 1980), p. 123.
25   Stilgoe, *Common Landscape*, p. 133. See also Fred Peterson, *Homes in the Heartland: Balloon Frame Farmhouses of the Upper Midwest* (Minneapolis: University of Minnesota Press, 2008).
26   Lewis, 'Axioms', p. 19. See, e.g., John Jakle and Keith Sculle, *The Gas Station in America* (Baltimore: Johns Hopkins University Press, 1994); Catherine Gudis, *Buyways: Billboards, Automobiles, and the American Landscape* (New York: Routledge, 2004); Pamela H. Simpson, *Cheap, Quick, and Easy: Imitative Architectural Materials, 1870–1930* (Knoxville: University of Tennessee Press, 1999). Work on these and many other subjects has been nurtured by the Vernacular Architecture Forum, founded in 1980.
27   Roy Rozenzweig and Elizabeth Blackmar, *The Park and the People: A History of Central Park* (Ithaca: Cornell University Press, 1992).
28   Jackson, 'Conclusion', p. 114.
29   I have written in more detail about zoning, its physical form and cultural influence, in Marina Moskowitz, *Standard of Living: The Measure of the Middle Class in Modern America* (Baltimore: Johns Hopkins University Press, 2004).
30   Although many historians and geographers have commented on the United States National Survey, the writing of Hildegard Binder Johnson remains the classic work on the subject. Hildegard Binder Johnson, *Order Upon the Land: The US Rectangular Land Survey in the Upper Mississippi Country* (New York: Oxford University Press, 1976).
31   Hildegard Binder Johnson, 'Towards a National Landscape', in Conzen (ed.), *Making of American Landscape*, pp. 127–45.
32   J.B. Jackson, 'The Order of a Landscape: Reason and Religion in Newtonian America', in Meinig (ed.), *The Interpretation of Ordinary Landscapes*, pp. 153–63.
33   Ibid., pp. 158–60.
34   D.W. Meinig, 'The Beholding Eye: Ten Versions of the Same Scene', in Meinig (ed.), *The Interpretation of Ordinary Landscapes*, pp. 33–48, quotation, p. 43.
35   Questions such as these are useful for the interpretation of any cultural documents; my thanks to Jean-Christophe Agnew, Cathy Gudis and Elspeth Brown for contributing to the evolving list of queries I use in both research and teaching.
36   S. Lewis, *Main Street* (New York: Harcourt, Brace & Company, 1920); D.W. Holdsworth, 'Landscape and Archives as Text', in Groth and Bressi (eds), *Understanding Ordinary Landscapes*, pp. 44–55.
37   Meinig, 'Beholding Eye', p. 44.

4 Draping the body and dressing the home

The material culture of textiles and clothes in the Atlantic world, *c*.1500–1800

Beverly Lemire

Why examine chintz bedding as evidence of global trade? Why consider a weaver's loom or a petticoat when analysing social practice? What evidence can be teased out from common artefacts as indicators of past societies? These questions, and many others, have shaped new scholarship over recent decades and made respectable the use of material objects in historical analysis. Anthropologists, archaeologists and museum curators have long employed artefacts in their work, but the questions they posed were often different from those debated by historians. Art historians always engaged with objects of different sorts.[1] But with those exceptions, historians typically privileged written records above all else as sources of information and inspiration. Two major trajectories of historical enquiry led to the merger of object study and history: the first was the intense examination of consumer practices and the changing material environment. Many studies depended on probate inventories in the early modern era, listing the goods of the deceased and, almost inevitably, some researchers turned to objects to augment their understanding. The second dynamic force was women's history.[2] Historians of women's work and women's worlds brought a new perspective to the study of daily life, particularly the creation and uses of textiles; in combination with cultural studies, researchers in these fields incorporated new perspectives in the reading of historical objects.

This chapter will explore the methodologies and historical findings arising from the commonest of material forms in the Atlantic world: textiles and clothing. A study of these goods illuminates the major structures of daily life and charts their changes. From the early modern to the dawn of the modern times, textiles for home or personal apparel represented the most important investments for the majority of the population. These goods were also imbued with complex economic and cultural meanings. Interactions between societies, East and West, as well as the evolving colonial projects in the Americas, can be discerned through the trade, use and evolution of materials, as well as through the needlework that constructed everyday items. In this way, baskets, petticoats and curtains open new vistas on the past.

Bringing sense to global trade

As sensate beings we respond to touch, sight, taste and smell. Our responses are of course shaped by the norms of our society, as moulded by our age, experience, ethnicity and our sex. Recognizing the importance of the sensory in past societies has opened up a plethora of new research from the social history of smell, to the historical genesis of comfort in the long eighteenth century.[3] As students of history we attain a clearer vision of the past through critical interpretations of the common goods made, owned and used in past societies. Objects defined and expressed priorities for historical actors with meanings we can attempt to recover with careful attention and a receptive eye that engages both written evidence and material forms. In the great movements of history we must also be aware of the changing material accessories that embellish and accompanied past lives; these offer different perspectives on processes of change.

Profound forces reshaped early modern Europe, among which was an expansion in global trade that brought diverse cargoes to these shores in volumes never previously equalled. Asia provided stunning new additions to the world of goods known and understood by Europeans. In 1500, scarcity and the threat of scarcity defined Europe's physical environment, a constant feature of life for ordinary and even middle-ranked people. Keith Wrightson describes the flow of resources for English families about 1500 as providing 'for most people a fairly bare living'.[4] Within this economy, commodities of all sorts were carefully husbanded, while reuse and recycling were normal strategies deployed to eke out every element of value from the goods at hand. These sensible imperatives defined everyday practice among virtually all households, regardless of social rank. The shadow of dearth persisted stubbornly, retreating slowly over the next three centuries, with some regions more affected than others, even as the balance began to swing towards greater abundance. In more and more regions of Europe the environment was transfigured as a result of new commercial structures as well as new agricultural and industrial initiatives. The market was already a significant factor in 1500, whether local or international, and would bode larger and larger in people's lives, whether rural or urban. The new system of global trade marked a qualitative break with all past European experience, as with each generation larger quantities of Asian merchandise restructured concepts of material life in the West and added a new dynamism to Europe's economy and society. Indian cottons exemplify this transformation, exceptional fabrics that had no equivalents among existing European textiles. Consider the bed curtain shown in Figure 4.1. Painted and printed in colourfast, washable dyes, one of an infinite range of qualities, weights and prices, Indian cottons realigned the consumer markets in Europe and its growing colonies.

The initial area of life affected was the home. As the first European agents in India, the Portuguese and then the Spanish incorporated Indian textiles in their furnishings most readily; and, from them, the style spread to other regions, along with knowledge of the new trade goods. The flow was buoyed by the power of Iberian political and aesthetic authority in the sixteenth century, illustrated in the 1568 inventory of the Dutch Stadholder, which included items such as 'Couvertures d'Espaigne', suggesting the Iberian fashion for Indian quilts.[5] The port of Southampton in southern England absorbed these influences sooner than most areas of England outside London. Among Southampton's prosperous commercial classes, Indian calicoes joined other decorative exotics by the mid-sixteenth

Figure 4.1 Bed curtain, *c*.1700, painted, dyed cotton (chintz), Coromandel Coast, India, for European market. IS. 121–1950. Courtesy of Victoria and Albert Museum, London.

century, like 'Turkye carpet', 'Venes [Venice] carpet', 'a great Loking glasse', as well as tapestry of various sorts – the Netherlands as well as other commercial centres of Europe were similarly affected. The calico cushions, cupboard cloth, coverlets, curtains and the like that appear in Southampton probate inventories in the 1550s speak to the attraction of goods associated with this dynamic foreign trade, as well as the vaunted erudition of the purchaser in touch with Asia, if only by association.[6] Public rooms occasionally displayed calico cushions or table carpets. But the commonest venue where these textiles were showcased was the bedroom. Several processes were becoming intertwined. First, there was a growing differentiation of space-specific household activities, thus sleeping became increasingly associated with separate bedrooms, as opposed to a multi-purpose living space that included a couch or bed. In the wealthier regions of southern England and northwest continental Europe records show a greater number of rooms in homes built between 1600 and 1750, as well as an increased specialization of these rooms. Bedrooms were also being furnished more lavishly, with a growing array of bedclothes and soft furnishings.[7] Second, this evolution of domestic space took place as Indian cottons became a greater and greater influence on the aesthetic composition of bedchambers.

We may well ask why Western Europeans wished to configure their most private and intimate space with fabrics from Asia. Among the wealthy commercial and political elites there was a fashion well in place by 1600 to remodel their sleeping chambers with hangings, bed curtains, quilts, coverlets, window curtains and cushions, all reflecting Asian motifs. The hybrid designs from India were among the most popular, and cottons were also less expensive than silks. As the English East India Company got under way in the early seventeenth century, records from London auctions reveal the feverish demand for these goods. Even calico goods that were 'somewhat defective and stayned' were bought without qualm, so keen were English buyers.[8] Dutch tastes followed the same trend, with quilts and bed hangings flowing into Amsterdam over the seventeenth century. Figure 4.1 is an example of a chintz bed curtain from about 1700, made of painted and dyed cotton, from the south-east coast of India, decorated with a tree of life motif that was immensely popular during the seventeenth century. The limbs of the tree are embellished with richly stylized blossoms, improbable in their assortment, overflowing with an organic vigour, gracefully executed. The border of this piece is filled with an undulating floral vine, suggestive of verdant gardens and the new botanic species brought from distant shores now transforming the landscapes of Europe. This hanging is typical of the calicos and chintzes carried to Europe and it brings the energy of an imaginary garden into the home, carrying with it associations that were both alien and familiar.[9] Europe remained a predominantly rural society, with metaphors and practical knowledge still deeply indebted to botanic lore and customary practice. The flowering of the tree of life had clear associations with fecundity, a logical adjunct to the bedroom. Jack Goody traces the evolution of floral culture in Europe and the antipathy of the early Church to customary plebeian celebrations incorporating flowers, leaves and vines as emblems of life. As he notes, floral culture had a resurgence in the Renaissance, through a combination of influences that included elite and common cultural forms, as well as the force of commercialization. As the artistic use of floral motifs increased, flowers themselves were cultivated more assiduously and marketed as a commodity; they were also featured in flower paintings that were a particular speciality of the seventeenth-century Netherlands.[10] Arjun Appadurai observes that 'a commodity is a thoroughly socialized thing'.[11] The bed curtain (Figure 4.1) exemplifies the dynamic trade in cottons, but we must also be aware of the context of its traffic, the influences shaping the reception of these goods in Europe and the mechanism of social practice that would have affected its use. The influx of Indian floral patterned cottons tapped into deep wells of cultural association among the common folk, as well as new passions for botany and gardens and a preoccupation with Asian commodities among the learned and affluent classes. Goody observes that, 'Part of the [rising] culture of abundance is the growth in the market of flowers from a local to a world scale.'[12] This painted chintz bed hanging epitomizes these forces.

The design applied to the curtain shows its Indian origins, modified for European tastes; the cut along one side of the cloth suggests at least a part of its functional life in its English home(s). Perhaps this excision represents an adjustment to fit furniture; perhaps it came about to patch another hanging, a common strategy of thrifty housewives. The characteristics of this hanging extend beyond its imperfect present state – in fact, its imperfections encourage us to consider its materiality and the ways in which its 'social life' was shaped.[13] Indian cottons poured into Europe through the seventeenth and early eighteenth centuries, when all varieties of linen were in greater demand. Light fabrics like linens were also amassing new meanings as an element of dress, epitomizing cleanliness in the show at cuff and collar, as well as being suggestive of the body itself when glimpsed between the slashes in a gentleman's doublet or behind an open waistcoat.[14] The elements of bedding also multiplied over the seventeenth and eighteenth centuries, and cottons gradually became a part of this greater comfort, utility and ease. One anonymous author, J.F., produced a guide, in 1696, to the huge range of linens and cottons sold throughout the cities and countryside of England: *The Merchant's Ware-house Laid Open: Or, the Plain-dealing Linen Draper. Shewing how to buy all sorts of Linnen and Indian goods* … . He insisted on the usefulness of his small book, not just for those in the trade, but 'for all persons whatsoever', recognizing that rich and poor alike spent money on these goods, the rich in great quantities and the poor in smaller. But the poor also were inspired 'to procure a little clean Linnen'. Cataloguing these textiles alphabetically, he lists the commonest fabrics sold including calicoes 'of general use with us'. He describes chintzes in some detail, extolling their 'very fine Colours' and designs 'either of Birds, Beasts, or Imagery'. More practically, he assures his readers of something many shoppers already knew, that whether used in clothing or 'Quilts for the Beds' these could be 'washed never so often, [and they] still retain their colours [until] they are worn to pieces'.[15] The capacity of printed and painted cottons to survive and thrive through repeated laundering was a hidden asset, not immediately evident when we look at the bed curtain in Figure 4.1 – that feature could be discerned only through practice. But J.F. identified a critical reputational facet of this cloth. The techniques employed by Indian artisans to fix these colours were likewise indecipherable to Europeans of that age. But these aspects of the fabric, as well as its drape, pattern and weight, were essential components explaining another element behind the widespread appetite for this commodity.

The Dutch and English East India Companies encouraged a trade in everyday domestic textiles for plebeian buyers, with cheaper varieties for the less affluent. One order from England to India requested quilts and bedding made 'strong, but none too dear … you know our Poorest people in England lye without any Curtains or Vallances'. The letter writer speculated that, 'Possibly some of these things may gain that repute here as may give us cause of greater enlargement in them hereafter.'[16] Cargos arriving in London in 1685 included 2,400 quilts among their stock; many other quilts were also made up in London, Amsterdam and other centres, using printed calico as the top piece. Between 1675 and 1725, there was a marked increase in the ownership of new kinds of goods across much of the English population.[17] This phenomenon ties in to what John Crowley sees as a growing preoccupation with comfort over the long eighteenth century, and Crowley notes how many authors 'sought to evaluate the relations of body, material culture and environment in the name of physical comfort'.[18] Comforts are, of course, historically contingent, and in this period were concerned with modifying the cold and damp of the autumn and winter seasons that came with chimney fires, poorly glazed windows, or windows not glazed at all. Innovations and amendments to the home and dress were designed to buffer the sometime harsh physical world. Cushioned chairs, beds curtained and heaped with quilts, washable bedding to counter bugs, bodily fluids, smoke and soot – each element of the domestic agenda could augment or detract from the comfort and care of the family. Tomas Maldonado and John Cullars consider that 'the ideology of comfort appears closely involved with at least two parallel categories: hygiene and order'.[19] Directions that explained how best to prepare a woman's bed prior to childbirth illustrates this point, showing as well that the transformation in material culture was under way by 1700. In this instance, the author specified the essential bedding for the travails ahead, these being a 'Quilt [rather] than a Feather-bed, having upon it Linnen and other [bed] Cloaths'.[20] Crowley observes that 'Physical comfort – self-conscious satisfaction with the relationship between one's body and its immediate physical environment – was an innovative aspect of Anglo-American culture [of this era].'[21] Doubtless this attention to comfort extended beyond the Anglo-American sphere, to include at least the Netherlands and other regions of Europe. Many sleeping spaces might still be rudimentary by our standards, at least for those with limited means; for those in the growing middle ranks, however, bed chambers were more common and the bed itself a more substantial piece of furniture. As well, the bedclothes and draperies that modulated this space were lighter, washable and more aesthetically pleasing and, most importantly, increasingly affordable.

The generations of trade that began in the sixteenth century transformed domestic life with new comforts and embellishments. This was not unique to one region of Europe, but affected the continent in general and most particularly the dynamic north-west, spreading across the Atlantic world. My illustrations come in large part from English records, but specialists in American, Canadian and Latin American history have charted similar processes, though with distinct regional forms and local chronologies. Records from the Old Bailey, London's busiest court, enable us to track the wider use of Indian calico quilts from the late seventeenth and through the eighteenth centuries, as textiles and clothing were among the most common items stolen.[22] Variations in the common commodities appearing in these records reflect shifts in material life. In this case, both before and even after the ban on cottons in 1720, calico quilts and bed curtains, 'Indian' quilts and generic quilts, were stolen in significant numbers, speaking to their prevalence in the bedrooms of Londoners, whether owned by lodging house keepers, shopkeepers, gentlemen or nobles.[23] In May 1746, the widow Mary White, living in lodgings near Somerset House, in her words: 'lost the Bed Cloaths all off my Bed'. Mary White had a seeming hand-to-mouth existence, depending for her income on plain needlework. But her life was not devoid of consolations or small pleasures. Along with the pair of blankets she owned a quilt valued at 10½ shillings and a calico cover, which gave added charm.[24] If this was an Indian calico, it would have been at least 20 years old and acquired before the ban in 1720. But, even if old, the printed colours would still have showed richly. The simple catalogue of her bedding illustrates the ways in which even some of the humblest people managed to enhance their dwellings, hinting at the pleasure such women might take in simple luxuries. The few eighteenth-century cotton quilts that survive in museum collections reflect the growing ownership of these household accessories, by people from across the social spectrum. Use and reuse of everyday textiles was often followed by the amassing of scraps into new domestic accessories, like patchwork quilts. By the 1760s, the British cotton industry was engulfed in technological change, with the result that more and more of the everyday fabrics used in gowns, aprons, shirts, breeches and jackets came from British manufacturers. British cottons, the first industrial product, ultimately became the source for most functional textiles – the growing numbers of cotton patchwork quilts that survive from the 1780s onwards reflect this next stage in the democratization of cotton, and the rise in domestic comforts.

Laurel Ulrich reminds us that, 'The history of textiles is fundamentally a story about international commerce in goods and ideas.'[25] Mary White's quilt, like the bed curtain in Figure 4.1, was part of this process of profound material change that linked Indian manufacturers with European consumers; this process also introduced new concepts of comfort into Western households, changing expectations and experiences. By the 1700s, the market was a vital part of this equation. Men and women constructing or remodelling a home depended on the links developed over the past centuries, with trade routes at once very distant, encompassing the globe, yet as familiar as the general stores or door-to-door pedlars serving local neighbourhoods. Exotics also evolved in line with the developing fashion cycles, familiar adjuncts to furnishings and dress, rather than exceptional rarities. In this way calico quilts and chintz curtains became part of the idiom of Western domestic furnishings, 'thoroughly socialized' to the communities they served.

Material forms and historical practice

Scholars have reaped rich rewards in their examinations of objects, applying various methodologies and theories in pursuit of a deeper understanding of history. Textiles and clothing have formed a growing focus of study not least for their deep resonance in past societies and past practices; they also served to transfer memories across time and space. 'Clothing ... reminds', as Ann Rosalind Jones and Peter Stallybrass contend, noting how 'material reminders ... [can be] working even when what is recalled is absent or dead'.[26] But what exactly is being recalled has been contentious.

Laurel Thatcher Ulrich offers up a virtual museum of artefacts to a critical re-evaluation, reassessing the meanings once attached to individual objects by nineteenth-century Americans assembling a colonial heritage. Central to her project is the evidence that can be gleaned from objects themselves, the social contexts of their constructions, as well as the issues that inspired their preservation. In this way Ulrich reconfigures the colonial world and the creation of its history.[27] Seven of the eleven objects studied in *The Age of Homespun* are textiles or clothing, from a needlework chimneypiece to a linen tablecloth, each revealing patterns of practice often deeply embedded with gender and ethnic factors arising from that period. The 'Indian basket' examined from this collection, for example, was said by its initial collector to reflect on the trading patterns in late seventeenth-century Narragensett Bay (what became Rhode Island). Using the substance of the basket as a guide (bark fibre and wool blanket threads), Ulrich reconstructs the time in which the basket was made and came into the hands of its colonial owner. Contending economic systems were part of this story: one which produced the wide-ranging and exceptional basketry of the indigenous peoples of the Northeast, and the other the flourishing capitalist system of manufacture in England that generated blankets in such numbers that they could be used as international trade goods. Through the basket Ulrich traces a system of gendered knowledge very different from that understood by Europeans, where skilled Algonkian women basket makers could identify fibres of all sorts fit for different types of weaving. The wool threads in the basket have lost their original colours, but were most likely used to highlight design elements, probably coming from a woven blanket, part of the trade pattern then in place. The basket speaks to a nascent system of exchange among women from the two communities, a carefully made basket traded for food or other needed goods, in uncertain times when the traditional resources available to the Algonkian were being eroded. This basket changed hands during a period of heightened tensions between settlers and native peoples, when the land-hunger among the former led to open war and a massacre of the Narragensett in the midst of this conflict. Ulrich notes that this is 'a story about exploitation as well as exchange, social disruption as well as entrepreneurship, violence as well as aesthetics'.[28] In this single basket, preserved by a later family member who abhorred the rate of change in mid-nineteenth-century America, Ulrich uncovers complex intersections of time, place, materials and power.[29] This example in itself is suggestive of the windows opened by a judicious study of material evidence, and the demands made on the researcher to follow up every thread.

In Adrienne Hood's study of textile production in Pennsylvania, threads are not only followed but counted in a meticulous treatment of the colonial weavers' craft distinct to this region and period. The New England model of textile production is perhaps the most widely known for the colonial and early republican eras, where young women with informally acquired skills produced needed fabrics both for personal use and for trade, in combination with other tasks. Hood found a different pattern in Pennsylvania, where rich agricultural lands discouraged mixed employment among settlers and enabled professional male immigrant weavers to thrive. To decipher the evidence from this period, this researcher had to master the complexities of fibre processing and preparation, as well as the complex mechanics of weaving itself. Students of material culture will encounter demands that push them beyond the written descriptions of events or the carefully documented counting of assets. In these cases, other skills must be acquired, demanding close observation and detailed comparisons of like objects in order to understand the nature and characteristics of their topic, to be able to trace change over time, or note the unique from the commonplace. The development of connoisseurship skills in a chosen subject (even at a rudimentary level) requires repeated thoughtful examinations of many items of a certain kind and date, in addition to study of works by experts. Reading cannot take the place of actual object study and digital equivalents do not suffice, however helpful. In many instances the object's common features as well as anomalies inspire new research.

Colonial America has left a generous legacy of documentary records in regional archives, as well as a surprising number of objects in local historical societies and museums, from spinning wheels to treadle looms. Hood needed to know the productive capacity of the looms listed in probate inventories, as well as the textile needs of the Pennsylvania communities they served. Only a detailed knowledge of the weaving process and the looms themselves, based on practical experience with equipment from this era, enabled her to work out the skills level and productivity of this distinctive set of weavers. Not only did Hood determine their distinctive employment practices, but she also showed how fully embedded Pennsylvania was in the Atlantic market. Fashionable textiles, like calicos and chintz, were as hotly desired in Philadelphia as in London; utilitarian fabrics, however, could be purchased locally, from specialist producers.[30] In addition to the many cultural theories that can inform and illuminate interpretations of objects and practice, there are also critical methodologies that are time-consuming to acquire. But, as Hood observes,

> By applying my practical and historical knowledge to the artifacts, I realized the depth of information embedded in the tools, fibers, colour, weave structure, and texture of handwoven fabrics. ... the artifacts could yield a different kind of historical insight unavailable from written sources alone.[31]

These examples illustrate the techniques brought to bear in historical material culture studies. They also demonstrate the ways in which the objects themselves illuminate issues of skill, gender practice, ethnicity and global trade as expressed in different times and places. A close reading of objects, particularly those routinely made and widely used, can create unexpected vantage points from which to assess the historical terrain. The garments that draped the body, protecting, adorning and negotiating its place in society are ambassadors from the past. Eighteenth-century costume collections at major museums contain a wealth of exquisite apparel – brocade gowns, embroidered muslin aprons, decorative stays, beautifully buckled shoes, silk coats, waistcoats and breeches – and rather less of the routine attire that comprised the wardrobes of the non-elite. The first garment acquired by Colonial Williamsburg, for example, was a brocaded silk gown. Linda Baumgarten, curator at Colonial Williamsburg, writes that: 'Survival of this or any artifact for hundreds of years usually favors the beautiful and the unusual.'[32] Yet the impact of social and cultural history over the past generation has encouraged the collecting and analysis of less celebrated articles as well as more intensive study of garments customarily hidden from view. Pockets were among the most discreet of garments, gendered in their form, they were typically tied around the waists of women and girls, and were a mainstay of female dress through the eighteenth and well into the nineteenth century. Worn over the shift, but under the gown or petticoat, access to these capacious soft bags came through the side slits in the external garment. Tie pockets, as these were called, were emblematic forms of female dress, typically made in pairs and commonly decorated for the evident private pleasure of the wearer (Figure 4.2). Embroidered, occasionally dated and signed, the makers of these pockets reveal

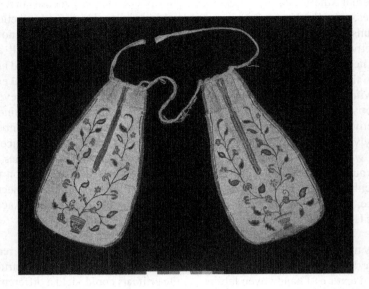

Figure 4.2 Pair of tie-on pockets, 1700–1725. Linen hand sewn with linen thread. Embroidered with wool and attached to linen tape. T. 697: B, C–1913. Courtesy of Victoria and Albert Museum, London.

their exuberance in the practicality of female dress, whether or not this was on public display.[33]

Barbara Burman has explored the rich cultural and functional history of pockets. Their gradual disappearance with the rise of what Burman calls later nineteenth-century 'disciplinary pockets' in new tailored styles of dress occasioned complaints from at least one writer. Reflecting on the lost pockets of her youth, one artist recalled the 'lovely hoards I kept in them'. This writer demanded, 'Why mayn't we have Pockets? Who forbids it? We have got Women's Suffrage, but why must we still always be inferior to Men?'[34] Consider the size of these pockets at between 12 and 20 inches in length and the volume that could be stored in each, or the organization that could be established between the right- and left-hand pocket. Pockets resonated with personal and cultural meanings. Little surprise, then, that Burman has identified a resistance to the force of fashion and a determined use of tie-on pockets despite the evolving shape and tailoring of women's dress over the nineteenth century. Burman observes that in, 'the act of making the pocket and the additional time and handicraft invested in the needlework surface decoration, a woman created an object embodying a cluster of values, including thrift'.[35] Many with experience of these pockets were apparently loath to give them up. Ultimately, however, women acceded to the transformation of their private space and adapted their carrying technology, clutching bags of various sorts in their hands or draping them on their shoulders, accepting the limitations of small sewn-in pockets with little capacity and less practical worth. A close scrutiny of these once ubiquitous objects prods us to reflect on the intersections of dress forms and discipline, with no single easy conclusion.

Petticoats were garments employed both for public display and practical concealment. Covering the lower half of women's bodies, they were relatively voluminous over the course of the long eighteenth century, sometimes suspended from hoops, but in all instances defining the physical dimensions of the woman so enveloped. There are no neutral elements of dress; every facet might elicit comment or stir political dissension. The popularity of the hooped petticoat occasioned a sharp rebuke by an anonymous author in 1745 that termed the style an 'enormous abomination', and denounced the resulting inconveniences he claimed to have suffered including at church. There, he complained of 'the Crowd and Embarassment [sic] of these ungodly Hoops ... One ... dashes against me and almost breaks my Shins: Two, or Three more attack me in the Rear, banging my Hams, and the Calves of my Legs.' The disgruntled writer concluded: 'For my part, I wonder how the Wearers of them have the Confidence to look Us, or even One another in the Face.'[36] No occasion for a dispute on matters of dress could be missed; within a short time a second author, employing the pseudonym 'Jack Lovelass', jumped into the fray. He argued for a toleration of fashionable hoop-wearing by the 'Tradesmen's Wives and Daughters' ridiculed by the first author, since they 'very frequently [have] Fortunes superior to the Daughters of many Persons of Quality'. Lovelass likewise observed the value of a fashion that would 'promote the Consumption of all the several Silks, Linnens, and Stuffs worn above the Hoops, almost all of which being manufactur'd at Home'.[37]

The politics of apparel might serve as ammunition for duelling authors entertaining literary Londoners; or social politics might be more subtly demonstrated in the body of the apparel itself. Some years ago I began a study of the ready-made clothing trade in the long eighteenth century. It was quickly apparent from the documentary evidence that the growth of the military from the mid-seventeenth century had encouraged the contracting of clothing in extraordinary volumes to dress England's soldiers and sailors. Tens of thousands of shirts, jackets and the like were produced through a system of subcontracting that employed untold thousands of women in networks of production that depended not at all on new mechanical technologies, but on systems of production that extended manufacturing capacity in advance of new machines. The other element essential to the functioning of this system was a gender division of labour: the employment of a largely female workforce paid at rates consistently lower than those paid men with similar skill sets. Seamstresses and needlewomen collected in corners of London where rents were cheap; the nature of their work enhanced their anonymity for they were not building ships or crafting gold, activities traditionally associated with tightly organized bodies of male workers, admired for their demonstrated expertise. These seamstresses were uncelebrated and largely unnamed, the labour associated with their production conducted in virtual obscurity. Their use of needle and thread was as naturally a part of their lot as caring for children or the cooking of meals.

Military contracting grew exponentially over the eighteenth century. One contractor, Charles James, sold over half a million items to the navy between 1760 and

1770 – shirts, trousers, frocks, drawers – over a quarter million shirts being delivered in a two-year period.[38] Very few articles made for the army and navy survive to this day, but in those ordinary goods that do remain, the common fabrics and long running stitches speak of production at speed.[39] Testifying about his trade, about 1800, one contractor estimated he employed between 1,000 and 1,200 workers to make his shirts, but he was not sure of the exact number. He responded, 'It is impossible to guess, I could not state the number within five hundred; we employ a great number [in different London] … parishes, and how many of the poor are employed upon our work it is impossible for me to tell.'[40] Uncovering the characteristics of the early ready-made trade provides insights into shifting forms of consumerism, as well as employment patterns of a predominantly, though not exclusively, female labour force. Other ready-wear sectors also developed for the market, well before the more celebrated appearance of factory production, catalogues and department stores after 1850. Petticoats make another appearance in this story, with characteristics in some respects very different from those of naval slops or the cheap, ready-made shirting that kitted out regiments. The pervasive features of the garments themselves illuminate another part of the ready-to-wear trade and the circumstances of their creation.

Most major costume collections, like that at the Royal Ontario Museum, Toronto, the Museum of London, and the Victoria and Albert Museum, London, will contain dozens of quilted petticoats, most of which are silks of various sorts – too valuable to be discarded and more likely to be treasured than similar wool items, though a few of those also remain. Close study of these articles reveals important elements in their construction, patterns of stitchery and the social environment of their manufacture. The first feature that stands out is how easily these petticoats were adjusted, tied with tapes around the waist to fit the slender or more generous frame; the full dimensions of the garment would also be determined by any hoop underneath. Quilting, as we have seen, was a well-known technique enhancing the warmth of two fabric layers, with padding either of wool or cotton sandwiched between and stitched in place. And there can be little doubt that these were comfortable garments, warm, softly draping the lower body, with flourishes in either the stitching or fabric combinations. The quilting itself added a stylistic dimension, particularly as the petticoat was so prominent a part of women's dress. A simple diamond patterns, such as seen in Figure 4.3, was a common motif and easy to make. But among the many surviving silk and satin quilted petticoats there was a standard array of ornamental stitchery on the bottom third of the garment – floral or architectural forms being most common – with plain geometric or semi-circular patterning on the top two-thirds. The construction techniques of the quilted petticoats were virtually identical, with occasional variations in the backing fabrics, while the decorative designs employed in the quilting were also surprisingly similar, suggesting common inspiration, or common cartoons to direct the stitching. In addition, the quilting, while fluidly executed, left much of the ground untouched. Close scrutiny of these objects also suggests a division of labour, with less expert hands tackling simpler tasks like the stitching of waist tapes, for example. These garments rarely demonstrate the highest standard of quilting and typically reflect a

Figure 4.3 Diamond quilted silk petticoat, lined with wool, hand sewn, 1740–1750. T. 306–1982. Courtesy of Victoria and Albert Museum, London.

standard form that, while attractive, is not meticulous. Value evidently lay in the colour and quality of the top fabric selected and in the novelty of the design quilted on the bottom, if any.

Placing these garments in conjunction with documentary sources, it becomes evident that ready-to-wear articles were not only produced for the lowest end of the market. The broad range of middling and genteel shopper were also provided with items like quilted petticoats that could be prepared in advance for the growing numbers of Londoners, goods easily shipped to provincial or overseas customers. Specialist 'petticoat warehouses' sprang up in London in the last quarter of the century and began competing on the price, quality and variety of their products in the pages of the daily newspapers. One owner announced 'a very large assortment of fresh quilted [petti]coats, in new and elegant patterns, never before quilted'. A competitor went one step further, announcing that if his stock was 'not found superior to any offered the public [he] will take them [back] again, and return the money with pleasure'.[41] His last claim was perhaps overstated. But the advertisements sketch the context wherein needlewomen, whether born in the capital or newly arrived, could find employment quilting 'elegant patterns' or stitching basic apparel. Both kinds of work were plentiful over the long eighteenth century. And both kinds of work could be called sweated labour: relatively poorly paid, outside the standard of male guild employment practices, with a workforce vulnerable to the extremes of market pressures, both when work was abundant and when it was scarce.

One of the more startling features of this pattern of work is how early the practices now associated with nineteenth- and twentieth-century sweated labour were put in place. Contracted military garb in the seventeenth century set the stage for a system that grew in size and in profitability. Typically excluded from male tailoring guilds, needlewomen were attacked by tailors for their work, leading to organized nationwide campaigns by journeymen tailors at the beginning of the eighteenth century. In 1702, the journeymen tailors sought to quash the ready-made trade and to bar women from needlework in this sector, without success. Gender tensions simmered throughout that century and into the next, between representatives of the tailors' guild, and then the tailors' union, and the generations of women who worked for wages with their needle. An advertisement by a tailor in the late 1700s documents these gender politics. The announcement asserts that the ready-made clothes at this outlet were 'Not made by Women, as is customary at the Warehouses, but by the best Workmen that can be got'.[42] Sailors' shirts and women's quilted petticoats reflect the scope of ready-made production in the eighteenth century, and suggest as well the working conditions under which these garments were created. In the 1830s a strike broke out at a time of heightened agitation for a general trades union for all wage earners. Once again the question was raised about women working in the needle trades, with the traditional tailors' representative actively hostile to those of the other sex making clothing. Followers of the English reformer and socialist Robert Owen proposed a system of equal wages for equal work, regardless of sex, a proposition hotly rejected by the tailors' union.[43] In the following decade the plight of needlewomen once again become part of public debate, with the publication in 1843 of 'The Song of the Shirt', lamenting the plight of poor needlewomen. Sweated labour would be rediscovered several times over the nineteenth century and again in the centuries to follow.[44] 'Clothing ... reminds', wrote Jones and Stallybrass of an earlier century. Looking at the running stitches seaming an eighteenth-century shirt or racing across the front of a quilted petticoat, the social politics of dress are brought vividly to mind.

Conclusion

In this chapter I have outlined some of the ways in which a close study of artefacts can animate historical enquiry. The tools, tableware or tapestries of an earlier age bring evidence of human priorities and passions; deployed as evidence in combination with theoretical interpretations and documentary sources their study can yield exceptional results. There was always intent in the creation of these objects; none was created outside the patterns of its day. These items were made, repaired, remodelled and recycled within the conditions and the context of their societies, revealing in their forms the imperatives of men's and women's lives, suggesting the particular pleasures or grinding discomforts that marked at least part of their lived experience.

As students of history we approach these objects with sharp eyes and a keen desire to uncover the past, but we must be aware that the physical features cannot in themselves create a narrative. Moreover, stark descriptions of artefacts are not enough; we must venture into analysis and explanation, blending these material forms into the wider currents of historical scholarship. Many historians come to this study at an initial disadvantage, as our schooling privileges education in literate, numerate and narrative forms of expression. Historians, seeking to understand and explain past societies, are faced with choices as to the evidence they employ among the scattered remnants that survive. Choosing to employ material evidence can bring unique insights absent from many written records. Textiles and clothing are among the most personal relics of the past, some even holding the body's impression in the worn fibres of a coat or the distorted drape of a quilt. Products of regional and global trade, local skills and gendered markets, these artefacts are shaped by the complexities of their time of creation, their history of use and period of collection. Approaching these objects with questions, answers will be forthcoming for the diligent and, as a result, history will be more richly conceived.

Notes

1 For an outstanding example of an art historical treatment of material objects, see Ruth B. Phillips, *Trading Identities: The Souvenir in Native North American Art from the Northeast, 1700–1900* (Seattle and London: University of Washington Press, 1998).

2 There is a vast array of works charting the shifting material worlds of early modern Europe and colonial North America. Among these are: Joan Thirsk, *Economic Policy and Projects: The Development of a Consumer Society in Early Modern England* (Oxford: Clarendon Press, 1978); A.D. Van der Woude and Aton Schuurman (eds), *Probate Inventories. A New Source for the Historical Study of Wealth, Material Culture and Agricultural Development* (Wageningen: A.A.G. Bijdragen, 1980); Arthur Ray, 'Indians as Consumers in the Eighteenth-century Trade', in Carol Judd and Arthur Ray (eds), *Old Trails and New Directions: Papers in the Third North American Fur Trade Conference* (Toronto, 1980); Neil McKendrick, John Brewer and J.H. Plumb, *The Birth of a Consumer Society: The Commercialization of Eighteenth-century England* (London: Hutchinson, 1983); Lorna Weatherill, *Consumer Behaviour and Material Culture in Britain, 1660–1760* (London: Routledge, 1988); Lois Green Carr and Lorena S. Walsh, 'The Standard of Living in the Colonial Chesapeake', *William and Mary Quarterly*, 45, 1 (1988), pp. 135–59; M. Baulant, A.J. Schuurman and P. Servais (eds), *Inventaires pres-deces et ventes de meubles: Apports à une histoire de la vie économique et quotidienne XIVe–XIXe siècle* (Louvain-la Neuve: Academia, 1988); Beverly Lemire, *Fashion's Favourite: The Cotton Trade and the Consumer in Britain, 1660–1800* (Oxford: Oxford University Press, 1991); John Brewer and Roy Porter (eds), *Consumption and the World of Goods* (London: Routledge, 1993); Stana Nenadic, 'Middle-rank Consumers and Domestic Culture in Edinburgh and Glasgow 1720–1840', *Past and Present*, 145 (1994), pp. 122–56; Daniel Roche, *The Culture of Clothing: Dress and Fashion in the Ancien Regime* (Cambridge: Cambridge University Press, 1994); Cary Carson, Ronald Hoffman and Peter J. Albert (eds), *Of Consuming*

Interests: The Style of Life in the Eighteenth Century (Charlottesville: University Press of Virginia, 1994); Ann Smart Martin and J. Ritchie Garrison, 'Shaping the Field: The Multi-disciplinary Perspectives of Material Culture', in Ann Smart Martin and J. Ritchie Garrison (eds), *American Material Culture: The Shape of the Field* (Winterthur, DE: Henry Francis du Pont Museum, 1997); Laurel Thatcher Ulrich, *The Age of Homespun: Objects and Stories in the Creation of an American Myth* (New York: Knopf, 2001); T.H. Breen, *The Marketplace of Revolution: How Consumer Politics Shaped American Independence* (New York: Oxford University Press, 2004); Mark Overton, Jane Whittle, Darron Dean and Andrew Hann, *Production and Consumption in England Households, 1600–1750* (London: Routledge, 2004); Toby Barnard, *Making the Grand Figure: Lives and Possessions in Ireland 1641–1770* (New Haven, CT: Yale University Press, 2004); Susan M. Stabile, *Memory's Daughters: The Material Culture of Remembrance in Eighteenth-century America* (Ithaca, NY: Cornell University Press, 2004); Cory Willmott, 'From Stroud to Strouds: The Hidden History of a British Fur Trade Textile', *Textile History*, 36 (2005); John Styles and Amanda Vickery (eds), *Gender, Taste, and Material Culture in Britain and North America, 1700–1830* (New Haven, CT: Yale University Press, 2006).

3 Alain Corbin, *The Foul and the Fragrant: Odour and the French Social Imagination* (Cambridge, MA: Harvard University Press, 1986); John E. Crowley, *The Invention of Comfort: Sensibilities and Design in Early Modern Britain and Early America* (Baltimore, MD: Johns Hopkins University Press, 2000).

4 Keith Wrightson, *Earthly Necessities: Economic Lives in Early Modern Britain* (New Haven, CT: Yale University Press, 2000), p. 53.

5 An Moonen, *'t is al Beddegoet: Nederlandse Antieke Quilts 1650–1900* (Uitgeverij Terra: Warnsveld, 1986), p. 7. I thank Marijke Kerkhoven for translating notes from this text for me.

6 Edward Roberts and Karen Parker (eds), *Southampton Probate Inventories, 1497–1575*, vol. I (Southampton: Southampton University Press, 1992) vol. I, pp. 65–70, 150–2, 159–62, 165–7; vol. II, pp. 244–52, 346–7, 358–9.

7 Mark Overton, Jane Whittle, Darron Dean and Andrew Hann, *Production and Consumption in English Households, 1600–1750* (London: Routledge, 2004), pp. 110–13, 125; Weatherill, *Consumer Behaviour and Material*, pp. 159–61; see also, H. Dibbits, 'Between Society and Family Values: The Linen Cupboard in Early Modern Households', in A. Schuurman and P. Spierenburg (eds), *Private Domain, Public Enquiry: Families and Life-styles in the Netherlands and Europe, 1550 to the Present* (Hilversum: Verloren, 1996), pp. 125–45.

8 John Irwin and Margaret Hall, *Indian Embroideries*, vol. II (Ahmedabad: Calico Museum of Textiles, 1973), p. 2.

9 Beverly Lemire, 'Domesticating the Exotic: Floral Culture and the East India Calico Trade with England, c.1600–1800', *Textile: The Journal of Cloth and Culture*, 1, 1 (2003), pp. 65–85.

10 Jack Goody, *The Culture of Flowers* (Cambridge: Cambridge University Press, 1993), pp. 164–90.

11 Arjun Appadurai, *The Social Life of Things. Commodities in Cultural Perspective* (Cambridge: Cambridge University Press, 1986), p. 6.

12 Goody, *Culture of Flowers*, p. 205.

13 'Social life' is a term applied to material goods by Appadurai.

14 Daniel Roche, *The Culture of Clothing: Dress and Fashion in the Ancien Regime*, transl. Jean Birrell (Cambridge: Cambridge University Press, 1994), Chapter 7.

15 F.J., *The Merchant's Ware-house Laid Open: Or, the Plain-dealing Linen Draper. Shewing how to buy all sorts of Linnen and Indian goods ...* (London: John Sprint and George Conyers, 1696), pp. ii–iii, 6–7.

16 Lemire, *Fashion's Favourite*, p. 17.

17 Weatherill, *Consumer Behaviour and Material Culture*, pp. 25–32.

18 John E. Crowley, 'The Sensibility of Comfort', *American Historical Review*, 104, 3 (1999), p. 751.

19 Tomas Maldonado and John Cullares, 'The Idea of Comfort', *Design Issues*, 8, 1 (1991), p. 39.

20 John Pechey, *A general treatise of the diseases of maids, bigbellied women, child-bed-women, and widows together with the best methods of preventing or curing the same* (1696), p. 126.

21 Crowley, 'The Sensibility of Comfort', p. 750.

22 For example, see Beverly Lemire, 'The Theft of Clothing and Popular Consumerism in Eighteenth Century England', *Journal of Social History*, 24, 2 (1990), pp. 255–76; Garthine Walker, 'Women, Theft and the World of Stolen Goods', in Jenny Kermode and Garthine Walker (eds), *Women, Crime and the Courts in Early Modern England* (London: University College London Press, 1994), Chapter 4, pp. 81–105.

23 For example: 8 May 1695, Proceedings of the Old Bailey Ref: tl6950508-26; 2 July 1684, Proceedings of the Old Bailey Ref: tl6840702-38; 6 September 1693, Proceedings of the Old Bailey Ref: tl6930906-34; 13 October 1708, Proceedings of the Old Bailey Ref: tl7081013-27; 7 December 1709, Proceedings of the Old Bailey Ref: tl7091207-41; 2 June 1715, Proceedings of the Old Bailey Ref: tl7150602-37; 3 March 1720, Proceedings of the Old Bailey Ref: tl7200303-17; 25 April 1726, Proceedings of the Old Bailey Ref: tl7260425-2. At http://www.oldbaileyonline.org/, accessed 4 October 2007.

24 15 May 1746, Proceedings of the Old Bailey Ref: tl7460515-23, http://www.oldbaileyonline.org/, accessed 4 October 2007.

25 Ulrich, *Age of Homespun*, p. 414.

26 Ann Rosalind Jones and Peter Stallybrass, *Renaissance Clothing and the Materials of Memory* (Cambridge: Cambridge University Press, 2000), p. 3.

27 Ulrich, *Age of Homespun*.

28 Ibid., p. 414.

29 Ibid., Chapter 1, pp. 41–74.

30 Adrienne Hood, *The Weaver's Craft: Cloth, Commerce, and Industry in Early Pennsylvania* (Philadelphia: University of Pennsylvania Press, 2003), pp. 1–15, 85–111.

31 Hood, *Weaver's Craft*, p. 3.

32 Linda Baumgarten, *What Clothes Reveal: The Language of Clothing in Colonial and Federal America* (Colonial Williamsburg Foundation, in association with New Haven, CT, and London: Yale University Press, 2002), p. 2.

33 Barbara Burman, 'Pocketing the Difference: Gender and Pockets in Nineteenth-century Britain', *Gender and History*, 14, 3 (2002), pp. 447–51.

34 Quoted in Burman, 'Pocketing the Difference', p. 447.

35 Burman, 'Pocketing the Difference', pp. 451–2.

36 A.W., Esq., *The enormous abomination of the hoop-petticoat, as the fashion now is, and has been for about these two years fully display'd: in some reflexions upon it, humbly offer'd to the consideration of both sexes; especially the female* (London: 1745), pp. 14–15.

37 Jack Lovelass, *The hoop-petticoat vindicated, in answer to The enormous abomination of the hoop-petticoat. By the ladies most humble servant Jack Lovelass* (London: 1745), pp. 22–3.

38 Beverly Lemire, *Dress, Culture and Commerce: The English Clothing Trade before the Factory, 1660–1800* (Basingstoke, UK: Macmillan Press, 1997), pp. 19–20.

39 The single shirt listed in the National Maritime Museum collection (cotton/linen, 1807, F.2156-0A) is described as 'non-regulation' and features a fashionable cut and quality of fabric not typical outside the officer class. At www.nmm.ac.uk/collections/, accessed 7 November 2007.

40 Lemire, *Dress, Culture and Commerce*, p. 71.

41 *The Gazetteer and New Daily Advertiser*, 14 January 1779, 20 January 1779.

42 Lemire, *Dress, Culture and Commerce*, pp. 72–3.
43 Barbara Taylor, "'The Men are as Bad as their Masters ...'": Socialism, Feminism and Sexual Antagonism in the London Tailoring Trade in the 1830s' in Judith L. Newton, Mary P. Ryan and Judith R. Walkowitz (eds), *Sex and Class in Women's History* (London: Routledge & Kegan Paul, 1983), pp. 187–220.
44 For the full text of 'The Song of the Shirt', see http://www.victorianweb.org/authors/hood/shirt.html.

5 Using buildings to understand social history

Britain and Ireland in the seventeenth century[1]

Anne Laurence

The contribution made by early modern country houses and vernacular architecture to the study of the built heritage of England might seem to be relatively uncontested, confined perhaps to the redating of some Renaissance detail or redefining the regional incidence of a particular kind of king-post. In fact, at both the level of grand narrative and at the level of counting and measuring the remains there is controversy. And once the history of the built heritage of Britain and Ireland as a whole is taken into account, the whole subject assumes a much more varied character. In this chapter I shall outline some of these debates and then look at how the study of domestic building across the whole British Isles can enhance our understanding of the social and economic history of the four nations, concluding with some observations about how we view such buildings today.

The grand narrative I want to open with is that of the 'great rebuilding', its use by historians, its dating and incidence. I shall then discuss some problems of relying upon surviving buildings for evidence of the domestic building of the past. I shall conclude with a comparative study of two types of building development in different parts of Britain and Ireland as an example of how domestic building may be used to enhance the study of society and the economy in the seventeenth century.

The great rebuilding

In the 1950s W.G. Hoskins noted that there was 'a revolution in the housing of a considerable part of the population' of England during the period 1570 to 1640, but especially concentrated in the period 1575–1625: this he named 'the great rebuilding'.[2] Hoskins identified this as the substantial modernization or rebuilding of many medieval buildings and, at the same time, the great increase in household furnishings and equipment. He described this as a primarily rural phenomenon not because he did not believe that it also took place in towns but because, through subsequent redevelopment, the evidence is largely lacking in urban building. Hoskins used the evidence of surviving buildings for the alterations to houses, and documents such as inventories for furnishings and equipment. He also identified regional differences in the timing of the great rebuilding, though he believed that it was something that most social classes took up.[3]

Hoskins' work was challenged by R. Machin, who, examining the statistics for the numbers of houses rebuilt, determined that a far greater number of houses had been substantially reconstructed in the period 1660–1739 and argued that 'the great rebuilding' should be located round the year 1700 rather than round the year 1600.[4] He also tried to establish a chronology from the late Middle Ages, when impermanent buildings were replaced by more substantial structures, to the seventeenth century, when houses were constructed from pattern books. Colin Platt discusses both rebuildings, and locates the second rebuilding partly in towns.[5]

Since then, there has been a body of work that has taken up Hoskins' assumption, accepting that rebuilding took place, and investigating regional variations in timing and scale. Houses, such as those of the impoverished Welsh gentry, which had consisted of a tall hall, a passage and a very small amount of private space, were, from the late sixteenth century, being converted into two-storey dwellings by inserting a floor and staircase and building a chimney at one end of the former hall.[6] This process is also seen in the south-west of England, where fifteenth-century hall houses were adapted in considerable numbers.[7] In some houses the open roof was covered in by the installation of a plaster ceiling in the upper room. Although many of these houses are by their appearance of the sixteenth or seventeenth century, smoke-blackened roof timbers are evidence that there was once an open hearth and a single hall. In new houses of the seventeenth century, the hall assumed much less importance.[8] A study of building in Boughton Monchelsea, Kent, shows that the bulk of reconstruction in the village took place considerably earlier than the late sixteenth century.[9] A study of building and rebuilding in Ingatestone, Essex, suggests that by the end of the sixteenth century most houses no longer had a hall with a central hearth, but had at least one chimney commonly of brick, that two-storey halls had often had a floor inserted, that many windows were glazed, and that there was a marked reduction in the number of houses with separate kitchens.[10] However, the timing of these modifications did not amount to a great rebuilding but to a small peak in a building continuum lasting 400 years.

Hoskins' greatest contribution was not so much to identify a time and place for a great rebuilding, but to see evidence in building of social changes, to do with traditions of hospitality, with alterations in the way households used their houses, with social and family relationships, with new pursuits and amusements. Old-fashioned hospitality took place in public, in the hall, mixing all social classes. Servants mixed freely with their masters in the public areas of the house; the private rooms, parlours and closets were for women. The modern way, becoming more common from the mid-seventeenth century, was for the servants to be relegated to separate quarters in the house. Roger North noted that, from the time of Charles II, hardly any houses had been built in which members of the household of all ranks mingled.[11] Privacy started as being the privilege of the gentry and gradually worked its way down the scale to lesser members of the household.[12]

Sociability increasingly took place among people of similar social standing in suites of rooms with ceremonial approaches and enfilades, and dining became a socially exclusive affair. New pursuits called for dedicated rooms. Libraries followed larger collections of books. Closets (which feature particularly in the biographies and autobiographies of godly men and women as places where they carried out their daily religious duties) were used for private or semi-private occupations such as reading, prayer and meditation. Galleries were used to display collections of paintings and for musical events.

But the new styles, plans and forms did not spread evenly at the same time. There was certainly a trickle-down effect from London, but different regions showed great variations in the extent of rebuilding. In Northamptonshire 64 per cent of pre-1660 houses survived without complete rebuilding in the late seventeenth or eighteenth centuries, while in Suffolk the figure was as low as 21 per cent but there was very little new building until after 1770.[13]

This discussion of the great rebuilding takes it as axiomatic that such a thing existed, but Matthew Johnson has challenged the nature of the narrative on several fronts. He argues that Hoskins was writing at a time when historians such a R.H. Tawney and Christopher Hill viewed the period from the late sixteenth century to 1640 as seminal in the development of English class relations and economic life. The appeal of Hoskins' thesis was that not only did it take vernacular building into the wider study of history, but also meshed neatly with a narrative of social and economic development.[14] But, Johnson notes, Hoskins developed his thesis impressionistically, relying heavily on evidence from the south-west of England, without attempting to quantify the extent of rebuilding, and without examining the possibility of differential development in different parts of the country.[15] Nevertheless, the idea that the buildings in which people lived can tell us about more intangible aspects of human life owes a very great debt to Hoskins' original formulation.

But how did this play out in other parts of the Britain and in Ireland? We have seen that there is evidence for gentry rebuilding in Wales, especially on the border with England, peaking in the 1630s and then again in the 1670s but remaining high in the early eighteenth century probably because of high agricultural prices.[16] The economies of Scotland and Ireland were separate from that of England (though in both cases England was an important trading partner) and the cultural influences on building in both countries came from different directions. We shall see later that concerns of defence loomed much larger in the architectural vocabulary of the gentry and nobility of both those countries than they did in England, while comfort was a comparative latecomer. At the same time, social relations in both countries were different to those in England. Male retainers, often with a semi-military relationship to their patrons, persisted long after their disappearance in England. In Scotland building was certainly influenced by French and Dutch models, through the country's traditional links with France and the Netherlands unmediated by London, so one might expect there to see these influences earlier than in the English provinces most distant from the metropolis. In Ireland, Dublin had become by the early eighteenth century a significant centre of culture. Wealthy Irishmen went on the grand tour, and to build in a correctly scholarly style became the badge of a gentleman; but while architects such as Vanbrugh and Talman imported Baroque styles into England in the later seventeenth century, the Catholic associations were too much for the Protestant ruling class in Ireland who adopted, from the early eighteenth century, a more austere classicism.[17]

Surviving buildings and documentary sources

Students of history who wish to connect buildings with social and economic developments are naturally heavily dependent on the buildings that remain standing. But can we draw any conclusions about whether such buildings are representative?

One problem has been dating houses. Machin, using buildings with date plaques, located the great rebuilding 50 years later than Hoskins. Johnson compared surviving buildings in Suffolk with Hearth Tax returns to estimate the survival rate. C.R.J. Currie, in a study based on Swavesey, Cambridgeshire, attempted to devise a model to predict the proportion of houses surviving from any particular era taking into account age, building materials and variations in settlement patterns. He concluded that the survival of early buildings was random and unrelated to the original quality of the building (that is to say that houses built of cob or with timber frames were not intrinsically less likely to survive than brick or stone houses, all other things being equal).[18] Cob and timber-framed houses were more vulnerable to fire, but not more vulnerable to rot and fungus or to fashionable remodelling. And brick and stone houses were much more likely to be dated than cob or timber-framed houses. In the end, he did not succeed in creating a model that related surviving houses to the frequency with which their building types occurred in earlier times. But what he has done is to offer a critical perspective on the use of surviving buildings for estimating what may or may not have been typical.

As well as losses from fire, decay and fashion, there have been more recent losses from industrialization, urbanization and war. Apart from bombing during the Second World War, the civil wars of the seventeenth century led to considerable destruction in such towns as Banbury and Gloucester, and damage to fortified country houses such as Basing House; the material destruction was probably much greater in seventeenth-century Ireland.[19] Some Irish country houses were destroyed during the War of Independence (1916–21) and the Civil War (1922–23), but far more were lost simply by being allowed to fall into dereliction in the period from the creation of the Free State in 1922 until the arrival of greater prosperity following Ireland's entry to the European Union in 1973.[20] Impoverished Irish governments saw little electoral advantage in restoring or averting the decay of the relics of Anglo-Irish landlordism at a time when the National Trust was active in England and Wales.

There can be difficulties in interpreting the fabric of what does survive: the merchants of Oxford, faced with narrow city sites in the seventeenth century, chose to build old-fashioned jettied houses, using elaborately carved timber for ostentatious display rather than stone (which was readily available).[21] In the eighteenth century older houses in the city were refronted to give them a modern appearance.[22] Sherwood and Pevsner's descriptions of Oxford High Street and of Burford High Street mention a number of buildings with fronts newer than the main accommodation.[23]

We can be misled in other ways: a dated plaque attached to the old grammar school in Burford came from a different building.[24] Two examples of disputed dates or attributions are Wilton House, Wiltshire, and Beaulieau House, Co. Louth. Wilton House, largely rebuilt by the 4th Earl of Pembroke, was long attributed to

Figure 5.1 Beaulieau House, near Drogheda, Co. Louth. The house was probably built by Sir Henry Tichbourne (*c.*1581–1667), during the 1660s, but what we see may be the rebuilding by his grandson, another Sir Henry. © The Open University.

Inigo Jones until several discoveries made it certain that Isaac de Caus had executed the south front, at least as clerk of the works, though we do not know how much he contributed to the actual design and the extent of his role is contested.[25] By tradition Beaulieu (Figure 5.1) was built shortly after the Restoration in 1660, an early date for a house of this style even in London.[26] The builder was supposedly Sir Henry Tichbourne, a Londoner who had served with the English forces in Ireland in the 1640s and 1650s and consolidated his land grant at the Restoration. After his death in 1667, his son completed the house and made alterations. However, correspondence recently discovered suggests that the house may have been substantially built in the period 1710–20.[27]

Important though the evidence of the built fabric is, by itself what it can tell us is relatively limited; it is the combination of the fabric with documentary evidence that makes the real contribution of material culture to our understanding of early modern societies. Ryan's study of Ingatestone uses a survey made for the local landlord dating from 1556 and a detailed local map of 1601 to estimate changes that took place in the buildings between those two dates.[28] Favourite sources for historians are wills and inventories, which tell us what individuals owned at their death and may list the rooms of their houses. Maurice Howard's caveats about the use of inventories as evidence for the disposition of space within houses are repeated by

Nicholas Cooper.[29] Both remind us that the designation of rooms in inventories is highly problematic; often they are identified by the name of the occupant rather than by function. Even if we cannot identify how individual rooms were used, we can certainly note from the second half of the seventeenth century the increasing prevalence of household textiles, of plate, and of household equipment associated with new products, foodstuffs and sociability (chocolate pots, coffee pots, tea pots, porcelain, tobacco implements), which have implications for the arrangement of the household.

Contemporary commentaries are another important source, but need to be used with an understanding of the regional and class biases of the authors. William Harrison, whose description of England was first published in 1577, mentioned a variety of innovations and changes: the use of stoves, the greater plentifulness and cheapness of glass for windows, the separation of the dairy and stables from the house, the acquisition of furnishings such as carpets, linen and plate by even 'the lowest sort in our South Country', the spread of chimneys and beds.[30] Gerard Boate used his account of building materials in Ireland to comment on the greater civility of the English:

> The gray free-stone which is found very abundantly in most parts of the land ... hath been used by the English, to all the Churches, Castles, and Edifaces, which since the Conquest have been builded by them; For the Irish themselves, never had the skill nor industry to erect any considerable buildings of Free-stone, Brick, or other the like materials, their dwellings being very poor and contemptible cottages ... . This sort of Gray Free-stone in Ireland hath a bad qualitie, that it draweth the moysture of the air continually to it .... To mend this inconvenience the English did wainscot those walls with oak or other boards, or line them with a thin crust of brick .... In every part of Ireland there is found a kind of clay very fit for to make bricks ... though the Irish never had the wit or industrie to make use of it for either of these two ends .... The Brick have been little used in Ireland even among the English themselves for a great while; but of late years they began to be very common.[31]

Many commentators wrote to decry the changes of the time. Robert Reyce commented not only on the decay of castles in Suffolk but also on the fact that the government did not consider the security of the commonwealth to be impaired by this neglect.[32] Edward Waterhouse believed it was 'high time to advertise the too too extravagancy of England'.[33] Other writers, particularly visitors who described Scotland and Ireland and more distant locations, produced travel literature to amaze and amuse their readers rather than offering dispassionate descriptions of what they saw. John Ray, a visitor to Scotland in the 1660s remarked on the lack of glass in the windows, of plaster ceilings and of linen.[34] While Thomas Kirke wrote in 1679 that 'all the gentlemen's houses [in Scotland] are strong castles ... [that] look more like prisons than houses of reception'.[35] Fynes Moryson and other visitors, writing about Ireland in the early seventeenth century, commented on the persistence of the custom of 'coshering' by which Irish lords and their followers (and even some of the Old English) went on a progress, living off their tenants, sleeping round a fire in what must have been a central hall.[36] Sir James Ware, who described Ireland in 1654, claimed that the only brick and stone buildings belonged to religious houses and a few castles built in imitation of castles built by the English.[37] The anonymous author of *A Brief Character of Ireland* (1692) claimed that Irish castles were purely defensive and unsuitable for permanent habitation.[38] Descriptions such as these provide an interesting insight into attitudes, but they are often too full of the writer's prejudices about what constitutes civilized living to be adequate sources for the history of buildings in the country.

Understanding the built heritage, then, involves not only a knowledge of surviving buildings, but also a sense of how typical what survives might be. Additional documentary material, both specific to a house and its occupants, and more generalized contemporary commentary, greatly improve the quality of what it is possible to say about both the life of the occupants and the buildings themselves. An additional technique is comparison.

Defence and security

The comparative history of the British Isles in the seventeenth century has largely been restricted to 'the British problem' of the Wars of the Three Kingdoms in the

Figure 5.2 Monea Castle, Co. Fermanagh, built in 1618 in the Scottish style by the Rev. Malcolm Hamilton, a Scottish planter, Rector of Devenish and Church of Ireland Archbishop of Cashel 1623–9. © The Open University.

Figure 5.3 Coppinger's Court, Co. Cork, built *c*.1618 by Sir Walter Coppinger, a member of an Old English family from Cork city who had bought the land from penurious Gaelic Irish families. © The Open University.

1640s and 1650s – the politics of the English Civil War and the simultaneous conflicts in Wales, Scotland and Ireland. There has been little comparative social history of England and Wales, Scotland and Ireland. A study of the buildings of the British Isles can help us to develop such a comparative history. The domestic life of these islands read through its vernacular buildings and the buildings of people of higher social status offers important insights into the social, economic and cultural history of the period. Two particular characteristics of early modern domestic building – or their absence – highlight not only significant differences in the social lives of people in the different nations, but in different regions: the architectural attributes of defence and the use of building for display.

The contrast between the architecture of Monea Castle, Co. Fermanagh (Figure 5.2) and Coppinger's Court, Co. Cork (Figure 5.3) is striking. Monea is apparently a traditional tower house, with slit windows and a walled enclosure (a bawn), built in the Scottish style, in the part of Ulster settled by emigrants from Scotland. Coppinger's Court is a large house of a type that might in England be described as a manor house, originally with a bawn forming a courtyard for the entrance front, built in the southern province of Munster, a more peaceful, prosperous and urbanized region than Ulster, settled extensively by descendants of the Norman settlers of the twelfth century (known as the Old English), who declared their loyalty to the crown despite many of them remaining Catholic after the Reformation.[39]

The two houses were built in 1618 and their architecture reflects both the political differences between Ulster and Munster and cultural differences between the builders. Ulster had been a stronghold of the great Gaelic lordships and of Catholic resistance to the Tudor monarchy. Following the defeat of the Earls of Tyrone and Tyrconnell after the Nine Years War, and their flight to the continent in 1611, much of their land and that of their supporters was confiscated by the government and awarded under what was known as a plantation scheme to Protestant settlers (or planters) from both England and Scotland. The Catholic Irish population had been much depleted by the war, but Catholics, most living at subsistence level, outnumbered the planters; there were few ports or towns; and much of the territory was inaccessible. For grants of land of over 1,000 acres planters were required to erect a bawn; grants of over 2,000 acres specified that planters build a castle (meaning a fortified stone dwelling).[40] The definition of both a bawn and a castle was somewhat vague, but the intention was clearly that everyone should maintain a minimum defensive capability.[41] By contrast, Cork was a predominantly Old English region, a late participant in the rebellions against the Tudors and, though much of the region had been laid waste during the Desmond rebellion, it had ports and towns. The Munster plantation, which began in the 1580s, was to settle English Protestants on lands confiscated from the Earl of Desmond and his followers after the suppression of the rebellion in 1583.[42]

The cultures from which the planters came were significant. The Scots planters in Ulster came from a society in Scotland in which semi-fortified tower houses were, as we shall see, a current building type. The English were much more familiar with domestic architecture based on manor houses with no defensive features.[43] Whether or not Scots buildings of this date really were defensible is questionable, but status was still measured by the presence of crenellations, machicolations, slit windows, gun ports and a defended entrance, suggesting that the owner of the house was of high military status. By contrast, Old English families' Munster houses carried only the most vestigial emblems of defence: Coppinger's court has purely decorative machicolations along the side walls.[44]

By the time of the Restoration of the monarchy in 1660, builders in Ireland were abandoning even these allusions to defence. Houses such as Beaulieu, Co. Louth, and Eyrecourt, Co. Galway, resembled the latest building in England. But their builders' optimism was premature. Charleville, Co. Cork, the house erected in 1661 by the 1st Earl of Orrery, which had reputedly cost £20,000, was burnt down in 1690 during the Williamite wars. Another casualty was Sir John Perceval's house at Burton, Co. Cork, built in the Dutch style in the 1660s and improved by his descendants in the 1670s, which was burnt by James II's troops retreating after their defeat at the battle of the Boyne in 1690.[45] Poorer landlords resorted to restoring or building additions onto older structures. 'Several builders in Ireland have incommoded their new houses by striving to preserve some incurable or smoky castle', wrote Sir Robert Southwell in 1686.[46]

Despite the union of the crowns in 1603, the Anglo-Scottish border was another region where semi-defensive buildings were still being erected in the early seventeenth century. Bastle houses, or pele towers – very basic square stone structures

Figure 5.4 Woodhouses bastle house, Northumberland, 1602. © The Open University.

Figure 5.5 Mervinslaw pele tower, Roxburghshire, late sixteenth century. © The Open University.

with space for grain or livestock on the ground floor and human occupation on the first floor – were a common building type.[47] These buildings were for security against cattle rustling rather than defence against cross-border military raids and reflected the lawlessness of the region. They also show how similar the life and economy of the population was on both sides of the border, dependent primarily on rearing and trading cattle on the poor upland pastures. Woodhouses bastle house (Figure 5.4) and Mervinslaw pele tower (Figure 5.5) are very similar buildings, designed to serve the same functions, on different sides of the frontier.

It is instructive to compare these simple buildings with gentry domestic building at the same period. In Northumberland, south of the border, defensible buildings were being adapted to provide comfortable domestic spaces without defensive features. The owners of tower houses such as Chipchase Castle (with a fourteenth-century tower and a house of 1621) and, on a more modest scale, Kirkheaton (Figure 5.6) built living quarters onto the side of older tower houses, providing well-lit and heated accommodation over two or three floors with no concern with defence.

By contrast, in 1600, John Charteris and his wife Agnes Maxwell commissioned a fine new tower house in Dumfriesshire. The fittings of Amisfield Tower (Figure 5.7) are unusually intact because the owners built a new house nearby in the modern style in 1631. Like Monea the tower was not equipped for real military

Figure 5.6 Kirkheaton House, Northumberland. Late medieval tower; early seventeenth century house. © The Open University.

Figure 5.7 Amisfield Tower, Dumfriesshire 1600. © The Open University.

action, but was for show. The elaborate carving and the arrangement of the cap houses on the roof were decorative rather than functional. But, like Monea, it was a building that, at a pinch, could be defended: the ground floor was vaulted to give the upper structure strength (and as a precaution against fire, as the kitchen was usually positioned here), and the windows were small.[48] Compare this with the comment of Robert Reyce, writing in 1618 that 'at this day there is in Suffolk no castle fully standing, or at leastwise none fortified or defensible', and that ancient moated houses were being replaced by houses sited 'where they may be further seen, have best prospect, sweetest air and greatest pleasure ... all for outward show'.[49]

These buildings illustrate the point that different parts of the British Isles shared some building traditions, often dictated by economic and political conditions, but that divergences from them might occur because of quite local changes in circumstances or, just as important, perceptions. By the seventeenth century Northumbrian gentry had ceased to feel that their status depended on military show, but rather upon demonstrating themselves to be part of a cultivated metropolitan elite. But, in Scotland, military tradition remained a significant part of noble and gentle culture and continued to define subjects' relations with the monarch, though castle design remained anachronistic and did not catch up with developments in artillery.[50]

Fortified buildings in the Highlands found a use not only during the wars of the 1640s and 1650s, but in the aftermath of the Glorious Revolution in the 1690s and in the Jacobite rebellions of 1715 and 1745. But not all Scots buildings retained a fortified aspect: the same contrasts that can be seen in Ireland in Monea castle and Coppinger's Court are to be found in Scotland. In Moray in 1640 Sir Alexander Innes was building a tower house at Coxton, while his kinsman Sir Robert Innes was building Innes House nearby in the style of the new lairds' houses, an L-shaped building, with a tower staircase at the angle with little of the imagery of fortification.[51] The Dutch captain, John Slezer, who published a collection of engravings of Scotland in 1693 commented upon the Scots' 'capacity to erect such superb edifices as that kingdom abounds with' in spite of their addiction to military occupations.[52]

Building as display

The analysis of buildings in this way relies upon some knowledge of architectural style, but also upon an understanding of the economic, social and political circumstances in which they were erected and used. It asks such questions as 'What impression did the patron want to make?', 'Why did s/he choose to build in this way?' It is concerned not merely with the appearance of buildings, but with function and use of space. Bastle houses and pele towers were highly functional, using local materials (chiefly stone in a locality not well provided with timber) to create secure dwellings and protection for livestock in a regional economy where wealth was primarily held in cattle. Tower houses were also functional, but as can be seen from the adaptation of Kirkheaton, the defensive capability was lost when their original function was superseded by a greater concern for comfort.

But why did not owners simply knock down their towers and build new houses, perhaps recycling the building materials?[53] There was little military need for defence. It was partly the poverty of Scots landowners in the later seventeenth and early eighteenth centuries that compelled them to adapt older houses rather than to build new ones.[54] A richer builder, Alexander Seton 1st Earl of Dunfermline, referred to Pinkie House, after his substantial rebuilding there in 1613, as his 'villa': 'here there is nothing warlike, even for defence' reads the inscription on the house.[55]

Houses are not simply functional, they are evidence of owners' taste, discernment and aspirations; they substantiated owners' social standing. Builders frequently added their coats of arms as a declaration of status and ancestry. But since the origins of noble status lay with military obligations to the monarch, and buildings with defensive features had to be licensed, a signifier of nobility was military motifs. The Earls of Kellie were not anciently noble. Thomas Erskine 1st Earl of Kellie bought Kellie Castle (Figure 5.8) in 1617 and joined two older towers with a new range with first-floor dormer windows and possibly added the larger windows for the main hall.[56] His grandson, the 3rd Earl of Kellie, constable of the royal palace at Holyrood, employed craftsmen who were working on Charles II's new palace, to create a modern suite of rooms with panelling, lavish decorative and

Figure 5.8 Kellie Castle, Fife, a fifteenth-century tower house joined to a sixteenth-century tower by Lord Oliphant's new range *c*.1603–7. The 3rd Earl of Kellie remodelled the interior apartments in the 1670s using craftsmen working on Charles II's new palace at Holyrood. James Lorimer restored the house in the 1870s. © The Open University.

heraldic plasterwork and inset paintings. The earlier tower houses were retained as a symbol of the family's lineage and nobility.[57] Yet at the very moment the 3rd Earl's alterations were being carried out, the Earl of Strathmore remarked that castellated houses 'truly are quite out of fashion, as feuds are, ... the country being generally more civilised than it was of ancient times'.[58]

Two builders for whom ancestry was particularly important were Abigail Sherard, Lady Leitrim and Lady Anne Clifford, Countess of Pembroke and Montgomery. Abigail Sherard was the wife of William Sherard, a Leicestershire gentleman who was created Lord Leitrim in 1627. She restored the Sherard family house at Stapleford, Leicestershire, gothicizing an earlier building and decorating it with coats of arms and sculpture representing purported Sherard ancestors such as Gilbert de Clare and William the Conqueror.[59] Lady Anne Clifford, who in 1643 after decades of litigation inherited the estates of her father, the Earl of Cumberland, set about restoring the castles and churches on her ancestral lands. Unlike Abigail Sherard who celebrated her husband's noble status, Anne Clifford, married twice, celebrated her father's family. Even before the civil war, the life of the military nobleman in a castle was obsolete in England. Her restorations were certainly about family pride; as wife of the Earl of Pembroke she had lived at

Wilton, one of the most modern and fashionable houses of its time, yet much of her restoration was simply reinstating medieval work, as at Brougham and Brough. Even at Skipton, which was substantially rebuilt as a house in the late 1650s, the style of the windows and doors is of the sixteenth century and the most important room is the great hall. However, she frequently asserted that she had rebuilt castles and churches from a state of ruination when the evidence of the surviving fabric suggests that rather more remained of the original building than she claimed.[60] Both women were closely concerned with family and lineage: Abigail Sherard commissioned a genealogy of the Sherard family and Lady Anne Clifford commissioned a family tree to form part of her own monument at Appleby church.

Lady Anne Clifford's castles were out of sympathy with the times with their military display and old-fashioned organization of space within. They retained the medieval great hall and private apartments, which segregated occupants by sex rather than status, and where privacy was not a significant consideration. By the 1650s, even the prodigy houses of Elizabethan and Jacobean courtiers, which were built around a great hall but had plenty of private space as well, were looking old-fashioned. In this respect the nobility followed the gentry, retaining the two-storey hall as a sign of status longer than those of lower rank.[61] As great halls declined, so the number and variety of secondary rooms increased – dining rooms, closets and parlours, for example – with fireplaces and reached by staircases. Separate quarters for servants were constructed and the circulation was rearranged so that servants could move around the house out of sight through hidden passages and staircases, an arrangement that would have been impossible in a house such as Amisfield.

Lavish display served a function for both the *nouveaux riches* and for older families who wanted to maintain publicly their grandeur. It could express aspiration or self-confidence. A family's quality, its honour, standing and reputation were reinforced by various kinds of conspicuous show from houses to clothes to hospitality and the number of servants kept.[62] During the seventeenth century there was a decline in the number of retainers and, in particular, in the numbers of male servants, and those there were tended to be of lower social status.[63] At the same time changes in traditions of hospitality and the pursuits of the gentry and others left their mark on their houses. The messages sent out by buildings and their decoration and arrangement were not lost on contemporaries: in the late seventeenth century Roger North wrote of how 'the justness or imperfection of [the builder's] mind will appear in them', not least because the gentleman was expected to take a close interest in the commission.[64] Indeed, for much of the period there was no such thing as a professional architect; instead gentlemen took an interest in architecture, though few showed the expertise of Roger Pratt, Hugh May or even Roger North.[65]

Presenting the country house in the twenty-first century

How do we, as citizens of the twenty-first century, view these buildings now? Interest in the English country house has developed far beyond simple accounts of life in the country house or architectural descriptions.[66] Mark Girouard's pioneering work brought together the architects and craftsmen of houses with the history of the families that used the houses. He looked at how houses represented power, the pretensions and ambitions of their owners and users, and at how architecture (style, motifs, the use of space) was deployed to convey important messages about the owner.[67] In his discussion of the mason and builder, Robert Smythson, he raised questions about what the unique architectural features of Hardwick Hall owed to its patron, Elizabeth Countess of Shrewsbury.[68] His work brought to a much wider audience a way of looking at the country house – and, by extension, the built environment – which took into account the social and economic history of which this was a part.

An important element in the literature has been the discussion of space, especially in relation to gender. One of the most effective analyses of the country house and its use in early modern England is Alice Friedman's study of Wollaton Hall and the Willoughby family. Friedman makes a point essential to considering buildings as material evidence of the past:

> The form of a building embodies a contradiction: it is the actualization of the social relationships, material resources, needs, and talents of a particular patron, architect, household, or group of builders at a fixed point in time, but it is expected to outlive them and to remain useful and meaningful long after they are gone ... . [E]ach generation both changes the buildings that it inherits and builds new ones of its own, expressing and accommodating the relationships, habits of mind and beliefs which are all part of their distinctive culture.[69]

These habits of mind and beliefs are not simply personal, individual; institutional concerns affect our understanding of built heritage: many of the older buildings with whose interiors we are familiar have undergone an extensive process of restoration in which many contemporary cultural assumptions about the display of the past are evident. In England, the foundation of the National Trust, in 1895, is now seen as an emblem of the value the English place upon their built heritage and rural landscape. It is easy to forget that the philanthropic founders were acting out of fear that both were about to disappear beneath the inexorable progress of industrialization and urbanization. But it was also an organization that depended upon a relatively wealthy population: the Trust does not normally accept properties into its care without a substantial endowment for maintenance. The National Trust for Scotland was founded in 1931 on similar terms. But the Republic of Ireland has never had such a body (the English National Trust has the care of some properties in Northern Ireland). Country houses have not been seen there as an inherently valuable part of that nation's heritage (as early Christian sites such as Cashel and prehistoric sites such as Newgrange have been seen).[70] Rather they have been seen as representing a regime that had to be cast off before the country could find its identity as a nation state. It is only relatively recently that an appreciation of the skill and artistry of Irish craftsmen has given these sites value, an appreciation fostered by the work of the Irish Georgian Society.

Thus viewing the built heritage is overlaid with cultural assumptions that differ between the nations of these islands. Just as the earlier history of these nations affects the survival of buildings, their style, function and form, so does the more recent history inflect the value that such remains have. But some of these differences, as we have seen with defended buildings, are not particular to one side of a border or another; the study of them illustrates that the built heritage reveals a social history that crosses national borders, a culture that does not necessarily coincide with political borders.[71]

Notes

1   I am grateful for permission from the Open University to use pictures from material originally filmed for the course A220 Princes and Peoples: France and the British Isles 1620–1714.

2   W.G. Hoskins, 'The Rebuilding of Rural England 1570–1640', *Past and Present*, 4 (1953), p. 44.

3   Ibid., pp. 44–59.

4   R. Machin, 'The Great Rebuilding: A Reassessment', *Past and Present*, 77 (1977), pp. 33–56.

5   Colin Platt, *The Great Rebuildings of Tudor and Stuart England* (London: UCL Press, 1994), pp. 134–5.

6   Eric Mercer, 'The Houses of the Gentry', *Past and Present*, 5 (1954), pp. 14–15; Nicholas Cooper, *Houses of the Gentry 1480–1680* (New Haven and London: Yale University Press, 1999), p. 282.

7   Hoskins, 'The Rebuilding of Rural England', p. 45.

8   Mercer, 'The Houses of the Gentry', pp. 17, 24.

9   Sarah Pearson, 'Boughton Monchelsea: The Pattern of Building in a Central Kent Parish', *Architectural History*, 44 (2001), pp. 387, 392.

10   Pat Ryan, 'The Buildings of Rural Ingatestone, Essex, 1536–1601: "Great Rebuilding" or "housing revolution"?', *Vernacular Architecture*, 31 (2000), pp. 18–19.

11   Felicity Heal and Clive Holmes, *The Gentry in England and Wales 1500–1700* (Basingstoke: Macmillan, 1994), p. 301.

12   Hoskins, 'The Rebuilding of Rural England', p. 54.

13   Richard Wilson and Alan Mackley, *Creating Paradise: The Building of the English Country House 1660–1880* (London: Hambledon and London, 2000), p. 207.

14   Matthew Johnson, 'Rethinking the Great Rebuilding', *Oxford Journal of Archaeology*, 21 (1993), p. 121.

15   Ibid., pp. 120–2.

16   Peter Smith, 'Introduction to Rural Building in Wales', in M.W. Barley (ed.), *The Buildings of the Countryside 1500–1750: Chapters from the Agrarian History of England and Wales vol. 5* (Cambridge: Cambridge University Press, 1990), p. 184.

17   Rolf Loeber, 'Early Classicism in Ireland: Architecture Before the Georgian Era', *Architectural History*, 22 (1979), p. 60.

18   C.R.J. Currie, 'Time and Chance: Modelling the Attrition of Old Houses', *Vernacular Architecture*, 19 (1988), pp. 1–9.

19   Stephen Porter, *Destruction in the English Civil Wars* (Stroud: Alan Sutton, 1994), pp. 64, 75, 77.

20   The Knight of Glin, David J. Griffin, Nicholas K. Robinson, *Vanishing Country Houses of Ireland* (Dublin: Irish Architectural Archive & the Irish Georgian Society, 1988), 'Introduction: A Patchwork of Irish Houses'; Terence Dooley, *The Decline of the 'Big House' in Ireland: A Study of Irish Landed Families* (Dublin: Wolfhound Press, 2001), p. 276.

21 'Early Modern Oxford', *A History of the County of Oxford: Volume 4: The City of Oxford* (1979), pp. 85–101. At: http://www.british-history.ac.uk/report.aspx?compid=22804&strquery=salter, accessed 16 December 2007.

22 'Modern Oxford', in *A History of the County of Oxford: Volume 4: The City of Oxford* (1979), pp. 188–208. At: http://www.british-history.ac.uk/report.aspx?compid=22805, accessed 16 December 2007.

23 Jennifer Sherwood and Nikolaus Pevsner, *The Buildings of England: Oxfordshire* (Harmondsworth: Penguin Books, 1974), pp. 307–10, 513–19.

24 Sherwood and Pevsner, *Oxfordshire*, p. 509.

25 A.A. Tait, 'Isaac de Caus and the South Front of Wilton House', *Burlington Magazine*, 106, February (1964), p. 74; John Heward, 'The Restoration of the South Front of Wilton House: The Development of the House Reconsidered', *Architectural History*, 35 (1992), pp. 82, 83, 97; Timothy Mowl and Brian Earnshaw, *Architecture without Kings: the Rise of Puritan Classicism under Cromwell* (Manchester: Manchester University Press, 1995), pp. 31ff.

26 Christine Casey and Alastair Rowan, *The Buildings of Ireland: North Leinster* (London: Penguin, 1993), pp. 155–6.

27 Ibid., p. 155.

28 Ryan, 'The Buildings of Rural Ingatestone', p. 11.

29 Maurice Howard, 'Inventories, Surveys and the History of Great Houses 1480–1640', *Architectural History*, 41 (1998), pp. 20–2; Nicholas Cooper, *Houses of the Gentry*, p. 247.

30 William Harrison, *The Description of England*, ed. George Edelen (New York: Dover Publications, 1994), pp. 197, 199, 200, 201.

31 Gerard Boate, *Ireland's Naturall History ... published by Samuel Hartlib* (London, 1657), pp. 148–60.

32 Robert Reyce, *Breviary of Suffolk* (1618), from Lawrence Stone, *Social Change and Revolution in England 1540–1640* (London: Longman, 1965), p. 127.

33 Edward Waterhouse, *The Gentleman's Monitor* (London, 1665), Epistle dedicatory unpaginated.

34 John Ray, 'Selected Remains', in Hume Brown (ed.), *Early Travellers in Scotland* (1891; Edinburgh: Mercat Press, 1978), p. 231.

35 Thomas Kirke, 'A Modern Account of Scotland' in Brown (ed.), *Early Travellers in Scotland*, p. 259.

36 Fynes Moryson, 'Description of Ireland', in C. Litton Falkiner (ed.), *Illustrations of Irish History and Topography* (London: Longmans Green and Co., 1904), p. 232; *A Geographicall Description of the Kingdom of Ireland ... By a Well-willer to the Peace of Both Kingdoms* (London, 1642), p. 28.

37 Sir James Ware, *The Antiquities and History of Ireland* (London, 1654; in Latin, 1705), p. 37.

38 *A Brief Character of Ireland* (London, 1692), p. 37.

39 An even more striking contrast is seen in Derryhiveny Castle (1643) and Eyrecourt Castle (after 1660), both in Co. Galway. Derryhiveny is a traditional Irish tower house, with slit windows and a walled enclosure or bawn, while Eyrecourt is a comfortable, symmetrical Dutch-style house with large windows of some time after 1660. General references to Irish houses come from Mark Bence-Jones, *A Guide to Irish Country Houses*, revised edn (London: Constable, 1988).

40 Philip Robinson, *The Plantation of Ulster* (1984; Belfast: Ulster Historical Foundation, 1994), Chapter 6; M. Perceval-Maxwell, *The Scottish Migration to Ulster in the Reign of James I* (1973; Belfast: Ulster Historical Foundation, 1990), pp. 16–18.

41 Robinson, *Plantation of Ulster*, pp. 131–2.

42 Michael Mac Carthy-Morrogh, *The Munster Plantation: English Migration to Southern Ireland 1583–1641* (Oxford: Clarendon Press, 1986), Chapter 1.

43 Robinson, *Plantation of Ulster*, p. 133.

44 Niall McCullough and Valerie Mulvin, *The Lost Tradition: The Nature of Architecture in Ireland* (Dublin: Gandon Editions, 1987), p. 48.

45 Toby Barnard, 'Boyle, Roger, First Earl of Orrery (1621–1679)', *Oxford Dictionary of National Biography* (Oxford: Oxford University Press, Sept. 2004; online edn, May 2006, at: http://www.oxforddnb.com/view/article/3138, accessed 21 December 2007); Toby Barnard, *Making the Grand Figure: Lives and Possessions in Ireland 1641–1770* (New Haven and London: Yale University Press, 2004), p. 25; the Knight of Glin and James Peill, *Irish Furniture* (New Haven and London: Yale University Press, 2007), pp. 25–6.

46 Quoted in Barnard, *Making the Grand Figure*, p. 26.

47 Ian and Kathleen Whyte, *The Changing Scottish Landscape 1500–1800* (London: Routledge, 1991), p. 87.

48 Ibid., pp. 85–6.

49 Robert Reyce, *Breviary of Suffolk* (1618), from Lawrence Stone, *Social Change and Revolution in England 1540–1640* (London: Longman, 1965), pp. 127–8.

50 Keith M. Brown, *Noble Society in Scotland: Wealth, Family and Culture, from the Reformation to the Revolution* (Edinburgh: Edinburgh University Press, 2004), pp. 2–3; Whyte and Whyte, *Changing Scottish Landscape*, p. 92.

51 Ibid., pp. 94–5.

52 *Theatrum Scotiae* (1693), quoted in Deborah Howard, 'Dutch Influence in Scottish Architecture', in Julia Lloyd Williams, *Dutch Art and Scotland: A Reflection of Taste* (Edinburgh: National Gallery of Scotland, 1992), p. 44. In the eighteenth century Scots began to revert to the tower house as a model, with the earliest houses (such as Inveraray castle) in the Scots baronial style.

53 Donald Woodward, '"Swords into ploughshares": recycling in pre-industrial England', *Economic History Review*, 2nd series, 38 (1985), pp. 175–91 discusses the reuse of building materials.

54 Whyte and Whyte, *Changing Scottish Landscape*, p. 99.

55 Deborah Howard, *Scottish Architecture: Reformation to Restoration 1560–1600* (Edinburgh: Edinburgh University Press, 1995), p. 51.

56 David Macgibbon and Thomas Ross, *The Castellated and Domestic Architecture of Scotland from the Twelfth to the Eighteenth Century*, 5 vols (1887–92; reprint Edinburgh: Mercat Press, 1999), vol. 2, p. 130.

57 The detailed building history of Kellie Castle is confused by Lorimer's restoration.

58 G. Donaldson, *Scotland: James V–James VII*, Edinburgh History of Scotland, vol. 3 (Edinburgh: Oliver & Boyd, 1968), p. 396.

59 The addition by her son of a large, symmetrical house of 1670–80 dwarfs the earlier work.

60 Compare the accounts in D.J.H. Clifford (ed.), *The Diaries of Lady Anne Clifford* (Stroud: Alan Sutton, 1990) and the inscriptions on the buildings with accounts in the *Buildings of England* and other reference works.

61 Cooper, *Houses of the Gentry*, pp. 277, 279.

62 Heal and Holmes, *The Gentry*, pp. 137–8.

63 Bridget Hill, *Servants: English Domestics in the Eighteenth Century* (Oxford: Clarendon Press, 1996), pp. 30, 43; M.W. Barley 'Rural Building in England 1640–1750' in M.W. Barley (ed.), *The Buildings of the Countryside*, p. 101. The dating of the feminization of domestic service is contested. Heal and Holmes, *The Gentry*, p. 140.

64 Quoted in Heal and Holmes, *The Gentry*, p. 298.

65 Wilson and Mackley, *Creating Paradise*, p. 114.

66 See particularly, Kari Boyd McBride, *Country House Discourse: A Cultural Study of Landscape and Legitimacy* (Aldershot: Ashgate, 2001).

67 Mark Girouard, *Life in the English Country House: A Social and Architectural History* (New Haven and London: Yale University Press).

68   Mark Girouard, *Robert Smythson and the Architecture of the Elizabethan Era* (London: Country Life, 1966), p. 129.

69   Alice T. Friedman, *House and Household in Elizabethan England: Wollaton Hall and the Willoughby Family* (Chicago and London: University of Chicago Press, 1989), p. 4.

70   David C. Harvey, 'Heritages Pasts and Heritages Presents: Temporality, Meaning and the Scope of Heritage Studies', *International Journal of Heritage Studies*, 7 (2001), p. 335.

71   Adrian Green, 'Houses in North-eastern England: Regionality and the British Beyond. *c.*1660–1750', in Susan Lawrence (ed.), *Archaeologies of the British: Explorations of Identity in Great Britain and its Colonies 1600–1945* (London: Routledge, 2003), p. 71.

6   Object biographies

From production to consumption

Karin Dannehl

Imagine a kitchen in a household of middling rank in around 1700. In this hive of activity several hours would be spent every day to prepare and preserve the food that sustained its members.[1] At its centre was the fire, and above the fire hung the cooking pot.[2] Our sketch of domestic industry is filled with smells, noise, heat and utensils. The objects that sustained the activities invite further investigation, for their existence suggests that our kitchen cameo is only a small part of a much bigger picture. What were they? If they were objects required by those who laboured in the kitchen, how did they come to be at the workers' disposal? On what basis were decisions of acquisition made? How were the objects designed and made? How sold? How repaired? What happened when they came to the end of their useful life?

Such questions relate to biographical turning points or stages in the life cycle of the objects found in the kitchen. In asking them, we set ourselves the task of considering the complete trajectory of an object from production to consumption. This chapter offers an introduction to the concept of object biography and the life cycle model, two concepts that, it will be argued, can be useful tools when handling the methodological challenges of an object-focused historical enquiry. The aim is not to give a full exposition of what different authors have said and how different fields view the biography approach to objects of the past. Rather, the chapter is pitched to show how the two concepts differ, how they might be applied and what challenges you might encounter in applying them. The example of eighteenth-century cooking vessels serves to link the abstract discussion back to the study of an actual object type. Since the biography highlights exceptional features while the life cycle study puts the focus on generic features, the two methods complement each other. Combining them into a hybrid methodology for exploring an artefact promises the highest returns.

The chapter is subdivided into six sections that will start with a look at definitions, and then move on to the general theme of the life story approach and the question of context before discussing the example study and potential sources. The sixth section is a discussion of the key findings.

Biography and life cycle model

Let us take a closer look at the definitions of the terms biography and life cycle. Not only will their meaning becoming clearer, a better understanding of the terminology will also make us appreciate their specific advantages and disadvantages. The *Oxford English Dictionary Online* recognizes three types of biography, essentially moving from the literary genres of history to any written record of life histories, and shifting from a focus on human life to include those of animals or plants.[3] At the base lies the notion of a story that traces an evolutionary development, and as such it can be transferred from a living organism to an object. As a literary genre the biography takes the shape of a story in an organized and structured fashion, starting at the beginning and ending at the end. Traditionally, it traces a life story that is considered to be complete, in other words, a life that concluded with the death of its subject, in order to trace the history of the subject and to show its exceptional character within its own time.[4] When applied to objects the biography offers the same features: a tightly defined, finite time frame, the focus on the subject against a context, and the express purpose of highlighting exceptional or unusual features. This leaves us with a problem. Many of the objects that the historian may want to investigate may be of interest not for their highly unusual value and hence unique life story, but precisely for their generic qualities. Such objects tend to be, at least at their point of making, fairly ordinary, and were for example the products of batch or mass production for everyday use. If our aim is to investigate the generic and more segmented elements of their life story, then they require a different approach.

One possible answer comes in the form of the life cycle model. Although equally premised on a life story, the life cycle model focuses on what is generic in the cycle more than potential peculiarities. Its definition from the *Oxford English Dictionary Online* first relates to the biological life cycle, a 'series of developments that an organism undergoes in the course of its progress from the egg to the adult state'. It also covers the account of such a development, and is applied to 'the course of human, cultural, ... existence from birth or beginning through development and productivity to decay and death or ending'. The expression is in fact frequently transferred to capture the total of developmental stages, for example in commerce, where it denotes a product life cycle from exploration to growth and maturity through to decline.[5] Used in a wide range of disciplines, life cycle models postulate a beginning and an end, with an intervening period of growth and decline,[6] where start and finish respectively mark a generational change.[7]

A sub-category of the life cycle model is the life cycle assessment study. Such a study sets out to examine the entire life cycle of the product, including extraction and processing of raw materials, manufacturing, transportation and distribution, use, re-use, maintenance, recycling and final disposal.[8] The insights derived from the approach are instructive. They show, for instance, that the greatest degree of uniformity in the life cycle of a product is naturally found at the point of production, where technical knowledge of making tends to be relatively standardized, while the greatest variation is found at the user end of the career path or life cycle, where users' individuality, their freedom of choice, and the specific parameters within which they use an object will determine a great range of uses, or performances. At the 'production pole' an object is least likely to follow an idiosyncratic career, deviating from that of other objects of the same kind and make, since the place of production itself is likely to be the most culturally standardized. In so far as recipes for fabrication tend to work thus, workshops and manufactories act as repositories storing such technical production knowledge.[9] Initially used to compare products, applications of life cycle assessment studies came to include government policy, strategic planning, marketing, consumer education, process improvement and product design.[10]

Users and detractors alike have noted that life cycle assessment studies can be taken too far by including more and more stages of the product's impact, making investigation and assessment unwieldy.[11] Since models are used for the express reason that they may represent reality in the form of a simplified abstraction, they must make compromises in order to be functional.[12] Both the life cycle study and the life cycle assessment are designed to deal with much shorter periods of time than a historical treatment would require, and both postulate a linear development in that they reduce the life cycle to a linear interdependence of its stages. In their treatment, few of these stages come close to the depth and breadth expected of contextual analysis in history. Moreover, for a life cycle assessment study, full access to comprehensive evidence is assumed, a situation that is rarely if ever found with objects from the past. It is no surprise to find that many of the stages suggested in industrial studies of this type cannot be reproduced for the eighteenth-century case study, so that neither the life cycle model nor its relation, the life cycle assessment, can simply be transferred from industry to history.

Object life stories: trajectories through different contexts

Let us now consider what some of the proponents of objects' life stories have said. One of them is Kopytoff, whose particular interest is the process of commodification. Kopytoff compares the object's trajectory with that of a human slave who moves into the 'commodity stage'. The slave loses the status of commodity when bought but usually remains a potential commodity for the rest of his or her existence. Much the same applies to an object.[13] In fact, the process of commoditization is a product of cultural shaping. Not only is an owner's decision to enter or withdraw an object from being or becoming a commodity made subsequently to the producer's decision to make a product for sale, it is frequently a societal decision rather than a personal one, and tied to the values that the members of the society in question share. Depending on the stages of an object's biography, and depending on the age of an object, this may mean different, culturally acceptable uses.[14]

Kopytoff's approach is essentially that of a biographer with a focus on individual objects, even though he limits his enquiry to the stage where the objects go through cycles of exchange. This leaves out the wide range of contexts that sociologists, anthropologists, archaeologists and historians have identified, and where objects can be possessions, exchange values, tools, acquisitions, signifiers of status, products and even cross boundaries between object categories – for example, between decorative object and work of art in the course of time.[15] For Dant, who also embeds object biographies into his analysis of material culture,[16] this shift in context is at least in part the result of human beings' changing relationship with an object over time.[17]

The huge potential for dramatic shifts in context for any given object is even more prominent in Cummings, another scholar who uses the term 'life' with regard to objects. Cummings emphasizes that objects have several contexts, functions and associations. Central to the historian's interest, objects not only exist in their manifestation as physical things, but also in the documentary appendage that accumulates with every stage of their life cycle.[18] In other words, humans accord objects a parallel existence in the 'discursive space', though the amount and survival of the materials documenting it may vary. There is room for these parallel lives to go in different directions and for objects to lead 'double' lives, one on paper and the other as an artefact. Consequently, the discursive material is not an unalloyed blessing. On the positive side, it enables the historian who, in contrast to archaeologists, may be in a better position to piece together the trajectory from production to consumption to go beyond the artefact, particularly where artefacts are not available. Historians' studies of object life stories, with documentary evidence at their disposal, are as a result not tethered to artefacts. On the other hand, it throws open the numerous contexts in which an object existed, potentially obliging the historian to address them all.

Contexts and challenges

Because different contexts equate with the different passages of an object's life story or biography, the challenges of context warrant further attention. Context affixes meaning to an expression or event, while something that is said or done 'out of context' is, as a result, also without a secure meaning. Where the surrounding words or circumstances are missing, the meaning becomes uncertain and deceptive. Historians seek to retrieve, describe and analyse context, and not surprisingly the extent to which this is feasible is subject to debate.[19] Some of the specific problems of context and contextualization are the focus of this section. Three areas in particular are relevant to the historian of objects: the difference between exceptional and utilitarian objects and the effect on contextual documentation, the dilemma of the humble object becoming exceptional, and the question of deciding on appropriate contexts.

In order to deal with objects, we need categories. Categories can be simple and relate to a single element – for example, size, material or age – or more complex categories that distinguish between social, cultural or economic roles of objects – for example, between luxury and everyday objects, decorative and functional objects. Categories seek to limit and define, and so it is no surprise to find that for every rule there are exceptions. In the present discussion, it is useful to distinguish between expensive, artistic or otherwise exceptional objects and utilitarian ones, which are likely to be less expensive, less likely to be valued for their aesthetic values because of how this social, cultural and economic baggage influences the biography and life cycle of the object. The exceptional object is invested with interest, and consequently with commentary, whereas the humble object tends not to receive much attention. A simple rule of thumb is that the more valuable an object, the more likely it is to accumulate a documentary record along the way.[20] An example will illustrate the difference. The maker's stamp on a piece of silver ware helps to identify the item as having come from a specific workshop, dating to at least the time period during which the maker, who can be verified from further sources such as masters' rolls, was active. Up until the end of the eighteenth century, small, tool-type articles rarely received the name or mark of the maker to help identification.[21] Base metal objects, with the exception of pewter ware, rarely bear marks.[22] The mechanism works both ways. The more discursive space an object is given, the more important and unique it becomes. The more important it is deemed to be, the more likely it is that its life story will be told, and the more important the full trajectory from production to consumption will become. The account will quite possibly be extended into the present times, because a precious object is more likely to be preserved, more likely to change hands, and most likely to be valued for this pedigree of ownership. The trajectory will thereby be biased towards an extended 'consumption stage' and will not necessarily give equal treatment to different stages of the object's existence. The humble object, by contrast, will be more likely to get used and used up, or returned as scrap to produce new objects, of similarly functional value that does not make them candidates for collectors' envy or museum displays. The case seems clear but the reality is more complex.

Given the large numbers of humdrum objects that once underwent the life cycle from production, distribution and consumption, and that have disappeared, those that have survived are, by virtue of their survival, exceptions. A collectors' guide spells out the incentive for collectors of humbler objects: 'To acquire even one old kitchen utensil or implement is to possess a piece of local and social history, of craftsmanship and, often, of beauty.'[23] The criteria may not be the ones a historian would like to see applied, but they illustrate how the boundaries between high art and craft, exceptional and everyday, are blurred.

This raises a dilemma for the researcher. If an everyday object is defined by being inconspicuous, then what are we to do on those occasions when they do appear – for example, in a comment by a diarist or as an artefact in a museum display. By dint of appearing, the humble object has become conspicuous. It is thereby at once removed from its regular contexts. For one, it did not undergo the final, the 'death', stage. In the case of our example, the cooking vessels, few survive because base metal was worth recycling. The pots that persisted have done so by chance and accident, and for reasons that can be very idiosyncratic. For example, although one may assume that a pot found in a field, filled with coins, was really intended to function as a pot for boiling despite its reassigned role as a safe, the new context of a hoard is likely to have to be taken into consideration. The problems do not end if the mundane object – intended for routine tasks and ultimately obsolescence and destruction – enters a collection and in a similar category to that of unique, expensive and exceptional objects. We also need to remember that the routines of use that may have involved the objects now on display have been removed purposefully to protect the artefacts from further wear and damage, precisely so that the object but not its context of use will be available for the historian, who is called upon at least in part to fill in the absent elements.[24] Museums' exhibition cases are sometimes little more than well-structured storage rooms, and even the most meticulously assembled period room – for all its verisimilitude – does not remove the need to reflect on this additional layer of context. This new context, in which the researcher finds the object, posits its own challenges. This means that many of the proposed models for studying material culture, at least in part because they tacitly assume but do not overtly stress context,[25] struggle to address the fundamental problem of classification. Similarly, the challenges of multiple contexts are rarely acknowledged, and there is no model aiding a systematic approach.[26] So context, yes – but which one?

The afterlife of an object will determine how much information about its prior existence there is, how changed the object is from use, wear and tear, as well as possibly deliberate alterations that may have occurred at any stage. Despite the blurred boundaries sketched above, biographical material – that is, material that relates to a specific specimen – is rarely available for everyday objects. They usually have not survived in great numbers and the various contexts through which they would have passed in their existence are not usually documented. These may be valid reasons not to make humble objects the protagonists of biographies, but thankfully there is an alternative approach: the life cycle study. The life cycle study gives recognition to the 'communication value between the observer and the original producing culture'[27] of small, utilitarian objects. By virtue of their large number they performed a large array of functions in the course of their useful life,[28] and concern has been replaced by enthusiasm about the kind of information they offer.[29] With the life cycle model it does not matter if their life stories may appear incomplete, either because there is no data to retrieve them, or because the trajectory itself was incomplete.

Armed with the earlier discussion of definitions, the initial evaluation of the two concepts and about the consideration of context, we can move on to the case study. In the following section, the example of the cooking pot will help to evaluate the options and the obstacles to such an investigation, why it is useful and what the historian may learn from approaching a class of objects with the help of the analytical aids of biography and life cycle.

Life stories from written sources: metal cooking pots

The student of hollow ware is fortunate in that, although eighteenth-century cooking pots were not natural protagonists in the recordings of diarists and writers, they do crop up in them, as well as in the documents produced by inventors, metal workers and foundry managers, newspaper copy writers and tradespeople, the authors of cookery books, and finally appraisers in charge of the chattels of the deceased. And, being made of metal, they occasionally even made it into pamphlets of those thundering the doom of the population poisoned by the pernicious effects of copper and brass. At all stages of the life cycle the biographer is likely to find some evidence.[30] The three overarching passages or stages of the generic metal cooking pot's life are production, distribution and consumption. First, a piece of domestic hollow ware would undergo the production stage, where design and the technology and skill of making featured. Second, it would move through the distribution stage and here questions of advertising and physical transportation would come to the fore, followed by sale and acquisition. The final passage would be the consumption stage, during which cycles of use and of restoring through cleaning and mending would have eventually led to scrapping and recycling of the metal pot, effectively returning its component materials to the distribution stage. An alternative route, and the one most likely followed by the artefact available to the historian, would have halted the use and consumption stage, or interrupted the life cycle at some point between production and using up, and led to the pot's preservation. This return to the distribution stage would have involved acquisition into a collection and subsequent return to the use stage with cycles of interpretation and investigation as a museum object.

There is room to flesh out the production aspect. A letter book and the documentation of a legal wrangle that accompanied a patent for producing cast iron hollow ware provide essential information for important stages in the overall history of metal hollow ware in England.[31] In early 1700 at the Coalbrookdale iron foundry in Shropshire, Abraham Darby succeeded in casting iron pots in sand, a process that was faster and cheaper than earlier techniques. His patent from 1707 granted him the right to keep his technique secret and to benefit from a royal monopoly for the exploitation of the process for 14 years.[32] This achievement is rated as an important breakthrough in industrial history. By the 1720s the then manager of the works, Richard Ford, was writing to keep the new owner, Nehemiah Champion, informed about the state of affairs and in particular the sale and distribution of the cast ware produced at Coalbrookdale. Large quantities of cast iron hollow ware were sent by barge on the River Severn down to Bristol, with complaints about faulty wares and the pressure of competition from foundries in Wales and further north peppering the correspondence. We note that the letter book and the court case do not relate to individual items of hollow ware. Instead, they assist us with aspects of generic life cycle stages, as well as the broader context of production at a give time, in this case the early eighteenth century.

Despite the survival of document evidence, some aspects remain extremely elusive: for instance, the connection between users and producers. Were there, for example, elements of consultation that may have resulted in changes in design? The artefacts sometimes show repairs that could be interpreted as traces of customization for the user, but available correspondence for hollow ware that mentions requests from end-consumers relates to hollow ware for industrial purposes. There is only the complaint from an early eighteenth-century wholesaler, Graffin Prankard, who cites the poor quality of the castings as the cause of his problems selling them, which indicates that consumers and users were not reduced to buying what was available.[33] Visual evidence, which would help to track changes in form and design, is also relatively scarce. Cookery books, such as Eliza Smith's, have frontispieces,[34] but still lifes and domestic scenes are mostly of Dutch origin and tend to use the lustre of highly polished copper vessels to add depth and the sparkle of light. Trade cards, a visual form of promotional literature with its heyday in the last third of the century, feature engravings of the shop sign but not often pots.[35] Perhaps most difficult is to show change over time because most documents that have been mentioned provide only brief glimpses, and the detail that is available – for example, about ownership at death from probate material for the early part of the century – is mostly not available for the latter. It means that the historian may have to make do with inserting his or her object case study into the broader but less specific historiography, for instance of changes in retailing, in advertising, in technology, and consumption, offering the supposition that cooking pots may have followed the trends observable for other aspects of eighteenth-century life. In the case of consumption, for instance, this meant an overall trend for more and more diverse objects owned by more and more people.

Beyond written records

To the historian the reconstruction of a story from documents is key. To the historian of objects, however, the physical experience of the three-dimensional thing that is packed with sensual information, has to be of at least as much importance. To pick up an artefact is to engage with the past on so direct and so immediate a level, it approaches something magical. The experiences of weight, surface texture, sound and smell are part of the physicality of objects. They are an essential part of what artefacts have to offer the historian, and can be experienced with many of our senses, including sight, touch, balance, hearing and smell. We do well to remember that most of the human body is surface, including inner surface areas such as nasal passages, the digestive tracts and the inside passages of ear and mouth. This vast tactile area determines human experience of the external, material world. Of this surface area tongue, fingers, nose and ears are only the most salient points. Effectively, the entire skeletal and muscular structures experience an impact with the material surrounds when it comes to lifting, moving, pulling and pushing, and they combine to restore equilibrium when the sense of balance is challenged through handling objects that can be picked up. Such is the power of touch that where an object is removed from access to the elementary senses, as is frequently the case with museum artefacts, the sense of seeing will be supplemented from memory with information of weight, shape and other experiences that handling the object would yield in an effort to complete the reduced experience.

Surviving examples of eighteenth-century cooking pots are not numerous. The metal constituted a valuable raw material, and when the heat of the embers and sanding had taken their toll, as is evident in surviving specimen, most of them would have been sold or exchanged for their scrap value. Such artefacts as have come to us show us the range of their shapes, capacity, their weight, the colour – rose-golden hues for copper, gold-like for brass and grey for cast iron – and the marks of use. They make tangible in what vessels the soups and stews would have been prepared, and what striking difference it made when the much lighter battery ware, in their graded sizes, took over towards the end of the eighteenth century. To experience this difference, it is necessary to touch and manipulate ideally both the artefact(s) and replicas thereof. The reason for this is that the artefact is irreplaceable but it also shows itself only in its present condition – possibly fragile, probably worn. A replica can aim to show the item as it may have looked and functioned when new, and, because it is a copy, it is not unique, but may be used for experimentation.

Re-enactment is a particular way of investigating the past, and its popular appeal of actors attired in period costume or the garb of Vikings, knights and Neanderthals has not always convinced more conventional historians of the seriousness of the pursuit. However, as will become evident, it is also a privileged form of getting to know some of the physical aspects of an object. Just as the excitement over a manuscript score or novel by an early author is permissible, the thrill of feeling the weight (or rather weightlessness) of a feather quill, the generic tool that would likely have been used to record it, or the weight of a cast iron skillet when filled with contents, should be equally acceptable. Re-enactment is unfortunately also a rather more resource-intensive form of research and most historians are unlikely to be able to carry it out for their own (case) studies.

Food ways[36] are programmes run by museums, using replica utensils with traditional ingredients and technology to demonstrate the cooking process and the final results to visitors. They are a prominent feature of 'living history' museums, and involve actors or demonstrators, frequently dressed in period costume to enact the work routines of people of a given period. The programmes also serve a research purpose in that they help to recapture practices and skills related to the use of domestic hollow ware, which for the most part went unrecorded. For example, in down-hearth cooking, women would frequently not wear shoes but continue to wear their long and fairly wide skirts. The present-day observer spots the fire hazard of a billowing skirt and the potential danger of burns to naked feet on hot bricks surrounding the fireplace. What is not evident at first glance is the inbuilt sensory alarm. Naked feet sense when they get too close to the live fire, and their owner is therefore likely to keep her distance from the flames. Wide, layered skirts, on the other hand, protect the legs from the heat. Demonstrators found that they felt the heat radiating from the fire much more on occasions when they practised wearing a pair of trousers or jeans. Because food ways aim to present a 'lived experience' they also aim to demonstrate within the right material context. Kitchens are reconstructed, or, if an original location is used, the kitchen furniture is displayed in such a way as to suggest the appearance of a working kitchen. The objects themselves may be originals or replicas, or a combination of the two, and in many cases the stock of utensils is an interpretation based on the collation of a number of kitchen inventories deemed representative for the type and size of kitchen to be reconstructed. Realism may go as far as a demonstrator picking a replica item out of the available array of utensils and proceeding to use it. Under these circumstances, display becomes a combination of preservation and frozen existence (the original artefacts on display) and fiction (the replica objects in use) but the compromise goes some way to creating an instructive experience. The best of them allow academic research, guided tours and touch-it sessions to go hand in hand.[37] The manager of the Odessa Houses in Delaware found that nothing compares with the hands-on, physical experience of the objects and the cooking methods.[38] To practise 'costume interpretation' is to perform tasks and activities in costume not merely for the benefit of visitors, but to put oneself into an environment that resembles as closely as possible that of an eighteenth-century man, woman or child. This way it is possible to experience the 'landscape of living', with all the caveats for which such an approach calls.[39]

Traditions and customs, experience and the economies of well-honed actions are all products of time spent in carrying out physical tasks and the development of physical skills.[40] Skill, on the other hand, can only be imperfectly described and, perhaps surprisingly, only with difficulty be retrieved through trial and error, because it is largely the result of a host of pressures operating upon the person acquiring them. Even where the historian has training in some of the specialists' fields – for example, metalworking – time–space–movement analyses and an assessment of the ergonomics for the eighteenth century can only be approximations. They elude precise investigation because we no longer have the precise conditions in which to carry out tasks.[41] Other stages – for example, distribution – are even more difficult to recover through re-enactment scenarios. The routines involved in supplying goods and in maintaining networks of middlemen and customers are too intangible and too reliant on a whole social fabric to be readily enacted. The same goes for the virtual supply of goods through advertising. It cannot be fully relived because the system of social references that made it work cannot be recreated. In other words, the value of re-enactment is limited to the more concrete, physical actions, as evident in the opening scene of the lively eighteenth-century kitchen with the cooking pot over the fire. And while using sensual knowledge may not be typical among historians, there are many gains to be had from doing so when dealing with material culture.

Towards a blended approach: mapping biographies and life cycle stages

One of the salient challenges for the historian is the balance of change versus continuity over time. Consider a busy kitchen, this time around 1800 – what has changed? The cooking pot is hanging above a range that burns coal as opposed to a down-hearth fireplace with logs of wood. What do the objects that can now be found in the kitchen tell us about the tasks performed here? What does it mean to enclose a fire, or to develop flat-bottomed saucepans that sit on hobs rather than skillets with three legs to position them in the hot embers? Once more the number of potential themes to be unpicked is large, and they invite the contemplation of themes as varied as production technology, domestic cooking technology, women's work, diversification of utensils and aspects of interior design.

These themes are as relevant for 1700 as they are for 1800, but historians are rarely interested in taking snapshots, and want to assess change and continuity over longer periods of time. How, for instance, can the gradual switch from copper and brass pots to cast iron, which occurred over the course of the eighteenth and early nineteenth centuries, and which is linked to new production processes, be mapped on to the biography of a specific artefact? And, conversely, how may specific life stories and the generic stages based on specimens available, and the macrohistory of an entire object category be combined? Infuriatingly, much, if not all, of the material that historians have at that their disposal provides mere glimpses, and this applies to documents as well as objects. By itself, an artefact is a time capsule that allows insight into only a relatively limited time period. Based on both documentary and artefactual evidence, snapshots may be turned into a sequence of stills, and some of the gaps filled in.

Adapting the biography approach and the life cycle model addresses this important issue of historical writing. The main aim is to present a chosen topic within its context based on evidence that will illuminate such context. In order to succeed, context and its evidence need to be handled in a particular way. Biography and life cycle support the identification of life cycle stages or areas to disentangle the various contextual elements. They encourage discussion of the stages or contexts that permit a more detailed treatment, while not denying the potential for further stages that have to remain untreated. Finally, because of their cyclical postulate, they assist in reassembling or reintegrating the stages.

When combined, the two approaches become a tool that can liaise between the material and the descriptive narrative on the one hand, and the interpretative and representational aspect of historical writing on the other.[42] They assist the historian in the task of focusing closely, in a first step, on the object or objects in question, to be able subsequently to integrate the detailed object history into a history that has a more broadly social, economic or other focus. In the example of cooking pots, the life cycle approach helps to bring out the triangle of influences between production, supply and consumption. A next step could lead towards explaining the changes that took place in the kitchens of eighteenth-century England. Ultimately, the combined biography and life cycle of the cooking pot can serve in discussions about rates of development in spheres as diverse as technological, industrial, retailing and consumer expansion during the eighteenth century.

Conclusion

The main challenge of the biography approach lies in the idiosyncratic nature of a biography, in other words its claim to uniqueness. At the core of the life cycle model, on the other hand, lies the idea of standardization. Its challenge resides in the fact that no object's existence is ever completely identical or entirely cyclical with a return to the origins. In their pure and rigid application neither concept is entirely suited to the historian's needs.

Both approaches are devices that stress the organic, and therefore unpredictable, element in all objects. They map the generic trajectory that purposefully produced objects were intended to undergo together with the idiosyncratic trajectory that is not part of the user's intention but part of the life story of particular objects. At times the biography (artefact specific), at other times the life cycle (generic object) and in a third instance a blended approach will yield the best results for making the complexities of the relationships between stages more transparent. And, as a framework, biography and life cycle models accommodate the gaps and offer the flexibility to integrate as few or as many stages or contexts as possible.

Indeed, the two approaches considered here concede and make a virtue out of the fact that objects can be elusive for the historian. Objects disappear or change their contexts and meanings, making access to earlier stages or biographical passages difficult. It may not be feasible, or indeed desirable, to investigate all stages of an object's life. Both the biography and the life cycle model highlight the gaps in the investigation as much as they assist with placing the pieces of the mosaic that are known. The likelihood that the empirical challenges are likely to increase with the age of the object means that some or most stages of the life cycle and greater or smaller sections of the biography of an object will remain obscure. In the absence of a continuous succession of material to support the research there is therefore no continuous story to be told. Wherever this is the case, the biography approach assists in mapping out the absent passages. Wherever an object is too humdrum and therefore elusive to yield a biography, there may be life cycle stages to be identified. While they may not be filled, except with generic placeholders, they position the object firmly within a more complete context of use and activity. Mapped onto each other, the life cycle model and the biography allow for the absences as well as the additions of contextual layers and materials, such as the artefact base upon which the historian of pots and pans may draw. Neither the life cycle model nor the biography is unproblematic but, coupled, they can assist the historian in dealing with the complexities and, above all, with the absences in a constructive manner. The view of the mosaic that biography and life cycle produce is partial and fractured, but from it the historian may gain insights into the interplay between the cultural meanings and values bestowed upon and through objects on the one hand, and the mechanical and physical boundaries of an object's life and the interplay between them.

Notes

1 An attempt at calculating the amount of time invested in different household tasks, such as cleaning, cooking and other domestic work, was undertaken by Lorna Weatherill, *Consumer Behaviour and Material Culture in Britain 1660–1760* (London and New York: Routledge, 1996), pp. 142–5.

2 For example, since the 1970s, Molly Harrison, *The Kitchen in History* (Reading: Osprey Publishing Limited, 1972); Doreen Yarwood, *The British Kitchen: Housewifery Since Roman Times* (London: B.T. Batsford, 1981); Una A. Robertson, *The Illustrated History of the Housewife 1650–1950* (Stroud: Sutton, 1999); Gilly Lehmann, *The British Housewife: Cookery Books, Cooking and Society in Eighteenth-century Britain* (Totnes: Prospect Books, 2003).

3 *Oxford English Dictionary Online*, available at http://dictionary.oed.com/entrance.dtl, under 'biography', accessed 17 January 2008.

4 *Bloomsbury Guide to English Literature* (London: Bloomsbury, 1992), under 'biography'.

5 See *Oxford English Dictionary Online*, under 'life cycle', 2. Citations: '1971 *Daily Telegraph*, 21 June 17/6 The four-stage life–cycle of every [manufactured] product exploration, growth, maturity, decline.'

6 For example, a plant's life cycle – e.g. grass from seed to seed-producing plant; an animal's life cycle – e.g. frog from spawn to fully grown frog capable of reproduction; a human life cycle – e.g. biological from birth to procreating adult, or from birth to death,

marked by cultural rites of passage such as baptism, communion/confirmation, marriage, parenthood and death. Life cycles also exist in medical research and chemistry.

7 In this form the life cycle study has a well-established tradition, and company and business history are two of the areas of historical writing where the approach is used. See, for example, Philippe Jobert and Michael Moss (eds), *The Birth and Death of Companies: An Historical Perspective*, papers delivered at a colloquium in Glasgow in September 1989 (Carnforth, Lancashire, and Park Ridge/New Jersey: Parthenon Publishing, 1990).

8 See SETAC (Society of Environmental Toxicology and Chemistry) 'Definitions of Life Cycle Assessment', in SETAC, *Guidelines for Life-cycle Assessment: A 'Code of Practice'* (Brussels: SETAC Publications, 1993). Available at: http://www.cfd.rmit.edu.au/dfe/lca1.html, accessed 4 December 2000. However, this online publication, based on a report edited by F. Consoli, D. Allen, I. Boustead, N. de Oude, J. Fava, R. Franklin, A.A. Jensen, R. Parrish, R. Perriman, D. Postlethwaite, B. Quay, J. Séguin and B. Vigon (eds) of a workshop organized by SETAC in Portugal, is no longer available.

9 Appadurai gives examples of production loci where greater trends towards variation are found. See Arjun Appadurai, 'Introduction: Commodities and the Politics Of Value' in Arjun Appadurai (ed.), *The Social Life of Things: Commodities in Cultural Perspective* (Cambridge, New York, Oakleigh: Cambridge University Press, 1992), p. 42.

10 The author of 'Life Cycle of a Steel Cooking Pan', for example, identifies ten stages, from the mining and transportation of raw materials to the cooking pan's use in the kitchen until its eventual consignment to the dustbin and the waste collection system. However, even his model could be expanded to include transport from the retailer's to the user's premises. See John Wright, 'Sustainable Resource Management: The Life Cycle of a Steel Cooking Pan', in John Wright, *Tipping the Balance: Sustainable Management of World Resources* (place of publication n.a.: Beckett Karlson, 1998), p. 42.

11 One example was Rob Goldberg, 'The Big Picture: Life Cycle Analysis' (Philadelphia, PA: The Academy of Natural Sciences, 1992). Available at: http://www. acnatsci.org, accessed 16 May 2000. However, his online publication is no longer available for consultation.

12 Ideally, models render complex interactions and interconnections accessible by simplifying them while at the same time drawing attention to the complexity that underpins them. See Mark Rees and John H. Lawton 'What Can Models Tell Us?' in Leslie Fowden, Terry Mansfield and John Stoddart (eds), *Plant Adaptation to Environmental Stress* (London: Chapman and Hall, 1993), p. 65.

13 Igor Kopytoff, 'The Cultural Biography of Things: commoditization as a process' in Appadurai (ed.), *The Social Life of Things*. In order to highlight the process and concomitant phases of commodification Kopytoff compares the effect of ownership and commodity status on things with that of slavery. His objective is not to emotionalize and dramatize the ownership of things by using a form of ownership that has become unacceptable within the Western cultural sphere, but instead uses its more readily accessible 'stages' of status to sensitize his readership towards ownership within the realm of things. See in particular pp. 64–5.

14 Kopytoff's examples are a Suku hut and a car. Depending on geographical and cultural arena, the biography of a car in Africa will be different from that of the same kind of vehicle in Europe. The Suku, on the other hand, have strong feelings about appropriate use of a hut, depending on its age. Thus using 'too old' a hut to accommodate guests is deemed inappropriate. See Kopytoff, 'The Cultural Biography of Things', pp. 66–8.

15 See, for example, Cornelius Holtorf 'Notes on the Life History of a Pot Sherd', *Journal of Material Culture*, 7, 1 (2002), pp. 49–71, who discusses life history approaches in archaeology, namely short life histories (the lives of things in the past until they are discarded) and long life histories study (the lives of things until the present) to demonstrate that the material essence of an object is far from eternal, but subject to interpretation. Far from being essential properties of objects, their material identities are the result of the relationship of people and objects, and consequently ascribed to them.

16 T. Dant, *Material Culture in the Social World: Values, Activities, Lifestyles* (Buckingham and Philadelphia: Open University Press, 1999), p. 142–4.

17 Ibid., p. 131.

18 Neil Cummings, 'Reading Things: The Alibi of Use' in Neil Cummings (ed.), *Reading Things* (London: Chance Books, 1993), p. 15.

19 Particular opposition to the idea of context comes from postmodernist historians. See, for example, contributions to Brian Fay, Philip Pomper and Richard T. Vann (eds), *History and Theory: Contemporary Readings* (Malden, MA, and Oxford: Blackwell, 1998).

20 For example, the tracing of the life story of the Koh-i-Noor diamond in Arndt. Mersmann, '"Diamonds are Forever" – Appropriations of the Koh-i-Noor: An Object Biography', *Journal for the Study of British Cultures*, 8, 2 (2001), pp. 175–91.

21 The practice only became more widespread in the nineteenth century, and particularly in America where American iron founders would have their names, or the names of their businesses or firms, moulded into all, including the small articles. See Alex Ames, *Collecting Cast Iron* (Ashbourne: Moorland, 1980), p. 13.

22 For the dating of brass, various techniques have been developed. Specialists differentiate between invasive and non-invasive techniques, but the difference between the documented and the undocumented object relative to the analysis is all the same considerable. An undocumented, non-authenticated artefact has to be treated with great circumspection. Dating techniques for metal objects draw on a database containing profiles of metal impurities, and this database is based on documented objects. Objects made of iron remain largely un-datable because iron is the metal with the fewest impurities and therefore the most difficult to date.

23 Geoffrey Warren, *Kitchen Bygones: A Collector's Guide* (London: Souvenir Press, 1984), p. 9.

24 A biography written from the 'numerous interpretations, often of a conflicting nature, making [the objects'] biography at times wholly schizophrenic' is the express purpose of Clifford Charles Lamberg-Karlovsky, 'The Biography of an Object: The Intercultural Style Vessels of the Third Millennium BC', in Steven D. Lubar and W. David Kingery (eds), *History from Things: Essays on Material Culture* (Washington and London: Smithsonian Institution Press, 1993), p. 272.

25 See W. John McIntyre, 'Artifacts as Sources for Material History Research', *Material History Bulletin*, Special Issue, 8 (1979), pp. 71–5, here p. 71, for reference to Edward McClung Fleming's article 'Artifact Study: A Proposed Model', published in *Winterthur Portfolio* in 1974. This model was further developed to enhance its usability and reflects the level of importance accorded to each quality through order of listing: material, construction, function, provenance and value. See also Anon, 'Research Reports: Towards a Material History Methodology', *Material History Bulletin*, 22 (1985), pp. 31–40, here pp. 31, 35 and 36.

26 But see Anon, 'Research Reports', pp. 31–40, for an attempt at a practical model.

27 Ibid., pp. 32–3.

28 See, for example, Henry Petroski, *The Evolution of Useful Things* (London: Pavilion, 1993), and Henry Petroski, *The Pencil: A History of Design and Circumstance* (New York: Alfred A. Knopf, 1990). The focus is not new to archaeologists, whose primary material consists predominantly of material objects, and who traditionally have seen their task in describing and classifying material objects.

29 Petroski, for example, insists that to study simple examples of engineering is as helpful, if not more helpful, as studying complex ones, such as space craft, because the principles of their development apply in either case, but are more easily demonstrated for simpler objects. See Henry Petroski, *To Engineer is Human: The Role of Failure in Successful Design* (New York: St Martin's Press, 1985). See also Susie West, 'Introduction' to Sarah Tarlow and Susie West (eds), *The Familiar Past? Archaeologies of Later Historical Britain* (London and New York: Routledge, 1999).

30 The example study is based on Karin Dannehl, 'A Life Cycle Study of Eighteenth-century Metal Cooking Vessels: A Reflexive Approach', unpublished thesis, University of Wolverhampton, 2005. More detailed references to primary source materials may be found there. The glimpse of how at least one contemporary viewed cooking pots with regard to health and safety is found in Anon, *Serious Reflections on the Manifold Dangers Attending the Use of Copper Vessels. And other utensils of copper and brass, in the preparation of all such solids and liquids as are designed for food to human bodies: in a letter to a friend M. Cooper* (London: publisher n.a., 1755). It permits us to reflect on the most salient change over time, which was the gradual, very uneven but all the same traceable switch from copper and brass to cast iron.

31 See Ironbridge Gorge Museum Trust (Coalbrookdale), Ford Letter book LAB/ASSOC/10, as well as the Coalbrookdale Company Stock Book 1728–1738 (piece number CBD MS 1) CBD 59/82/5. For court case material see: National Archives/PRO: PRO Chancery Depositions C 7/89/4 n.d. (1709–10); PRO Chancery Deposition C11/1721/15 (1716); PRO Chancery Deposition C11/1726/16 (1716); PRO Chancery Depositions C 11/1726/18 (1709) and PRO PROB 4/1311.

32 Patent No. 380, signed 18 April 1707, 'A new way of casting iron bellied potts, and other iron bellied ware in sand only', granted 'Abraham Darby, of our city of Bristol, Smith' the 'sole vse and benefit' of his invention.

33 See Somerset Record Office (Taunton), Dickenson MSS Do/DN/423 Graffin Prankard's Letter Book, letters dated 10 7mo (September) 1715 and 15 8mo (October) 1715. To judge by his correspondence, Prankard was never slow to voice his discontent if the wares were damaged or in poor condition.

34 Eliza Smith, *The Compleat Housewife or Accomplish'd Gentlewoman's Companion: being a collection of upwards of six hundred of the most approved receipts in cookery, pastry, confectionary, preserving, pickles, cakes, creams, jellies, made wines, cordials ...*, facsimile edition (London: Studio Editions, 1994). It was first published in 1727, and its 16th edition, with additions, was printed for C. Hitch and L. Hawes, etc., in London, 1758.

35 An exception is the tradecard by Elwell and Taylor, *c.*1760s, in the British Museum, Heal and Banks Collection, 85.99.

36 The section is based on interviews with demonstrators at the Odessa Houses, Delaware, and the Colonial Williamsburg Living History Museum in 2000. Debbie Buckson, manager of the Odessa Houses in Delaware, has a background in art history but she became increasingly involved in running the Odessa House Museums. Together with Susan Schmitt, she practises 'hearth cooking' dressed in period costume, including shift, stays and skirt. Much of their knowledge of how eighteenth-century kitchens and cooking worked has been acquired through trial and error. Girls at the time would have learned the skills required for cooking for a family through being around, through observation, just as boys would learn their fathers' trade, and from being given increasingly greater responsibility. Debbie herself, with no prior knowledge to bring to the task, trained with Harriet Stout at Jamestown Festival, who practises and demonstrates open hearth cooking there, and Susan Lukas in Pennsylvania.

37 Interview with Debbie Buckson in March 2000. As with all locations open to the public, a number of constraints upon 'authenticity' arise from contemporary, that is current, standards of health and safety. Authenticity may never rank above the safety of staff and visitors.

38 Ibid. The times for demonstration are 10 o'clock in the morning to 4 o'clock in the afternoon, and Debbie Buckson and Susan Schmitt point out that this panders to visitors' viewing preferences rather than eighteenth-century cooking practices. In an experiment with Susan Schmitt, roasting a chicken on the spit and boiling squash in a cast iron pot suspended over the fire, dressed in a long cotton skirts and barefoot, Schmitt commented on the fact that visitors preferred to see the roasting in operation. For this reason the chicken would tend to be left over the fire for longer than would be necessary for its optimum cooking.

39   Ibid.
40   Historic smithies, like their domestic counterpart, the kitchens, reveal much the same challenge. Alongside the educational objective, their aim is to rediscover old techniques, since the minutiae of everyday work and practice were not recorded. The training of apprentices, though a serious business for the master, took place as a matter of course and received reflection only through the pieces the apprentice would produce. Not only were smiths less likely to describe and record what they knew from experience, the smith's work, like the cook's, relies on the right timing for each step, making it impossible to interrupt a process to record it, or for an observer to dissect it into its constituent parts. The insights into the challenging task of retrieving past work processes were gained in April 2000 from Peter Ross, for 25 years master metal smith and demonstrator in the 'James Anderson Blacksmith Shop' at Colonial Williamsburg Living History Museum, Virginia, until 2004. See also, for example, Linda M. Hurcombe, *Archaeological Artefacts as Material Culture* (London and New York: Routledge, 2007), who discusses the practices of experimental archaeology to retrieve missing information about material remains.
41   Peter Ross observed that since the apprentices, whom he trains in his workshop – a historic smithy at Colonial Williamsburg – are apprentices in the twenty-first-century sense, he cannot exercise absolute control, nor does necessity impose the same pressure on them to perform, and to perform well, the tasks he gives them. He cannot recreate the conditions under which skills immediately related to efficiency would have developed. For instance, even the routine action of beating metal into a shape is conditioned by the fact that the worker had to get it right to ensure his livelihood, while the actor, although under pressure to deliver a good performance, is not under the same pressure to shape the piece of metal. Personal communication from Peter Ross in April 2000 and December 2002.
42   See C. Behan McCullagh, *The Truth of History* (London and New York: Routledge, 1998), pp. 167–9.

7 Regional identity and material culture

Helen Berry

The study of individual and group identity has become a popular theme in histori-cal research, in particular over the last 20 years.[1] It has most usually entailed the his-torian combing the archives for written records. If the unit of study is the nation state, this will involve research on the official records relating to the operation of power, such as legal documents, parliamentary proceedings and diplomatic papers; if the subject is the identity of individual persons, the historian may look for letters or diaries that record their subject's personal experiences. Whatever the unit of analysis, whether an entire nation or a single, private person (and the many other categories in between, such as a particular ethnic identity, gender or family group), the historian's focus, unlike that of the archaeologist or anthropologist, has tended to be upon the written word, in printed or manuscript form, rather than other sorts of material culture such as the built environment, art or manufactured goods. Where historians do use evidence from material culture in relation to questions of identity, it is fair to say that many notable examples use material culture to substantiate a hypothesis formed from detailed text-based research, rather than vice-versa.[2]

One reason for this is that academic historians are trained in the empirical tradi-tion of using archival or printed evidence, which embeds their professional focus upon text-based source criticism; they are experts at piecing together and interpret-ing historical documents. The historian places importance upon deploying a scep-tical approach to claims of accuracy in written texts, based upon factors such as the bias of the author, and the patchy survival of evidence, although (in common with other disciplines) he or she must now also wrestle since the rise of postmodernism with questions of 'truth' in history.[3]

The increasing trend towards specialization within disciplines has, in many instances, actually made it harder to find a common language to explore questions of identity in history across disciplinary boundaries, which is unfortunate given the mutual and overlapping concerns of researchers engaging with cultures in the past. Yet there are signs of an evolving cross-pollination of ideas and approaches. Creative dialogue across disciplines is sometimes achieved in very particular cir-cumstances, such as where a research project is conceived by a team of experts working collaboratively, or where an academic has received specialist training in two or more different disciplines.[4] Some of the most influential historians in the field of early modern history have been influenced by the methods of other disciplines, such as anthropology.[5] There is also now a large body of specialist literature in relatively new fields, such as design history, that offers fresh critical and analytical approaches.[6]

Historians faced with interpreting material culture as a route to finding out more about identity in history are perhaps closer than ever before to adopting the critical approaches of related disciplines. Between history and archaeology, for example, there is a common interest in interpreting material evidence, whether or not the 'artefact' in question contains evidence of written text. So, for example, historians are now aware, following the influence of 'new historicist' approaches in the 1980s, that texts should be regarded as a form of material culture, requiring attentiveness to their form and use.[7] Those historians who study printed sources such as books and newspapers frequently analyse them as material objects in their own right, not just for the information they contain in the printed word (which in itself can be subjected to 'multiple readings' and interpretations) but in the typeface, the quality of paper, the size of the book, the nature of the binding and the relationship of illustrations to printed words. When the historian, in the manner of an archaeologist or other object-centred researcher, treats a printed document as an artefact, new questions are opened up not just about the information ('text') it contains, but about how it was produced and distributed, who owned it, how they bought it and what it cost, how they read it, whether they lent it to someone else, why they bought it, and how they displayed or stored it; in short, what it meant to them.

Like other material traces of a society, written texts help to constitute identity through *culture*, a word that can evoke 'high art' notions of picture galleries and opera, but that at its most basic level means 'tillage', and is thus deeply connected to the idea of land (as in *cultivate*, with which *culture* shares a common linguistic root).[8] Identity and material culture (including texts) are thus intimately bound up with specific geographical areas; or, to put it another way, human identity is intimately connected with a sense of place, although there is often a mismatch between the different categories of identity imposed by organizational structures, such as local and national government. For example, national boundaries tend not to be coterminous with ethnic groups and their traditional patterns of land tenure (as is the case with many modern African nation states), or indeed the concept of land ownership, which may have no meaning for the peoples who live from the land (as is the case in nomadic societies, such as indigenous tribal peoples in North America or Australia). Even in those parts of the world where the concept of outright ownership of land is anathema, the intimate bond between peoples, societies and cultures, and their relationship to the land, remains an important and enduring one.[9] There are of course many other subdivisions between the nation state, the land and the populations who inhabit it, forming a complex web through which power is mediated. Between nation and person lie a multiplicity of real and virtual ties and allegiances; in England, for example, there is the parish, or county. One intermediary unit, which is the focus of this chapter, is the *region*, a meaningful unit of analysis found within many nation states – for example, in Western Europe, the Indian subcontinent and North America – which sometimes finds expression through political structures, but more often is defined according to topographical features such as a distinct type of farmland, divided from its neighbours by natural barriers such as mountain ranges, the sea or river networks.

Following a closer examination of the rationale for considering regions as 'cultural provinces', this chapter explores the case study of north-east England,[10] and one particular type of material culture produced in that region during the eighteenth century: high-design glassware. The intention is to open up the question of how historians can approach the subject of regional identity by using the kinds of questions other disciplines bring to bear upon material culture, thereby broadening their traditional focus upon textual sources in exciting new ways. The essay is necessarily a product of a broader interdisciplinary context of approaches to objects, including disciplines such as anthropology or design history. However, it is most firmly rooted mainly in analysis by and discussions with archaeologists, because (as has already been noted) archaeological theory is providing new perspectives on the relationship between land, culture, material goods and identity.

It is worthwhile therefore pausing to consider some pressing issues regarding the nature of identity, and what archaeologists can teach historians about the difficulties in interpreting an artefact. In the textbooks read in schools in the last quarter of the twentieth century, a straightforward relationship was often proposed between an object and what one could 'tell' about the people who produced it in an unfolding narrative of the evolution of human history. Thus there was smooth transition between successive 'ages', from Stone Age, to Bronze Age, Iron Age, and so on. Many archaeologists are now keen to stress, however, that the relationship between a society's material culture and its cultural identity is problematic, and the evolution of technological change ought not to be considered in a straightforwardly 'progressive' way, two principles that apply whatever the time period and culture under consideration.[11]

The modern analogy might be a hat, which, as a cultural artefact, may be suggestive of one particular type of identity performance by its one-time wearer, but there is no straightforward substitution of the hat for the person who wore it; a piece of headgear will not tell the interpreter about the 'essential' quality of its former owner. The most that can be said is a series of plausible inferences regarding the set of meanings that might be ascribed to the artefact (the hat) by whoever made it in a particular set of circumstances related to certain times and places.[12] What, for example, might be known about customary headgear in the location in which it was found? Was it worn by a man, woman or child? Was it buried with the person, and, if so, why? What did the fabric of which it was made, and ornamentation (if any) signify? Did it denote status? What did the design suggest about the trade networks in the area (was it a new fashion or influenced by far-distant cultures?) If from a period of 'history' rather than 'prehistory', are there written records that might provide more information about how the hat was worn, what it meant to its wearer, and its wider social meanings? Also, what other hats might there have been in the owner's wardrobe?

So many questions for just one (imaginary) hat. Yet this example does serve to illustrate the kinds of question that are the stock-in-trade of archaeologists as fruitful lines of enquiry about an artefact. Their questions may be grouped into two areas: the *material* and the *contextual*. The material questions consider the *form* of the object, i.e. its design, and what the artefact is made from, which could extend to a technical or scientific analysis of the substance from which it is made, the dyes used, where the fabric was made, even carbon dating to ascertain the approximate age. Contextual questions probe the *function* of the object – that is, the social and spatial aspects of the artefact (by whom, how and where was it worn). Some archaeologists propose that it is actually misleading to separate form, or 'style', from function in this way, since the two are intricately connected by repeated use.[13] Hence, a useful object can also signify social status in particular ways (the hat may protect the wearer from the rain, but also indicate he is the captain of a battalion), but, more than that, its use actually helps to *constitute* the status of the wearer. These observations are helpful in framing a set of questions that may be applied to identity, whether the study is focused upon an individual or a larger unit of analysis, such as a region, and to different types of artefact. A comparative approach is beyond the scope of the case study offered here, but it is offered in the hope that other historians and students may test whether the problems and principles of interpretation explored here are consistent in other time periods and regions, in different cultural contexts.

Curiously enough (given historians' relative neglect of material culture in modern times), there *was* a tradition of paying close attention to artefacts among those who wrote British history, but this took place before the rise of the modern historical profession in the twentieth century. Between the sixteenth and nineteenth centuries, 'antiquarianism' was a mainstream pursuit of amateur historians, comprising gentlemen-scholars and clergymen who used artefacts as the basis of their investigations, particularly into Romano-British history.[14] Robert Plot, the first Keeper of the Ashmolean Museum in Oxford, gathered material for his *Natural History of Oxfordshire* (1677) by sending letters to his network of correspondents throughout the county, enquiring: 'Are there any ancient *Sepulchers* hereabout of Men of *Gigantick* stature, *Roman Generals* or *others* of ancient times? has there ever been any ... *British, Roman, Saxon*, or *Danish* antiquities?'[15] Following the Union of the Scottish and English Parliaments in 1707, the search for 'authentic' British identity was invested in the interpretation of ancient history and the landscape itself. This was recognized through the grant of a Royal Charter by George II to the Society of Antiquaries in 1751, and in the expanding libraries of antiquarian history published in the second half of the eighteenth century.[16] The call by leading antiquarians such as Richard Gough for correspondents to write to him of 'our national Antiquities' constituted what Rosemary Sweet has called an 'antiquarian Republic of Letters'.[17] Towards the end of the eighteenth century, some antiquarians developed a romantic style of writing that celebrated the picturesque, a style that many Victorian historians later found at best quaint and at worst damnably unscientific.[18] The emergence of anthropology as a new discipline during the late nineteenth and early twentieth centuries diminished the study of material culture with the rise of the 'ethnographic monograph', directly observed studies of living indigenous peoples rather than the collection of artefacts.[19] So, with the rise of professionalized and distinct disciplines in modern universities, material culture came to be seen as the preserve of professional archaeologists and anthropologists during the course of the twentieth century.

In the 1960s and 1970s, however, a revived interest in local history, through which historians explored the relationship between people, identity and the land, brought archaeologists and historians back to a common research agenda. A seminal work for historians was W.G. Hoskin's *Making of the English Landscape* (1955). Hoskin was instrumental in opening the first university department in English Local History at the University of Leicester in 1965.[20] Another Leicester historian who was instrumental in the revival of local history, Charles Phythian-Adams, proposed a new model for considering regional history as distinctive *cultural provinces*, of which an identifiable local material culture is one element.[21] The idea of regions as cultural provinces is a useful analytical tool for thinking critically about the subdivisions of any particular geographical area, not just the British Isles, particularly in relation to the role of material culture in creating regional identity as a fluid and dynamic force involving the interrelationship of the land, its topographical features, such as mountains and watersheds (forming 'lines of punctuation in the landscape'),[22] and the processes of human interaction such as farming, settlement and industrialization. Thus, the distinctiveness of regional culture comprises not only 'indigenous' goods – for example, those made using locally available materials such as clay or metal ores, and fuelled by local resources such as coal or wood – but an entire range of artefacts resulting from regular trade networks and encounters with neighbouring regions and far-distant cultures (what Phythian-Adams calls the 'broad underlying axis of activity').[23]

Does using 'region' as a unit of analysis in relation to material culture therefore provide meaningful insights into questions of identity? Alan Everitt's approach to regional history suggests that the very idea of a region might become historically significant only at specific historical moments – for example, with the arrival of a regional railway network or even regional television broadcasting (which would make regional identity a very recent phenomenon indeed).[24] Nascent regional identity might certainly precede the specific language of regionalism; certain common cultural forms may make it rational and plausible for the historian to use 'region' before the term was commonly used by its inhabitants.[25] Phythian-Adams' model suggests this is indeed the case where there are consistent commonalities over time between the cultural productions of certain areas that are *distinctive* from other neighbouring domains, where the designation of 'cultural province' helps to illuminate that distinctiveness. The problem with this model, and one I shall be probing further in the specific case study that follows, is that the material culture of an area can be represented and interpreted for political reasons as a fixed, immanent regional identity; the idea of a 'cultural province' (although this was explicitly not Phythian-Adams' intention) can appear to endorse a particular model of what a region is, underpinning and bolstering the power of those who for a variety of reasons (which may include class politics, national or local 'pride') are invested in maintaining a particular story about the past as a means of constructing a certain identity that resists or refuses other, alternative stories. Here, material culture can be marshalled to provide a nostalgic, or even 'orientalist', view of a particular society, especially (but not exclusively) if the interpretation is by an outsider who has a certain agenda of their own.[26]

Material culture can have a powerful role to play in reinforcing or challenging preexisting notions of the past, and for that reason the question of how historical evidence is gathered, and who should interpret it, becomes a politically contentious one, whether in a local community, a wider region, or a nation as a whole. To take one specific example from the United States, the city of Annapolis, Maryland, has been the site since 1981 of a public archaeology project to revise the town's history as written by its culturally 'European' ruling elites. Excavations undertaken collaboratively by academic anthropologists from the University of Maryland, members of the Historic Annapolis Foundation and public volunteers have uncovered the previously hidden material culture of Annapolis's slave inhabitants which illuminate aspects of their everyday life in antebellum houses, such as their concealment of objects used in African 'hoodoo' religion within doorways and under floors.[27] To continue the comparison with continental North America, from Quebec to California, a similarly revisionist approach by archaeologists (among others) to re-evaluating tourism, museums and the heritage industry has placed a new contemporary emphasis upon 'people's history', with material culture playing a particular role in recovering the lives of those whose voices are traditionally missing from history.[28] Unearthing new material evidence of alternative identities can therefore profoundly disrupt the stories that are told locally about what makes a particular area – a town or indeed an entire region – distinctive, changing perceptions of the rootedness of contemporary identities in the past. In recent decades, the influence of new schools of thought regarding the nature of identity and subjectivity has dramatically changed the way history has been written, especially the underlying assumptions about the nature of identity itself. Instead of overarching narratives that confidently assert a single, widely accepted story of the evolution of particular national histories and characters, since the 1980s in particular, the emphasis has instead been upon plurality and contingency. In the wake of postmodern approaches to studying the past (which lent a particular emphasis to the changeable quality of individual subjectivity) we no longer have 'the history of the nation state', but 'histories of nation states', where identification with a particular nation (however it is defined) is just one of many identities a person may adopt in different situations. Thus, one individual may identify in different contexts as British or Scottish, a Rangers supporter, an animal rights campaigner, a Methodist, ethnically Asian, politically right- or left-wing. In this postmodern schema, identities are more analogous to the 'hats' discussed above, worn at different times and in varying contexts, in a way that emphasizes personal choice and agency.[29] However, in terms of the identities that are promoted, given prominence in the textual and material preservation, not all are given equal prominence: historically, the deeds and material culture of 'great white men' were valorized; at present, investment (especially by public funding bodies that support the heritage industry) is often in the everyday and allegedly 'inclusive' history of traditionally excluded minorities; the poor, women, ethnic minorities and children – 'allegedly' since these are also subject to the limitations of representation and selectivity.

This discussion of some of the most topical and critical debates in history and archaeology frames the case study to which we now proceed, which highlights the difficulties (and, it is hoped, benefits) resulting from one historian's attempt to synthesize several different types of textual and material evidence: primary and secondary literature on Georgian glass production and the glass industry in north-east England; documentary evidence concerning the technological innovation made by William Beilby that resulted in the production of a new type of enamelled glassware during the 1760s; 'Beilby glass', and an interpretation of this specific type of material culture. By showing how Beilby glass has been simultaneously rendered invisible locally in the north-east through general neglect of its historical importance, yet celebrated nationally and internationally as an example of 'British' fine art and a valuable stage in the evolution of glassware, the remainder of this chapter illustrates how material culture can provide new insights for historians into the tensions between the unequal values ascribed to eighteenth-century cultural production and the political character of regional identity construction.

The case study of Beilby glass that follows in the remainder of this chapter starts with a brief overview of the history of glassmaking in early modern England, before proceeding to examine in more detail the emergence of glass production on Tyneside, and the available contextual information about the workshop of the Beilby family. Having surveyed the documentary evidence that places these objects in their historical context, it then proceeds to consider the different approaches to interpreting the material evidence provided by surviving examples of Beilby glassware that are to be found in various public and private collections around the world, taking into account their ownership, use and variety of possible meanings. Drawing upon insights from archaeology, the case study also considers the disparity in prestige afforded these objects, conveyed through their different cultural settings and interpretations today.

By the start of the eighteenth century, England had become a European fashion leader in the production of high-quality drinking glasses made from lead or flint glass (as it was then called), the highest-quality glass that is still hand or machine cut and marketed as crystal today.[30] The process of introducing lead oxide into liquid glass (the 'melt') to improve the brilliance and lustre of the finished product was invented by an Englishman, George Ravenscroft, at his manufactory at the Savoy in London. Ravenscroft, who traded with Italian merchants, was aware of Venetian glassmaking techniques and employed Italian glassmakers who were skilled in making 'cristallo', alkali glass.[31] Ravenscroft patented his technique in 1674, but his monopoly ended in 1681, and by the end of the seventeenth century, lead glass was being made at 61 glasshouses in England, most of which were in London, but there were also four in the Bristol area, five around Stourbridge, and one in Newcastle.[32] Bristol was a noted centre of glass production – the first glasshouse was established in 1651, by one Edward Dagney or Dagnia, from a family of Italian origin.[33] In 1690, another member of the Dagnia family set up the first high-quality flint glass manufactory on the River Tyne.

The manufacture of Newcastle glass dated back to Elizabethan times, when Sir Robert Mansell owned the monopoly on glass production in the north. Local coal was found to be of suitable purity for glassmaking, with convenient sources of other ingredients required to make the liquid melt – furnaces were initially fired by wood, then later coal. Ease of access to maritime trading routes during the eighteenth century enabled transportation of raw ingredients and finished product. Alkali and silica were crucial ingredients needed for the manufacture of fine-quality plate glass, and were brought to the north-east on coal ships returning from London in the form of fine white sand from Lynn in Norfolk, soapers' ashes, Spanish barilla and saltpetre from London and Yarmouth.[34] The glassmaking industry diversified and proliferated, so that the area around Ouseburn in Newcastle became known as the Glasshouses. By 1736, the historian Henry Bourne recorded that three types of glass – Crown glass, plate glass and bottle glass – were produced in this area by seven main glasshouses, some of which also produced a small quantity of the highest-quality flint glass.[35] John Brand listed coal, lead, salt and glass as the principal exports from the River Tyne in 1789.[36] Between 1696 and 1737, at least three glasshouses also appeared on the River Wear.[37] By the start of the nineteenth century, glassmaking had helped to give the local landscapes of both Tyneside and Wearside an industrial character (Figure 7.1), bringing with it an enduring socio-economic and cultural legacy that shaped the modern identity of north-east England.

Figure 7.1 George Balmer (1806–1846), *Sunderland. The Bridge from the Westward* (undated), ref. J6820. The view shows the River Wear upstream of the cast-iron Wear Bridge (built 1793–96) On the right are the cone-shaped kilns of glassworks. By kind permission, Tyne and Wear Museums, Newcastle upon Tyne.

The flint glass produced by the Dagnia family on the Tyne was among the finest in Europe, and was exported to the continent where it was especially sought after by Dutch engravers. The Dagnias held the monopoly of fine glassmaking in Newcastle until 1728, when Joseph Airey and Isaac Cookson began to produce flint glass. Airey and Cookson have been credited with producing some of the highest-quality glass manufactured on Tyneside, and it was their glasshouse at Closegate in Newcastle that was a source of flint glassware that became known as 'Beilby glass' once decorated.[38]

The Newcastle glasshouses typically supplied the Beilby workshop with wine goblets, delicate liqueur glasses known as ratafia glasses, decanters and ale glasses, as well as larger one-off commissioned pieces such as commemorative punch bowls. Here, a description of their form is made possible through viewing surviving examples, or photographs of the same.[39] The drinking vessels that the Beilbys decorated are archetypal examples of what is known as Newcastle Light Baluster ware – recognizable by their distinctive, delicately tapering stems (or 'balusters'), and the inclusion of knops (beads of glass) midway down the stem. The evolution of this extremely light and delicate form was encouraged by the imposition of a government tax in 1745, which charged excise upon Crown plate and flint glass by weight, a levy that was doubled in 1777 in the wake of the American Declaration of Independence in 1776.[40] Apart from the unusually peaceful years when Walpole was Prime Minister, successive Hanoverian wars brought the need to raise taxes, and glass manufacturers were forced to think laterally in order to reduce their tax bill. The lighter the finished product, the less tax was imposed, encouraging some manufacturers to concentrate upon the lightweight but valuable high-design end of the market. The bowls of Newcastle Light Baluster ware wine glasses were typically bucket-shaped, or fluted. The technique of perfecting the inclusion of air bubbles, or 'tear drops', in the knop was also a distinctive feature of Newcastle glass. The Tyneside glassmakers also demonstrated their skill with air 'twists' running through the stem, achieved through blowing air bubbles into the molten glass – a technique that originated in the Low Countries, and was especially popular between *c.* 1730 and 1760.[41] Tyneside glass blowers later added white and (later) coloured glass to the stem, forming what was known as an 'opaque twist'.

Further evidence derived from documentary sources is useful in providing contextual detail about how Beilby glass was produced from the undecorated vessels supplied from the Newcastle glasshouses. The Beilby workshop was a family concern. The best-known member of the Beilby family is Ralph Beilby, the engraver who was master to, and sometime business partner of, the famous wood engraver Thomas Bewick.[42] Ralph's father, William Beilby, had been a well-to-do goldsmith and jeweller in Durham, but lost his business. His third son, also William (b. 1740) was apprenticed at the age of 15 to a Birmingham enameller, John Hezeldine, who taught him his trade, and also brought him into contact with the glassmakers of Stourbridge. When William returned to his brother Ralph's workshop at Amen Corner next to St Nicholas's church, Newcastle, he saw the potential for applying the techniques he had learned in Birmingham to the high-quality lead and flint glass that was being manufactured in the glasshouses on the Tyne. William

Figure 7.2 Beilby goblet (*c.*1770), ref. 99.17BEIL. Bucket-shaped bowl and double series opaque twist in stem, white enamel upon Newcastle light baluster glass. By kind permission Huntington Library Art Collections, San Marino, California.

Beilby's technological and design innovation was to use the techniques of enamelling in white or colour that had previously been applied to metal and jewellery, and apply them to glass. Beilby's technique entailed mixing colour with a glass melt, or 'flux', which created a mud-like substance that could be hand painted onto the glass. It was then fired by placing it on a steel rod and inserting it into a furnace, a delicate process that involved lowering it through a ten-inch aperture into an eight-foot-long brick tunnel. A number of holes in the furnace allowed Beilby to monitor temperature: through much trial and error, he discovered the correct temperature for fusing the enamel to the glass without melting either substance.[43]

    The experimentation required for Beilby to perfect his technique was expensive, and it was never produced on a large scale. The period of Beilby glass production spans roughly 1760, when William returned home from Birmingham, until 1778, when he left the north-east for London. According to the memoirs of Thomas Bewick, William taught enamelling and painting to his sister Mary and younger brother Thomas in their workshop at Amen Corner, and was sometimes assisted by Ralph, his master.[44] The cost of producing high-design handmade and hand-decorated glassware in relation to the unit of production was extremely high, requiring the purchase of the best-quality flint glassware, the input of many hours of human labour and a high amount of wastage, as many glasses cracked or melted in the furnace before William perfected the right temperature for the enamelling process. Beilby glass has been described as a 'stunning technical achievement', but it was only ever affordable by the gentry and nobility.[45] Pieces were ordered by post or via personal callers to the Beilby workshop, like Edward Charlton, a member of the Northumberland gentry, who commissioned a Beilby goblet after calling into their workshop to place an order for engraving work.[46] There is, however, little accompanying documentation to provide further detail, for example, about exactly how much individual pieces cost (currently, for example, no trace has been found of business accounts, bills or correspondence mentioning the use of the glassware or documentary verification of who commissioned each piece, or how it was displayed or used).[47]

Which brings us back to the evidence that may be drawn from the surviving pieces of Beilby glassware. In terms of its design, Beilby glass drew upon European traditions in art, but applied them in a new medium that was distinctively British. The motifs are often extravagantly rococo – an influential late baroque style prevalent throughout eighteenth-century Europe that found fashion in a wide range of British arts – including architecture, furniture-making and musical composition, the common feature of these different expressions of rococo style being a love of ornamental embellishment. The decorative features deployed on Beilby glassware consisted most commonly of asymmetrical scroll and leaf motifs, and curling vines or hops, appropriate to the function of the vessel for containing wine or beer, executed in a white enamel that echoed the delicate opaque twists in the stem. The more ambitious and prestigious pieces, such as royal goblets and commemorative bowls, are attributed to the work of William Beilby, while his sister Mary and brother Thomas worked upon smaller pieces, such as drinking glasses with floral garlands, beehives and pastoral scenes.[48] The quality of these prestigious objects means that they were unlikely to have been used as everyday drinking vessels, and the likelihood that they were used for special ceremonial occasions is increased by the survival of pieces commissioned for special commemorative purposes, such as the Beilby goblet of 1763 bearing the royal coat of arms of George III, and a ship on the opposite side, with the words 'Success to the African Trade of Whitehaven', a commemorative piece that celebrated the launch of the slave ship *King George* that year.[49]

There are further clues in the design of each separate and distinctive piece of Beilby glass – not only the form of the vessels considered above, but in the decorative motifs and occasionally the words that were inscribed upon the surface, which are suggestive of the political leanings of the person for whom it was commissioned. There was much precedent in the history of high-design glass manufacture in the eighteenth century for 'Jacobite' glasses that were used to toast the Pretenders at secret gentlemen's clubs.[50] These were often engraved with Jacobite emblems such as the rose (indicating the secret 'sub rosa' allegiance of the drinker). The butterfly emblems on certain Beilby glasses have been interpreted occasionally as a Jacobite symbol, an allusion to how the Young Pretender would 'alight' on British soil. This is, however, speculative: very few of the Beilby pieces are signed, and it could merely have indicated provenance without intruding upon the visual impact of the piece.[51] The range of political allusions suggests the Beilby workshop engaged with a range of clients who had different commemorative functions in mind for their expensive glassware: the Claverings, a north-east gentry family who had long-standing Whig sympathies, commissioned a Beilby goblet bearing the legend 'Liberty and Clavering for ever'.[52]

Beilby glassware often appropriated the design motifs that were popular at the time in prints and landscape paintings, especially those that depicted classical ruins (see Figure 2). Anne Janowitz has argued that these were particularly pleasurable to Georgian connoisseurs, especially those who supported the Union of England and Scotland, and the settlement of the Hanoverian monarchy, since they invited meditations upon the decline of tyrannical absolutist government.[53] Classical ruins appealed to the taste of the gentry among whom the common experience of the Grand Tour to Italy and Greece was a material reference to their coming-of-age as men of taste.[54] Other motifs, such as Norman soldiers and heraldic shields, were similarly in tune with the popularity of gentlemanly pursuits such as antiquarianism, which, as has already been noted, was popular in mid- to late Georgian Britain. Beilby glassware was costly to make, and reflected the wealth and status of its owner; however, its kudos was not merely in its expensive price tag. Its presence in a display cabinet, or on a dinner table, would have evoked the fashionable themes of literary and historical texts, providing visual cues that would have been immediately evident to the educated dinner guest, and tangible confirmation of the cultivated taste of the host. Beilby glass did not just reflect status, however: its commission, ownership, display and (occasional?) use actually constituted polite gentility through dinner-table sociability that cemented the patronage of elite households, and ritualized communal celebrations among guilds and political allies of commercial and electoral success.

The history of glass production in north-east England forms an important part of its industrial heritage, and rates, along with coalmining and shipbuilding, as one of the industries that brought Tyneside and Wearside global economic importance during the nineteenth century. The history of the north-east's contribution to glassmaking until now has predominantly been the story of the manufacture of window glass, bottle glass, and industrial plate glass for large-scale engineering and construction purposes.[55] The first piece of plate glass in the world was manufactured in Sunderland, and, at its height, Newcastle and the surrounding area was one of the most notable centres for glassmaking in the world. A total of 41 out of the 126 glasshouses licensed by the Board of Excise in 1832 were located in the north-east;

in the same year, 64 per cent of the duty on English bottle glass was paid in the region.[56] Such statistics help to reinforce the region's industrial reputation and lend substance to its labour history. In fact, as has been shown, in the century before 1800, both quantity *and* quality were to be found among the north-east's glass producers, but this is not widely known or acknowledged.[57]

Recovering the history of Beilby glassware has been an exercise in interpreting artefacts and placing them in their socio-cultural context. But might disagreement over how to interpret these objects help to explain why they are not identified as part of the widely known history of the region where they were produced? Different experts tend to treat glassware in different ways, some as high-status art objects, others as mainly functional items whose decoration constitutes a 'craft' rather than an art.[58] The early modern distinction between 'useful' crafts, and the more prestigious, purely creative arts that filtered through to the nineteenth century and beyond was resisted by William Morris and his followers, but has never been successfully eradicated, in Britain at least.[59] When the cultural bias of privileging the cultural outputs of certain geographical locations (such as the metropolis, rather than the provinces) is added, then further inequalities in the interpretation of material culture emerge. For example, there is a long tradition in newspaper advertising of conferring prestige upon material goods solely on the basis that they are produced in, or imported from, London.[60] If we consider the example of Beilby glass explored here, the hierarchy imposed upon certain modes of cultural production is evident, even when considering a single piece of glass, from the fact that those highly skilled glassblowers who made the finest-quality glass by hand on Tyneside and Wearside did not have their names attributed to their art; the glassware they made is known only as 'Beilby glass' in its decorated form. Leslie Stephen, writing in the original *Dictionary Of National Biography* (1885), observed that Ralph Beilby became a silversmith, jeweller and seal-engraver under his father's tuition, and thereby 'acquired several *useful* arts and accomplishments'.[61] Alexander Koller's entry in the *New Dictionary of National Biography* acknowledges William Beilby's status as an 'artist' but describes the first results in white enamelling at the Closegate flint glasshouses as 'rather weak'.[62] One economic historian writing on the evolution of the glass industry on the Rivers Tyne and Wear from 1700 to 1900 wrote:

> There are no grounds at all for believing that ... enamellers [on glass] were anything more than skilled journeymen working for the glass houses; the polychrome armorial enamels executed by the Beilby brothers could perhaps be said to have transcended the cheap imitativeness of ordinary white enamelling ...[63]

Elsewhere, the author comments: 'at best white enamelled glass was only a poor and distinctively provincial imitation of engraved glass'.[64]

It says much about deeply engrained prejudices about the material culture of north-east England that the white enamelling techniques used by the Beilbys have been misunderstood in the region of their production as cheap 'provincial' imitations of the effects of hand engraving. The Beilbys, like Thomas Bewick, were never regarded as artists in their own lifetimes by London-based art connoisseurs, nor during the nineteenth century, as Leslie Stephen's comments in the Victorian *Dictionary of National Biography* illustrate. Certainly Bewick's *Memoirs* encouraged the romantic celebration of domestic production in the face of creeping industrialization, and even after he became famous he resisted metropolitan values, refusing to leave his home in the north-east and go to London, despite becoming famous nationally for his *History of Quadrupeds* (1790).[65] Yet the Beilbys' innovative application of enamelling upon glass in the 1760s was far from parochial: it reflected the spread of new technologies from the metropolis, and between one provincial British town and another through the practice of sending boys to be apprenticed in different parts of the country, to wherever there was a master craftsman with skills to impart. Beilby glassware was produced during the reign of George III, when a distinctively British style in the arts was emerging. Following the Hanoverian succession, the influence of German style was witnessed upon many artistic endeavours, from the music of Handel, to the manufacture of ruby red glassware by Mayer Oppenheim of Birmingham, which was patented in 1755.[66] The Beilbys regarded themselves less as rustic handicraftsmen and more as innovators: participants in the emergent national polite culture that marked urban sophistication throughout Britain. Ralph Beilby was a founder and active member of the Literary and Philosophical Society of Newcastle.[67] The addition by William Beilby of his signature on his most prestigious creations, such as a decanter produced in 1762 for the Common Council of Newcastle, showing the arms of the mayor, Sir Walter Blackett (now in the Victoria and Albert Museum, London), and a gilt-rimmed royal goblet with coat of arms and Prince of Wales feathers (now in the Fitzwilliam Museum, Cambridge) might suggest that he himself regarded his painting upon glass as art.[68] Like Wedgwood china or Chippendale furniture, Beilby glass is an exemplary model of Georgian design innovation.

Beilby glassware is now found among the finest art collections in the world; in addition to the British collections cited above, other notable examples are in the Philadelphia Museum of Art, the Corning Museum of Glass in New York, and the Huntington Art Collections, San Marino, California. Surviving complete pieces of Beilby glass command high prices at auction (should it make any difference to the historical interpretation that one Beilby glass sold in 2002 for several thousand pounds?).[69] The act of viewing, even occasionally handling, an historical artefact calls into play another layer of interpretation of which historians are almost always less mindful than archaeologists.[70] In the Laing Art Gallery in Newcastle upon Tyne, home of Beilby glass, 14 of some of the most striking surviving pieces are displayed in the local history gallery in a poorly lit wooden case below waist height, with almost no accompanying interpretative information. However, at the Victoria and Albert Museum in London, Ashmolean Museum in Oxford and Fitzwilliam Museum in Cambridge, Beilby glass takes its place in the narrative history of the evolution of design in English glassware according to a conventionally chronological story, with slightly more prominence. (Coincidentally, in both the Ashmolean and Fitzwilliam museums, Beilby glassware appears among other glass in rather 'in between' galleries located on staircases.)[71] By contrast, the Huntington gallery exhibition raises their status as exclusive and valuable art objects, finely lit and raised above eye level for maximum impact, spotlighted in a darkened room to highlight the lustre of the glass and the luminosity of the fine hand-painted enamelling. The accompanying glossy catalogue at the Huntington is illustrated with an example of an 'elegant Beilby goblet' from the prestigious Corning Museum of Glass in New York.[72] While this is partly a question of contrasting use of space and resources between the host institutions (a public art gallery in north-east England and a privately endowed art institute in California), it also speaks volumes about the way in which the global importance of Beilby glass is recognized mostly outside of its native region.

In conclusion, there are many locations throughout the world where archaeological inquiry or re-examination of the existing material culture has produced striking results in terms of a challenge to the dominant and in many respects highly politicized discourses about local history, and how this continues to influence local residents' self-perceptions of their heritage. On a national level, this presents a challenge to stereotypes regarding the contribution made by particular regions and communities to national life. Over time, this could lead to a re-evaluation of what is meant by national identity as an aggregate of regional identities that sometime collude, sometimes resist an overarching narrative about the people who are subsumed within a dominant culture. As has already been observed, the current tide is in favour of recovering the everyday, and the material culture of 'ordinary' people, particularly those who have been marginalized or oppressed. Yet this chapter proposes that high-design goods can present an equally challenging and indeed political problem if they do not 'fit' the pre-existing narrative, especially in a region like north-east England whose history and contemporary self-identity, in spite of recent urban regeneration, continues to be deeply invested in the story of its nineteenth-century working-class, industrial heritage.

Notes

The author would like to thank Karen Harvey for her editorial guidance, and a number of colleagues in the School of Historical Studies, Newcastle University, who have provided stimulating discussions, comments and additional references towards this chapter, particularly Scott Ashley, Chris Fowler, Kevin Greene and Elizabeth Kramer.

1   The literature on the history of identity is extensive: for examples, see Jonathan Barry and Henry French (eds), *Identity and Agency in England, 1500–1800* (Basingstoke: Palgrave Macmillan, 2004); Colin Kidd, *British Identities before Nationalism. Ethnicity and Nationhood in the Atlantic World, 1600–1800* (Cambridge: Cambridge University Press, 1999).

2   One of the most notable examples of this was Lawrence Stone, *The Family, Sex and Marriage in England* (London: Penguin, 1977), which used examples from art history to illustrate his hypothesis on the rise of affective marriage; another is Philippe Aries' *Centuries of Childhood*, transl. Robert Baldick (London: Cape, 1962), which used portraiture to support his theory that childhood was 'invented' in the eighteenth century.

3   Richard J. Evans, *In Defence of History* (London: Granta, 1997), was a passionate defence of the importance of establishing historical truth in the face of extreme

154   *Helen Berry*

postmodern scepticism at the possibility of establishing any relationship between truth and language.

See, for example, Adrian Green, 'Houses in North-eastern England: Regionality and the British Beyond, *c.*1600–1750', in Susan Lawrence (ed.), *Archaeologies of the British: Explorations of Identity in the United Kingdom and its Colonies, 1600–1945, One World Archaeology* (London: Routledge, 2003), no. 46, pp. 55–75.

See Keith Thomas, 'History and Anthropology', *Past & Present*, 24 (1963), pp. 3–24; Jack Goody and Alan Macfarlane are two well-known examples of anthropologists who have been highly influential in early modern historiography.

One of the most prominent examples is the *Journal of Design History*, founded in 1988.

James Raven, Naomi Tadmor and Helen Small (eds), *The Practice and Representation of Reading in England* (Cambridge: Cambridge University Press, 1996); Peter Burke (ed.), *New Perspectives on Historical Writing*, 2nd edn (University Park, Pennsylvania: Pennsylvania State University Press, 2001). For an archaeological perspective on this subject, see John Moreland, *Archaeology and Text* (London: Duckworth, 2001).

Raymond Williams, *Keywords. A Vocabulary of Culture and Society* (London: Croom Helm, 1976; 2nd edn 1983), p. 87. For a useful overview of recent developments in cultural history, see Karen Harvey, 'Introduction', in *idem* (ed.) *The Kiss in History* (Manchester: Manchester University Press, 2005).

For a discussion of these issues, see Anthony D. Smith, *The Ethnic Origins of Nations* (Oxford: Oxford University Press, 1986), especially Chapter 8, 'Legends and Landscapes'.

10 Defined here as the terrain incorporated into the modern counties of Northumberland, Tyne & Wear and County Durham.

11 'Processual' archaeology, as it is usually termed, was about 'systems theories', seeking patterns and laws that would provide an interpretative framework for the past. This was followed by 'post-processual' archaeology, which by contrast pays attention to issues such as context, experience and identity. See Kevin Greene, 'Roman Pottery: Models, Proxies and Economic Interpretation', *Journal of Roman Archaeology*, 18 (2005), pp. 33–6.

12 For studies of the relationship between style and identity in archaeology, see Polly Weissner, 'Reconsidering the Behavioural Basis for Style: A Case Study among the Kalahari San', *Journal of Anthropological Archaeology*, 3 (1984), pp. 190–234; R. Boast, 'A Small Company of Actors: A Critique of Style', *Journal of Material Culture*, 2 (1997), pp. 173–98.

13 Bryan Pfaffenberger, 'The Social Anthropology of Technology', *Annual Review of Archaeology*, 21 (1992), pp. 491–516. Reprinted in Victor Buchli (ed.), *Material Culture. Critical Concepts in the Social Sciences* (London: Routledge, 2004), vol. 3, pt 2, p. 506.

14 Rosemary Sweet, *Antiquaries: The Discovery of the Past in Eighteenth-century Britain* (London: Hambledon and London, 2004), especially Chapters 1–3.

15 Stuart Piggott, *Ruins in a Landscape. Essays in Antiquarianism* (Edinburgh: Edinburgh University Press, 1976), p. 108.

16 Joan Evans, *A History of the Society of Antiquaries* (Oxford: Oxford University Press, 1956), pp. 1–32.

17 Sweet, *Antiquaries*, p. 61.

18 In the late seventeenth century, Aubrey was the first to associate the stone circles of Britain with the druids. This theme was taken up by William Stukeley (1687–1765) in his *Stonehenge* (1740) and *Avebury* (1743). See Piggott, *Ruins*, p. 118.

19 Victor Buchli, 'Introduction', in *Material Culture*, vol. 1, pt 1, p. xx.

20 W.G. Hoskins, *The Making of the English Landscape* (Leicester: Leicester University Press, 1955).

21 Charles Phythian-Adams, 'Introduction: An Agenda for English Local History', in *idem* (ed.), *Societies, Cultures and Kinship, 1580–1850. Cultural Provinces and English*

Local History (Leicester and London: Leicester University Press, 1993), pp. 9–23. Interestingly, the archaeologist Gordon Childe prefigured this approach in the 1940s and 1950s with classic works such as *Prehistoric Communities of the British Isles* (London and Edinburgh: W. & R. Chambers, 1940). I am grateful to my colleagues Chris Fowler and Kevin Greene for highlighting this point.

22 Phythian-Adams, 'Agenda for English Local History', p. 10.

23 Ibid., p. 9.

24 Alan Everitt, 'Country, County and Town: Patterns of Regional Evolution in England', *Transactions of the Royal Historical Society*, 5th Ser., 29 (1979), pp. 79–108.

25 For a discussion of these issues, see Adrian Green and Tony Pollard, 'Introduction: Identifying Regions', in *idem* (eds), *Regional Identities in North-east England, 1300–2000* (Woodbridge: Boydell and Brewer, 2007).

26 See, for example, Elizabeth Kramer's case study of the Scottish painter E.A. Hornel (1864–1933), whose paintings depicted Japanese women wearing brightly coloured kimonos, reinforcing the 'timeless and exotic' quality of Japan at a time of monumental political upheaval in that country. See 'A Paradise of Pretty Girls: The Kimono and Perceptions of Japan', in Maria Hayward and Elizabeth Kramer (eds), *Textiles and Text. Re-establishing the Links Between Archival and Object-based Research* (London: Archetype, 2007).

27 The extensive bibliography of this ongoing project under the directorship of Mark P. Leone of the University of Maryland is at http://www.bsos.umd.edu/anth/aia/AboutAIA.htm.

28 See Richard Handler, *Nationalism and the Politics of Culture in Quebec* (Wisconsin: University of Wisconsin Press, 1988); Martha K. Norkunas, *The Politics of Public Memory. Tourism, History and Ethnicity in Monterey, California* (Albany: State University of New York Press, 1993).

29 The ramifications of reaction *against* contingent and fluid identity in contemporary religion and politics have been explored most recently by Amartya Sen in his *Identity and Violence: the Illusion of Destiny* (Harmondsworth: Penguin, 2006).

30 Maxine Berg, *Luxury and Pleasure in Eighteenth-century England* (Oxford: Oxford University Press, 2005), Chapter 4, 'Glass and Chinaware: The Glamour of the Polite Table', pp. 117–26, 254.

31 Sebastian Payne, 'Cracking the Origins of Lead Glass', *British Archaeology*, 86 (2006), p. 52.

32 Charles Truman, *An Introduction to English Glassware to 1900* (London: Victoria and Albert Museum, 1984), p. 10. Payne's figures are 88 glasshouses, 27 producing lead glass by 1696, 'Origins', p. 52.

33 Francis Buckley, 'The Early Glasshouses of Bristol', *Transactions of the Society of Glass Technology*, 9 (1925), p. 36.

34 Ibid., p. 7.

35 Henry Bourne, *History of Newcastle upon Tyne: or, the Ancient and Present State of that Town* (Newcastle upon Tyne, 1736), p. 145.

36 John Brand, *History and Antiquities of the Town and County of Newcastle upon Tyne* (London, 1789), vol. 2, pp. 36, 42–7.

37 Francis Buckley, 'Glasshouses on the Wear in the Eighteenth Century', *Transactions of the Society of Glass Technology*, 9 (1925), pp. 105–11.

38 James Rush, *A Beilby Odyssey* (Olney: Nelson and Saunders, 1987), pp. 53–5.

39 The most complete photographs are in ibid. The present author has also had the opportunity of handling a rare Beilby commemorative punch bowl in the Laing Art Gallery, Newcastle, for which thanks is due to Ms Ruth Percival, Assistant Keeper of Fine and Decorative Art, but owing to the fragility of the object it was an experience I would not wish to repeat.

40 Buckley, 'Glasshouses', p. 288.

41 Truman, *English Glassware*, pp. 11–12.

42   Jenny Uglow, *Nature's Engraver. A Life of Thomas Bewick* (London: Faber & Faber, 2006), Chapter 4.

43   Rush, *Beilby Odyssey*, pp. 56–7.

44   Thomas Bewick, *A Memoir of Thomas Bewick Written By Himself* (1st edition 1862, facsimile edition Newcastle upon Tyne: Frank Graham, 1974), pp. 56–7. Mary, the youngest Beilby sibling, has received scant attention as an artist in her own right. She is surely typical of middle-class eighteenth-century women who, although they did not have access to formal training or apprenticeships, worked alongside male relatives in the family business. Her life as a decorator of glass is reminiscent of that of Caroline Herschel, who helped her brother Sir William, later Astronomer Royal, by grinding glass lenses and other small tasks until, 'I became in time as useful a member of the workshop as a boy might be to his master in the first year of his a prenticeship' (Harry Ransom Humanities Research Center, University of Texas, Ms. MO677, autobiography of Caroline Herschel, vol. II, 1772–1788, f. 8, 1775).

45   Alexandra Marmion, 'Striking Innovation in British Glass', Catalogue of Loans from the Corning Museum of Glass, Corning, New York, from an exhibition at the Huntington Library, Art Collections and Botanical Gardens, San Marino, California, unpublished catalogue, 2001, n.p.

46   Rush, *Beilby Odyssey*, pp. 102–3.

47   Unfortunately the business papers in the Tyne and Wear Record Office (DT.Bew) and Victoria and Albert Museum (National Art Library MSL/1955/3250–62) do not contain details of this early period of the Beilby workshop's activity, but the later period when Thomas Bewick went into partnership with his former master, Ralph.

48   Rush, *Beilby Odyssey*, p. 60 and passim.

49   Ibid., p. 85.

50   G.B. Seddon, *The Jacobites and Their Drinking Glasses* (Woodbridge: Boydell and Brewer, 1995).

51   Rush, *Beilby Odyssey*, p. 58. See also Nigel Tattersfield, 'Fresh Light on the Ingenious Beilbys', in *Bewick Studies. Essays in Celebration of the 250th Anniversary of the Birth of Thomas Bewick, 1753–1828* (Cherryburn and London: The Bewick Society, 2003), p. 74.

52   H.T. Dickenson (ed.), *The Correspondence of Sir James Clavering* (Gateshead: Surtees Society, 1967), pp. ix–xii.

53   Anne Janowitz, *England's Ruins: Poetic Purpose and the National Landscape* (Oxford: Oxford University Press, 1990), passim.

54   See Jason Kelly, *Archaeology and Identity in the British Enlightenment: The Society of Dilettanti, 1732–1816* (forthcoming, 2009), Chapter 1, 'The Dilettanti Culture of the Eighteenth Century'.

55   The National Glass Centre in Sunderland *does* contain other aspects of the history of glassmaking in the region, but, unfortunately, few actual examples on display to accompany the textual commentary.

56   Ross, 'Development of the Glass Industry', I, pp. 1–2.

57   Maxine Berg notes that the high-quality drinking glasses made in the north-east were sent to London, where the social elites from that region ordered most of their tableware (*Luxury and Pleasure*, p. 122). This is an accurate generalization, to which the example of Beilby glass adds the caveat that a local trade in high-status glassware, which bypassed the capital, is also in evidence.

58   The vexed question of 'When is an artefact a work of art?' is explored by Alfred Gell, 'Vogel's Net: Traps as Artworks and Artworks as Traps', *Journal of Material Culture*, 1, 1 (1996), pp. 15–38.

59   See Debra Cohen, *Household Gods: The British and their Possessions* (New Haven and London: Yale University Press, 2006), Chapter 3 'Art at Home', for a discussion of Morris. In a global perspective, the distinction between fine art and decorative art is highly culturally specific: in Italy, it dates back to at least the Renaissance; in Japan,

unlike in many Western European countries, textiles can be regarded as fine art. I am grateful to Elizabeth Kramer for a discussion of these issues; for further reading, see her article, cited in n. 26.

60 See, for example, Helen Berry, 'Promoting Taste in the Provincial Press: National and Local Culture in Eighteenth-century Newcastle upon Tyne', *British Journal for Eighteenth-century Studies*, 25 (2002), pp. 1–17.

61 *Oxford Dictionary of National Biography* (Oxford, 1885), IV, p. 133.

62 'Beilby family (per. *c.*1755–1819)', *Oxford Dictionary of National Biography* (Oxford: Oxford University Press, 2004) available at: http://www.oxforddnb.com/view/article/73669, accessed 3 January 2008.

63 Catherine M. Ross, 'The Development of the Glass Industry on the Rivers Tyne and Wear, 1700–1900', Unpublished PhD dissertation, University of Newcastle, II, 2 (1982), p. 635.

64 Ibid., I, pp. 282–3.

65 Uglow, *Nature's Engraver*, p. 105.

66 The introduction of glass cutting into England is also credited to German innovation: see Ross, 'Development of the Glass Industry', II, n. 1, p. 635.

67 Uglow, *Nature's Engraver*, pp. 42–3, 52–3.

68 Rush, *Ingenious Beilbys*, pp. 60–8.

69 See, for example, http://www.sothebys.com/app/live/lot/LotDetail.jsp?lot_id=159361284, accessed 27 October 2008.

70 Perhaps this is because historians' traditional reliance upon written sources was supposed to engage the intellect, but not draw attention to other forms of bodily, sensory engagement, which inevitably adds complex additional questions regarding the subjectivity of the historian's analysis and the role of sense-data as a form of 'evidence'. This may in part explain the present author's discomfort at handling an actual piece of Beilby glass (see n. 39).

71 Fitzwilliam Museum, *Glass at the Fitzwilliam Museum, Cambridge* (Cambridge, 1978); Martine S. Newby, 'A Handlist of English Glass Displayed in the Department of Western Art, Ashmolean Museum, Oxford', unpublished catalogue, revised 2000. My thanks to Ms Newby for kindly providing a copy.

72 Marmion, 'Striking Innovation', n.p.

8 Objects and agency
Material culture and modernity in China

Frank Dikötter

Objects and agency

From exotic spices in medieval Europe to manufactured goods in the Trobriand Islands, 'foreign' has denoted 'superior' across a range of different societies, if only because exotic goods came from distant lands and were highly valued. During the nineteenth century, however, as elites around the world came to locate modernity in Europe, things local were increasingly rejected as signifiers of backwardness, while imported goods from France, England or Germany were embraced instead as prestige symbols: dominant groups in Asia, Africa and South America believed that modernity had to be brought home in order to propel one's country into the universe of 'civilized' nations and join a universal march towards a better future. 'Foreign' stood for 'modern' as Europe was viewed as the fountainhead of a new world of progress. In South America, republican elites embraced elegant shirts, woollen trousers and frock coats from Paris, while fine wines, fashion books and illustrated magazines were imported from Europe, grand pianos being hauled over steep mountain paths on muleback.[1] In Japan, kimonos and parasols were traded for derby hats and horn-rimmed spectacles, while beer and baseball rivalled sake and sumo in an exuberant imitation of life as it was lived in England.[2] These trends were by no means confined to Asia, Africa and South America, as a similar lure of the foreign appeared in parts of Europe (a fact conveniently overlooked by some historians of colonialism). In Italy, Victorian porcelain, including the new toilet bowl from Mr Crapper, along with entire carriages and coaches, and even English nannies, were imported. White flannels, English saddles and the riding coat, bastardized as *redingote* in France, all became common among European elites keen to identify with the forces of progress. In Germany, the habit of sending English shirts to London to be laundered and ironed was upheld by some until the bombing raids started under Nazi rule, as all over Europe 'people wanted the best, and the best was English'.[3]

Foreign, in Europe and out of Europe, was no longer merely exotic: to buy foreign was to be modern. In China – the focus of this chapter – modern commodities were eagerly embraced at all social levels, as contemporaries often observed. 'The Chinese have eagerly acquired all the technical discoveries of the foreigners; machine guns and trench mortars, flying machines and wireless telegraphs, thermos bottles and cinematographs, hair-cutting machines and fountain pens': so noted Johan Gunnar Andersson while travelling through China in 1928.[4] A local commentator writing a few years earlier went further, pointing out how in his country

> residences as well as public buildings are being built in the latest European style, together with modern fittings and fixtures for the interior. Foreign cooking, foreign wines, foreign games, foreign clothes, foreign customs – almost everything foreign is becoming fashionable.[5]

In his examination of the interaction between China and Europe, E.R. Hughes concluded: 'Such things as bicycles, thermos flasks, and electric torches are found in many villages, together with soap, matches, cigarettes and some tinned foods ... if they are useful they are adopted; if they are not useful they are ignored.'[6]

All too often these global changes have been explained in a reductionist way, which denies the agency and power of ordinary people in shaping the environments in which they live; larger, mysterious forces such as 'globalization' or 'capitalism' are instead identified as the vectors of economic change, portrayed more often than not in negative terms. Social scientists critical of the 'intrusion of the West', for instance, have interpreted the global circulation of commodities as the result of a market system that has no regard for the needs of local people. Serge Latouche, in *The Westernization of the World* (1995), has argued that the rise of the West to world domination has brought widespread social, cultural and material destruction, as 'oppressed people' reject eurocentric modes of development: globalization has led to acculturation, as a stable, tradition-bound regime of production is followed by a disorientated response to a new global mode of production.[7] 'Traditional Russia', argues Theodore von Laue in *The World Revolution of Westernization* (1987), was destroyed by imported gadgets, whether grand pianos or fine liquors.[8] The idea that a global economy inevitably leads to the destruction of local identities, as a homogenized consumer culture ruthlessly displaces previously autonomous cultural experiences in its subjugation of the world, has great appeal for those who equate globalization with Westernization. But local peoples have always creatively incorporated products and social forms for purposes other than those intended by their producers, as Frederick Errington and Deborah Gewertz demonstrate in the case of Papua New Guinea.[9] Marshall Sahlins, too, notes that local culture does not necessarily disappear under the impact of rapid change, as global homogeneity and local differentiation develop together: he refers to this process as the 'indigenization of modernity', a vision articulated around the arresting image of *lokua*, small fish living in reef ponds cut off from the sea at tidal lows but periodically replenished by ocean waters.[10]

Michel de Certeau, in an influential book on the practice of everyday life, noted that while 'mass culture' might tend towards homogenization, 'ordinary culture' displays a fundamental diversity of situations, interests and contexts despite an apparent uniformity of objects: pluralization, he noted, is born from ordinary usage.[11] His essay argued that the products imposed by a dominant economic order can undergo numerous transformations by the ways in which ordinary people make use of them. Indians in South America may have been unable to fight their colonial subjection, but they nevertheless often transformed the rituals, representations and laws imposed on them into something quite different to what their conquerors had in mind: 'They subverted them not by rejecting or altering them, but by using them with respect to ends and references foreign to the system they had no choice but to accept.'[12] He turned Michel Foucault upside down, showing how, at the everyday level, ordinary people are not so much subjected to an insidious form of discipline, but capable of resisting it by everyday acts of appropriation: Michel de Certeau analysed the ways in which consumers created the network of an antidiscipline. Invaluable as his approach may be, his notion of 'resistance' against a 'dominant social order' overstates the case: rarely can the world be divided into an oppressive 'system' from above and 'resistance' from below. Even in the case of colonialism in Africa, to quote the philosopher Kwame Appiah, 'to speak of "resistance" in this phase of colonial culture is already to overstate the ways in which the colonial state was invasive'.[13] Moreover, while de Certeau underlines that users are never passive, his focus is nonetheless on moments, practices, strategies or operations rather than on human beings in specific social situations – uses rather than users are invested with the power to generate change.

This chapter suggests that people operate from within a social universe in which things are understood, used and circulated in culturally specific ways. Material modernity in China was not a set of givens imposed by foreigners but a repertoire of new opportunities, a kit of tools that could be flexibly appropriated in a variety of imaginative ways. The local, in this process of cultural bricolage, was transformed just as much as the global was inflected to adjust to existing conditions: inculturation rather than acculturation accounts for the broad cultural and material changes that marked modern China. A host of factors – not all of which can be examined within the confines of this piece – influenced the different choices made by a variety of social groups in this process of appropriation, from taste, price, novelty and perceived usefulness to quality, availability and marketing. Impoverished pullers of rickshaws, those foreign-derived machines that enabled one man to do the work of two chair-carriers, used medical syringes to inject new opiates fabricated by virtue of the tools of modern chemistry, while homes in Shanghai's shantytown were erected with iron cans from Standard Oil. As much as the potato and tobacco were considered 'foreign' in the seventeenth century but had become part of 'tradition' by the late Qing, a whole range of imported goods became inextricably enmeshed in the warp and weft of everyday life in China, from the mansions of the wealthy to the shacks of the poor.

Copy culture

A first stereotype to be dispelled is the idea that 'hostility toward alien things' characterized modern China.[14] The opposite was true: in contrast to other parts of the world, such as Africa and South America, the material goods and technological innovations associated with foreign modernity were not merely imported for elite consumption, but were copied locally and quickly made available to much larger sections of the population. A long-standing tradition of manufacturing goods from foreign patterns, the use of component parts produced by individual workers in assembling complex objects, the spread of small enterprises in an expanding market from the sixteenth century onwards and the availability of cheap labour in a rapidly growing population: these different factors facilitated the domestication of foreign goods, as desirable objects from abroad were copied at low cost to address the needs of a large but relatively poor population. A two-tier economy appeared in which wealthy circles bought foreign goods and ordinary people welcomed cheap imitations, from the enamelled washbasin to the metallic flashlight. While lack of space does not allow us to analyse all the dimensions of this phenomenon, it should suffice to note that a nationalist movement of import substitution in the first decades of the twentieth century further encouraged copy culture: economic nationalism eased the transformation of 'foreign goods' into 'national goods' within less than half a century. A relatively low intake of foreign goods – in contrast to Russia, the Ottoman Empire, South America, Africa and Southeast Asia – was not an indication of a lack of interest in things foreign, let alone 'hostility to alien things', but rather a measure of their success, as they were quickly appropriated and transformed into local products.

While modernizing elites, by virtue of their closer familiarity with the foreign, most conspicuously started to appropriate foreign objects by the end of the Qing, ultimately ordinary people, thanks to their distance from the centres of power, were the least inhibited about acquiring new goods that were perceived to be meaningful and useful. Working men and women, by small if often tightly constrained choices on how their hard-earned money should be spent, incrementally changed the material landscape of modern China. In a country marked by opposition between the dearth of the many and the riches of the few, luxury imports were used by elites as visual evidence of social status, while cheap imitations satisfied the demand for new products among ordinary people: both were included in a culture that worshipped the tangible and craved the new. Carl Crow provided an example of the coexistence of expensive imports and cheap substitutes in the 1930s. Shops in any town in the Yangzi valley sold small batteries used in electric flashlights. If a customer asked for a foreign brand it would be offered, but if the price was felt to be too high, a locally produced battery with a similar name and virtually identical packaging would be sold instead.[15] Even foreign advertising agents with long experience of market conditions in China believed that the production of cheap imitations that could easily be distinguished from the original import was not the same as the counterfeiting of well-known brands by manufacturers in Japan: Japanese counterfeits aimed not so much to produce a cheaper variation of the import for buyers who could not afford the original, as to create such confusion that the genuine could not be told apart from the imitation.[16] Copy culture, in short, produced a two-tier economy that was at the heart of social differentiation: the rich and cost-conscious acquired imported goods to signify wealth and status, while the poor and cost-conscious were restricted to buying local imitations. Bicycles, radios, gramophones, cameras, sewing machines, thermos flasks, clocks, rubber shoes, aspirin, soap, fountain pens, matches, umbrellas, glass windows and mirrors – these and more were admired by people of all social backgrounds the moment they appeared, and rapidly copied to address local needs.

Resignification, differential usage and a glass world

While it is important to understand how worship of the tangible pushed ordinary people and social elites alike to embrace new commodities, first from abroad and then copied at home, we should also bear in mind that imported objects were adapted to local uses. A shared object often becomes the subject of resignification and differential use, even if the object itself imposes a limit on the possible uses. For reasons of space, this section will focus on one type of material only, namely glass. Ordinary glass may seem to be a fairly straightforward object, but a closer look shows how it acquired a range of meanings and uses in modern China. Europeans inextricably linked porcelain with China, to the extent that it was called 'china'; in China, glass came to be seen as a quintessential foreign substance. Zhang Deyi, one of the first imperial envoys to travel through France in the 1860s, noted that all the windows were made of glass rather than paper, bright and clear as crystal, unbreakable by wind and impermeable to rain.[17] When taking the train he marvelled at the glass windows, which could be slid up and down.[18] He was also elated by the beautiful glassware on display in a glass factory in Belgium, and commented that its sheer transparency and brightness 'opened his eyes and heart'. In a poetic mode, he even imagined a building in the middle of a lake with hundreds of glass rooms: 'I would call it the glass world, where people would live pure lives in empty rooms.'[19] His imagination was not far removed from that of ordinary farmers: a few decades later in Baisha town, Zhejiang province, local farmers referred to the only house with glass panes as the 'glass mirror house' (*bolijing wu*).[20] In Shanghai the *Shenbao* in 1912 suggested covering Nanjing Road with a huge glass roof, which could be opened in clement weather and closed against rain, allowing pedestrians to stroll down the street even on a rainy day.[21] Earlier in the century, far up north, ensconced behind the walls of the imperial palace, empress dowager Cixi insisted on having a conservatory; from farmer to empress, glass held a nation in thrall.[22]

Although plated glass was imported as early as the eighteenth century, stiff and strongly resistant oiled paper was commonly used to cover the windows. In the decades following the Nanjing treaty in 1842, glass windows were used more frequently by wealthy families, and broken glass was even imported and recycled in Canton and Shanghai.[23] The scholar Yang Jingting recorded in 1845 how glass windows were fashionable in Beijing: 'Rich families are very proud, as they no longer need to draw the curtains to see the arrival of visitors since they have installed glass windows.'[24] During the same period a poem judged glass to be 'as bright and as clear as ice, and as thin as a cicada's wings'.[25] Up north in Manchuria, glass windows installed in the 1880s brought sunshine during the cold winter months, as was observed appreciatively by Tai Susheng.[26] Yet even the wealthy dreaded future expense: unlike paper windows, glass could not be repaired.[27] Nonetheless by 1882 a trade representative noted that all new houses had glass windows in Jinjiang.[28] In

Shanghai, where trends in material culture would often be set, coloured glass windows were popular by the 1870s, and appeared in teahouses and bars.[29] Further south, rich families in Canton also replaced their windows with 'transparent tile' (*mingwa*), as glass panes were known locally.[30] Plated glass remained a luxury product for many decades, conspicuously displayed to indicate wealth and status: the most expensive room of an imperial institution in Suzhou, visited by William E. Geil on the eve of the 1911 revolution, had a glass window and a modern clock, purposely placed to convey an aura of luminous modernity.[31]

After the fall of the empire, however, cut glass was one of the few products that held even ordinary people in awe, and Paul Myron noted in his book on business opportunities in China that many paid high prices to obtain it.[32] The first glass factory in Shanghai opened in 1882, although most of the glass was imported from Belgium. Only with the onset of the First World War was local production encouraged, leading to the appearance of 770 glass factories during the republican period, the main centre being Boshan in Shandong province.[33] But in a country of dearth the quality of glass panes was often poor. Carl Crow even found it impossible, bar in a few modern buildings erected under foreign supervision, to find a window with no imperfect panes. Foreign window-glass factories found a sale for defective glass in China, known to the trade as 'China grade'.[34] Defective or not, glass was widely welcomed: in the many villages outside Beijing, three-quarters of all houses had glass windows in 1929, even if they were tiny; as one surprised observer commented, 'the more open a society is, the larger the surface covered by glass'.[35] Some foreigners were attached to the soft light allowed to stream through by the paper covering the lattice. Ida Pruitt judged glass to be 'hard and cold',[36] but the exact opposite conclusion was reached by Zhang Zhongxing (born 1909), who rhapsodized over the light that streamed through glass panes, banishing darkness even at night, when he could still watch the stars and the moon through the window like a modern incarnation of the Tang poet Li Bai.[37] He was not the first: the celebrated poet Yuan Mei had already praised the replacement of paper by glass in the eighteenth century, as '[I] can [now] wave to the moon without leaving my room, and [I] can see the snow without getting cold.'[38]

Glass also appeared in the looking glass, and its reflective power assured it huge appeal. Tens of thousands of them were imported in Jinjiang – and no doubt many other ports – as early as the 1880s.[39] Imported mirrors made of glass were considered much brighter, clearer and shinier than local ones made of copper or tin.[40] Mass production of the mirror in China reinforced rather than displaced cosmological conceptions about spatial relationships and spiritual forces. Spirit screens were traditionally used to prevent evil forces from entering a household, and were often placed inside or outside a doorway, often adorned by the *bagua*, or trigrammed mirror. The use of bronze mirrors as an all-purpose device for *fengshui* was even more widespread, and it has been noted how the 'mystical appeal of mirrors runs deep in Chinese history': hundreds were buried in ancient imperial tombs, as the polished demonifuges could reveal powers and spirits of earth beneath and heaven above.[41] In the countryside in the 1940s – for instance, in Zhonghechang – glass shops sold mirrors and decorative plaques etched with flowers that would blur the reflection of passing faces. These mirrors were sometimes used by the local farmers for purposes quite different from the ways of city people: after a birth, some believed, a demon could be frightened by seeing its ugliness reflected in a mirror, which was placed to bar entrance to the house.[42] *Bagua* mirrors can still be found throughout south China, placed outside the house to keep malign spirits from entering. In Kunming it is common for a small, round mirror, resembling a cheap shaving mirror, to adorn many houses, while larger ones, some rectangular or square, can also be found.[43] In the bathroom and the water closet both ancient cosmological concerns and modern notions of individuality happily coincided, as mirrors were welcomed in order to ensure that an otherwise windowless and enclosed space would not become a dead and stagnant area.[44] Mirrors could also be placed in other confined spaces, for instance an entrance, room or hall, while even restaurants and shops were keen to use mirrors to create a good flow of *qi* and money.[45]

Glass was also used in spectacles, and they too found a variety of usages. Spectacles were sometimes used less for their optical virtues as for their ability to display wealth and education. Like watches, they were imported from abroad as early as the eighteenth century, and like watches they were immediately copied by local artisans, as wearing spectacles became more common among well-to-do families. Yang Jingting observed in 1845 that some men in Beijing even pretended to be short-sighted and wore spectacles so that 'people would regard them as scholars'.[46] Such were the social connotations of glasses that during the late Qing an inferior would take them off when speaking to a superior as a sign of respect, very much as in Europe hats were doffed as a mark of courtesy (this part of social etiquette was still followed in parts of China in the 1920s).[47] By the turn of the century expensive spectacles could be found even in jewellery shops as a fashion accessory in Shanghai. A short poem published in a pictorial magazine in 1909 described the spectacle culture of Shanghai:

> Spectacles are such an ingenious invention, helping the eyes to have a rest and see more clearly. People love to buy a pair to make their eyes dazzle, whether the spectacles have plain glass, long- or short-sighted lenses. The most fashionable ones come in a slightly pointed shape with golden filigree frames and tinted glass lenses in wax yellow or black ink.[48]

It added that 'in recent years, from the wives of officials to mere prostitutes, all are often seen wearing [spectacles]'.[49] In the 1930s, readers interested in things modern were told that spectacles could be bought from shops even by those with perfect eyesight; glasses were a must in the everyday presentation of the modern self.[50]

The uses to which glasses could be put did not always accord with the intentions of their producers. In Chengdu, for instance, they were worn on windy days simply to protect the eyes against dust rather than to improve eyesight; in the north they must have been useful as protection against sandstorms.[51] In the 'civilized weddings' (*wenming jiehun*) of the republican era, a bride would no longer wear a headscarf to cover her face but use tinted glasses instead to hide her eyes.[52] Even more often, however, spectacles seem to have been used against the glare of the sun, much as Eskimos wore glasses against the blinding whiteness of the snow. Most lenses were made of a smoky quartz, although even colourless rock crystal had sufficient opacity to soften the light passing through the lenses. In the late 1920s the use of glasses against the sun was important enough for Crookes anti-glare glasses, later called Calobar lenses (they gave protection against UV and IR), to become popular in parts of the country, whether or not one suffered from poor eyesight.[53] Moreover, as Rudolf Hommel indicates, the dark colour of the glasses was also an aid 'to the almighty officials for scrutinizing with searching eyes without being detected in doing so'.[54]

Even the way in which spectacles were worn varied according to social context: while students placed the shafts firmly behind their ears, photographs show that ordinary people frequently had frames with straight iron shafts, which were placed against the head, or even bent up underneath a skull cap or against the ears like a claw, no doubt in order to avoid cutting into the ears.[55] Eileen Chang, a famous writer and social commentator in the 1940s, confirms that spectacles were used for ornament: 'The indiscriminate importation of things foreign went to such an extent that society girls and professional beauties wore spectacles for ornament, since spectacles were a sign of modernity.'[56] Not everyone, however, wore spectacles as a mere fashion statement: emperor Puyi as a boy already suffered from severe short sight and other ocular defects, and glasses made a huge difference to his comfort and well-being; he became so devoted to his spectacles that he refused to be parted from them for a moment, even to have a photograph taken or his portrait painted.[57]

Enchantment and the magic mirror

A craving for new objects ran through the social landscape of China, as modern commodities were embraced for their practicality, their fashionableness or their social distinctiveness. But a sense of enchantment also characterized the relationship between people and goods, one that is still to be found as one walks through popular markets in many parts of the world today. In modern China the ticking of clocks delighted myriads of people, while millions were fascinated by electricity. To a country that made an abundant display of lanterns carried on bamboo poles at traditional festivals and important social occasions, plentiful electric bulbs – to follow our glass theme – seemed both propitious and decorous. The sources are replete with examples of wealthy merchants and ordinary farmers marvelling at mechanical objects as if they were animate, whether it was the wonderful sight of a huge locomotive steaming by or the simple switching on of a light to expel darkness. Even the poor on occasion could 'have fun', for instance by attending free trials at greyhound races or strolling through busy streets and department stores.

Photography is a good example, which we shall follow in this section, building further on our focus on glass. All too often a narrow focus on images in advertising or publishing, analysed in isolation from social practices, fails to capture the diverse ways in which viewers themselves experienced new modes of visuality, and photography offers an exceptional opportunity to get much closer to the different ways in which images were used, to the negotiations that took place between photographers and sitters, to the multiple meanings of visual artefacts, and to the fragile and unstable links between image and context. After all, ordinary people were not merely spectators when it came to photographic imagery: they themselves produced an enormous amount of visual material by patronising the many photographic studios that mushroomed in large cities and small towns alike.

In China, initial reactions to the camera were generally positive, in contrast to the hoary notion that local people would run away from a camera. One of its first uses was observed in Canton in the 1840s by Zhou Shouchang:

> People sit on a platform and face a mirror, the artist captures their shadow from the light, immerses it into a solution, and embeds it with glass so that no gas can escape; beards, whiskers and clothes can all be discerned, and the result is extremely realistic, surpassing even what an excellent painter can achieve.[58]

Maybe his observations were based on the work of Jules Itier, who took a daguerreotype of governor-general Qiying in Canton in 1844; such was the interest in the camera that Itier had to take pictures of several other dignitaries, merchants and their family members.[59] The camera was also discovered in the 1860s by imperial envoys to the West: Linzhen referred to the camera as a 'magic mirror' (*shenjing*) and learned how to 'borrow light to capture flowers, birds and people'.[60] With an increased flow of goods and people during the last third of the nineteenth century, studios were gradually established in most large cities. By the 1920s, deep inside the hinterland, photographs appeared in the houses of farmers. In Jianying, a small village in the north of China, hardly any home did not have at least a few framed photographs of members of the family.[61] Skilled workers in Yunnan in the early 1940s had photographs of pin-up girls and of their families on the wall.[62]

Inside the many studios, efforts were often made to recreate a 'modern' atmosphere. In one case, a few years after the 1911 revolution, a long tea-table occupied the end of the room, a counterpane was used as tablecloth, and cups and saucers of German origin were placed on the table as for a school treat. Ready-made costumes for the benefit of customers dangled from hooks and nails, two foreign suits being in great demand, the collars and shirt fronts greasy and grey with use. A bouquet in a foreign glass vase, some walking sticks and English books completed the *mise en scène*.[63] Even in a studio in remote Xining in the mid-1930s, as Peter Fleming reports, a considerable number of Tibetans would pose wearing their Homburg hats and heavy boots with upturned toes; among the scrolls, spittoons and rickety chairs, they would stand rigidly in front of a faded, tattered backcloth with segments of outlandish architecture signalling modernity.[64] In the language of backdrops, foreign architecture was common, as posers either stood or sat in front of a huge mansion, often illuminated to project an aura of modernity, or inside, frequently with a staircase. More extravagant were the planes, cars and motorboats signifying wealth and progress. Gardens also made a regular appearance, as an illusion of space was created inside a crowded studio. Modern attire was popular in the large cities, although in the north photos of men in full gown and traditional cap remained common well into the 1930s. Not only did the language of backdrops play an important role, possibly more so than in Europe, but the way in which people posed could vary. In Europe the subject's eyes generally looked away from the camera in studio portraits, while the photo captured the upper part of the body only.[65] In China most people looked straight at the camera and were photographed in full, whether standing or sitting; clothes offered visual evidence of wealth and status, while full body photography captured a larger part of the all-important backdrop.

Photos were always related to wealth and status: the poor had small black-and-white portraits on simple cardboard mounts, while the rich had large portraits displayed in elaborate wood or bronze frames. Yet even ordinary mounts could vary enormously according to taste and demand, ranging from traditional decoration to art deco. Here, too, customers played a role in the fabrication of material culture, not only choosing the cardboard and frame according to taste and income, but sometimes appropriating the photograph even further by making the frame themselves, for instance with embroidery, a key cultural practice among women in imperial China. The use of calligraphy was also culturally specific to photographic practice in China; in a country where mastery of the written language was a sign of social distinction, the educated would add a carefully calligraphed verse on to a *carte-de-visite*, while scholars wrote entire poems or stories on to sepia-toned photos and added a red chop signature. Kang Youwei thus penned verses on the side of his photographic portrait.[66]

The camera was multivalent, capable both of reproducing established social norms and promoting new forms of identity. On the other hand, as the example of Sheng Cheng shows, the camera was instrumental in the exploration of the self. When sent to school in Nanjing a year before the fall of the empire, he discovered photography, as his 'reflection stayed fixed upon the mirror's face'. He had his picture taken several times to show his mother how he looked.[67] After 1911, photographs were liberally attached to the walls in student dormitories, although generally not those of parents, friends or lovers but of themselves – 'perhaps an expression of the students' interest in their own recently discovered personalities', as Olga Lang astutely observed.[68] In Hangzhou, photographers had signs in great gold characters announcing 'The Second I', apparently capitalizing on the discovery of the self.[69]

On the other hand, group pictures could foster a sense of community: traditional families were often large, and up to several dozen members all had to stand still and hold their breath after much arranging around and posing, including babies and small children.[70] In a country where lineage provided an overarching sense of identity, and family size was a matter of social prestige, collective portraits could be so large that they had to be taken outside, as the photo of the Jiang lineage from Hangzhou, in which 76 members are gathered, demonstrates.[71] Ritual ceremonies around ancestor worship, on the other hand, were greatly simplified by the discovery of photography, members of the family regularly coming together, bowing to the picture of the immediate progenitor, and making some simple offerings.[72] Funeral processions in northern cities would carry the enlargement of a photograph of the deceased in portable pavilions, which would be placed in the mourning hall next to candlesticks.[73]

Photographic images permeated everyday life, whether snapshots of ordinary sitters taken in studios and hung on walls, photos of the dead used in ancestral halls, portraits of political leaders displayed in public places, collective pictures of students, office workers or prison guards, images of criminals posted in railway stations, news photos reproduced in pictorial magazines, photos of courtesans printed on postcards, or amateur snapshots of babies exhibited by photography associations. As with other objects, some of their uses were suggested by the objects themselves, while others were more open to cultural inflection. Some of the techniques deployed in producing photos were peculiar to China, including the use of calligraphy to write traditional poems on to photos of people or landscapes, or the addition of a traditional red seal when a photographer signed his product. The extensive use of backdrops was also striking, as ordinary people would pose as if driving an expensive car, or even flying through the skies in a modern plane. Poor or rich, with few exceptions poses remained formal; the photo was a record of the person rather than the personality, and smiles remained rare until the 1930s.

Conclusion

In contrast to Japan, often seen as the spearhead of modernity outside Europe and the United States, it is striking how rapidly the foreign in China has been domesticated to blend into the local, so much so that both have often become indistinguishable from each other: the popular expression *zhongxi hebi*, meaning 'integrating Chinese and Western elements', had positive connotations.[74] In Japan a division between 'Japanese' (*wa*) and 'non-Japanese' (*yo*) objects is even reflected in everyday language, with two syllabaries commonly in use: *katakana* is specifically devoted to the transliteration of non-Japanese terms, while *hiragana* is used for Japanese words. Rooms with carpet, chairs and sofa, called *yoshitsu*, can coexist in the same house with a tatami-covered room with futon, called *washitzu*. The salience of this division often surprises outsiders, as even rice served in 'foreign' restaurants is referred to as *raisu* (written in *katakana*) while the same rice served in a local dining place is called *gohan* (written in *hiragana*). Boundaries between 'Japanese' and 'non-Japanese' are of course continuously shifting – sukiyaki, served by kimono-clad waitresses to guests sitting on tatami, was a dish borrowed from meat-eating Europeans – but they are constantly policed, vigilantly observed and widely acknowledged.[75] No comparable barriers have been erected in China, even if a sense of distinction between 'Chinese' and 'non-Chinese' is widespread; rather than contain the foreign, this distinction contributes to its spread, as local (*tu*) is often perceived as inferior and foreign (*yang*) as superior.

We could be bold and take this observation a step further. In a groundbreaking study of garage sales Gretchen Herrmann has shown how important the personal memories of objects can be for buyers and sellers in the United States. Not only do objects become part of an extended sense of self ('this was my dress'), as sellers are concerned about placing their possessions in good homes, but buyers, too, purchase goods with a similar view in mind: they will assure the sellers that their pretty dress or juice blender will be appreciated and treated with due care. The fact that the goods on offer have been used and have a history as somebody else's erstwhile possession is one of the principal attractions of the garage sale:

> Such shoppers may prefer garage sales to other outlets for secondhand goods such as rummage sales or flea markets precisely because, in the former, they encounter the original owners of what they have bought and so can claim to be taking away something of the previous owners with their purchases.[76]

Similar trends can be found in Europe: the fashion editor of *Elle* magazine, Maggie Alderson, has a house in Hastings full of second-hand stuff, as she loves the patina of age on things that have been used. She would even wear vintage clothes if she could, although this proves difficult because the fabrics have become stiff and women have changed in shape over time.[77] If second-hand markets are hard enough to find in China, where new is generally preferred to old (except for a limited number of goods considered to be collectables), the world of garage sales, including the notion that there is a sympathetic law of magical contagion by which objects transmit the relative success of their previous owners, seems even more alien outside of a Christian context. The newness of things, as Adrian Forty has pointed out, is often resisted by societies in which a free market has taken hold.[78] A much more pragmatic attitude towards material goods seems to prevail in China, where most consumers have bought the new and discarded the old without too many misgivings, for a very long time. Even deities demand material rewards such as temples, although when they lose their powers they, too, can be discarded by their devotees; while statues displayed on family altars are periodically thrown out, if the spirits have departed, thanks to the low cost of carving gods; a very pragmatic attitude thus extends even to sacred objects.[79] If an intrinsic element of a rapidly changing world is the capacity to overcome resistance to novelty, could China be more in tune with modernity than Europe?

Notes

1   This chapter relies heavily on, and extrapolates from the evidence presented in, Frank Dikötter, *Exotic Commodities: Modern Objects and Everyday Life in China* (New York: Columbia University Press, 2007); also published as *Things Modern: Material Culture and Everyday Life in China* (London: Hurst, 2007).
2   See two delightful books, namely Louis Frédéric, *La vie quotidienne au Japon au début de l'ère moderne (1868–1912)* (Paris: Hachette, 1984), and Edward Seidensticker, *Low City, High City: Tokyo from Edo to the Earthquake* (Cambridge, MA: Harvard University Press, 1991).
3   Luigi Barzini, *The Europeans* (Harmondsworth: Penguin, 1983), pp. 35–41; Luigi Barzini, *The Italians* (London: Hamish Hamilton, 1964), p. 59.
4   Johan Gunnar Andersson, *The Dragon and the Foreign Devils* (Boston: Little, Brown, 1928), pp. 242–3.
5   Min-ch'ien Tuk Zug Tyau, *China Awakened* (New York: Macmillan, 1922), p. 85.
6   E.R. Hughes, *The Invasion of China by the Western World* (London: Black, 1937), pp. 282, 287.
7   Serge Latouche, *The Westernization of the World* (London: Polity, 1995); see also Tony Spybey, *Globalization and World Society* (London: Polity, 1995).

8 Theodore H. von Laue, *The World Revolution of Westernization: The Twentieth Century in Global Perspective* (New York: Oxford University Press, 1987), pp. 43–5.

9 Frederick Errington and Deborah Gewertz, 'The Individuation of Tradition in a Papua New Guinean Modernity', *American Anthropologist*, 98, 1 (March 1996), pp. 114–26; see also the pioneering work by Daniel Miller, *Modernity: An Ethnographic Approach* (Oxford: Berg, 1994).

10 Marshall Sahlins, 'On the Anthropology Of Modernity; Or, Some Triumphs of Culture Over Despondency Theory', in Antony Hooper (ed.), *Culture and Sustainable Development in the Pacific* (Canberra: Asia Pacific Press, 2000).

11 Michel de Certeau, Luce Giard and Pierre Mayol, *The Practice of Everyday Life: Living and Cooking*, vol. 2 (Minneapolis: University of Minnesota Press, 1998), p. 256.

12 Michel de Certeau, *The Practice of Everyday Life* (Berkeley: University of California Press, 1984), p. xiii.

13 Kwame Anthony Appiah, *In My Father's House: Africa in the Philosophy of Culture* (Oxford: Oxford University Press, 1992), p. 9.

14 John K. Fairbank, Edwin O. Reischauer and Albert M. Craig, *East Asia: Tradition and Transformation* (Boston: Houghton Mifflin, 1973), p. 178.

15 Carl Crow, *Four Hundred Million Customers* (New York: Halcyon House, 1937), p. 271.

16 Ibid., p. 274.

17 Zhang Deyi, *Ou Mei huanyouji* (Travel diary to Europe and America) (Changsha: Yuelu shushe, 1985), p. 779.

18 Zhang Deyi, *Hanghai shuqi* (Travels abroad) (Changsha: Yuelu shushe, 1985), p. 484.

19 Ibid., pp. 570–1.

20 Cao Juren, *Wo yu wo de shijie* (I and my world) (Taipei: Longwen chubanshe, 1990), p. 36.

21 'Da bolizhao' (Big glass roof), *Shenbao*, 9 Feb. (1912), p. 8.

22 Lou Xuexi, *Beiping shi gongshangye gaikuang* (Conditions of industry and commerce in Beijing) (Beijing: Beiping shi shehuiju, 1932), p. 443.

23 Imperial Maritime Customs, *Catalogue spécial de la collection chinoise à l'exposition universelle, Paris, 1878* (Shanghai: Statistical Department of the Inspectorate General, 1878), p. 9.

24 Yang Jingting, 'Dumen zayong' (Miscellany verses on Beijing) in Lei Mengshui *et al.* (eds), *Zhonghua zhuzhici* (Bamboo verses of China) (Beijing: Beijing guji chubanshe, 1997), p. 181.

25 He Er, 'Yantai zhuzhici' (Bamboo verses on Beijing) in Lei, *Zhonghua zhuzhici*, vol. 1, p. 194.

26 Tai Susheng, 'Shenyang baiyong' (A hundred verses on Shenyang) in Lei, *Zhonghua zhuzhici*, vol. 1, p. 626.

27 'Report on the Trade of Newchwang, for the Year 1865', *Report on the Trade at the Ports of China for the Year 1865* (Shanghai: Imperial Maritime Customs' Press, 1866), p. 20.

28 'Report on the Trade of Chinkiang, for the Year 1882', *Report on the Trade at the Ports of China for the Year 1882* (Shanghai: Imperial Maritime Customs' Press, 1883), p. 141.

29 Wang Tao, *Yingruan zazhi* (Miscellany on Shanghai) (Shanghai: Shanghai guji chubanshe, 1989), p. 115.

30 Chen Kun, 'Lingnan zashi shichao' (Poems on various matters of Lingnan) in Lei, *Zhonghua zhuzhici*, vol. 4, p. 2846.

31 W.E. Geil, *Eighteen Capitals of China* (London: Constable, 1911), p. 171.

32 Paul Myron, *Our Chinese Chances through Europe's War* (Chicago: Linebarger, 1915), p. 171.

33 Liu Shanlin, *Xiyang feng: Xiyang faming zai Zhongguo* (Inventions from the West in China) (Shanghai: Shanghai guji chubanshe, 1999), p. 202; on Boshan glass, see

'Boshan boli gongshi zhi chengxiao' (The success of the Boshan Glassware Company), *Shenbao*, 29 June 1911, p. 2:2.

34 Crow, *Four Hundred Million Customers*, p. 269.

35 Li Jinghan, *Beiping jiaowai zhi xiangcun jiating* (Families in the villages of Beijing's suburbs) (Shanghai: Shangwu yinshuguan, 1929), p. 74.

36 Ida Pruitt, *A China Childhood* (San Francisco: Chinese Materials Center, 1978), p. 10.

37 Zhang Zhongxing, *Zhang Zhongxing juan* (On Zhang Zhongxing) (Beijing: Huawen chubanshe, 1998), pp. 460–2.

38 Yuan Mei, *Xiaocangshanfang shiwen ji* (Collection of writings and poems from the Xiaocang mountain studio) (Shanghai: Shanghai guji chubanshe, 1988), vol. 1, p. 353.

39 'Report on the Trade of Chinkiang, for the Year 1883', *Report on the Trade at the Ports of China for the Year 1883* (Shanghai: Imperial Maritime Customs' Press, 1884), p. 145.

40 *Tuhua ribao* (Pictorial daily) (Shanghai: Shangahi guji shudian, 1999), vol. 6, p. 125.

41 Sarah Rossbach, *Feng Shui: The Chinese Art of Placement* (New York: Dutton, 1983), pp. 68–75.

42 M.B. Treudley, *The Men and Women of Chung Ho Ch'ang* (Taipei: Orient Cultural Service, 1971), pp. 39, 178.

43 Piper R. Gaubatz, *Beyond the Great Wall: Urban Form and Transformation on the Chinese Frontiers* (Stanford, CA: Stanford University Press, 1996), pp. 143–4.

44 Derek Walters, *The Feng Shui Handbook: A Practical Guide to Chinese Geomancy* (London: Aquarian Press, 1991), p. 152.

45 Rossbach, *Feng Shui*, p. 107.

46 Yang Jingting, 'Dumen zayong' (Miscellany verses on Beijing) in Lei, *Zhonghua zhuzhici*, p. 181.

47 Imperial Maritime Customs, *Exposition universelle de Liège en 1905. Catalogue spécial des objets exposés dans la section chinoise* (Shanghai: Statistical Department of the Inspectorate General, 1905), p. 12; Elsie McCormick, *Audacious Angles on China* (New York: Appleton, 1924), p. 36.

48 *Tuhua ribao*, vol. 2, p. 68.

49 Ibid., p. 451.

50 'Modeng xuzhi' (Basics of modernity), *Beiyang huabao*, no. 663 (13 August 1931), p. 2.

51 Liu Shiliang, 'Chengdu Qingyanggong huashi zhuzhici' (Bamboo verses on the flower fair at the Qingyang temple in Chengdu) in Yang Xie *et al.*, *Chengdu zhuzhici* (Chengdu bamboo verses) (Chengdu: Sichuan renmin chubanshe, 1982), p. 88; see also Zhong Bin, 'Hankou xinnian zhuzhici' (Bamboo verses on New Year in Hankou), in Xu Mingting (ed.), *Wuhan zhuzhici* (Bamboo verses on Wuhan) (Wuhan: Hubei renmin chubanshe, 1999), pp. 277–8.

52 Shen Yun, 'Shenghu zhuzhici' (Bamboo verses on Shengze) in Lei, *Zhonghua zhuzhici*, vol. 3, p. 2071.

53 Luo Han, 'Hankou zhuzhici' (Bamboo verses on Hankou) in Xu, *Wuhan zhuzhici*, p. 246.

54 Rudolf P. Hommel, *China at Work* (New York: John Day, 1937), p. 196.

55 Heinz von Perckhammer, *Peking* (Berlin: Albertus Verlag, 1928), pp. 36, 94, 117.

56 Eileen Chang, 'Chinese Life and Fashions', *Twentieth Century*, 4, 1 (1943), p. 59.

57 Reginald F. Johnston, *Twilight in the Forbidden City* (Hong Kong: Oxford University Press, 1985), p. 273.

58 Zhou Shouchang, 'Guangdong zashu' (Notes on Guangdong) in *Siyitang rizha* (Diary of Siyitang) (orig. 1846 ; Beijing: Zhonghua shuju, 1987), p. 198.

59 Jules Itier, *Journal d'un voyage en Chine en 1843, 1844, 1845, 1846* (Paris: Dauvin et Fontaine, 1848–1853), vol. 1, p. 325, vol. 2, pp. 41, 113–14.

60 Linzhen, *Xihai jiyou cao* (Draft travel notes on the Western seas) (Beijing: Yuelu shushe, 1985), p. 38.

61 Jean Dickinson, *Observations on the Social Life of a North China Village* (Beijing: Department of Sociology, Yenching University, 1924), p. 12.

62 Shih Kuo-heng, *China enters the Machine Age* (Cambridge, MA: Harvard University Press, 1944), p. 99.
63 A.S. Roe, *Chance and Change in China* (London: Heinemann, 1920), pp. 114–15.
64 Peter Fleming, *News from Tartary: A Journey from Peking to Kashmir* (London: Jonathan Cape, 1936), p. 80.
65 For exceptions see Tom Phillips, *We are the People: Postcards from the Collection of Tom Phillips* (London: National Portrait Gallery, 2004).
66 See Jia Ping'ao, *Lao Xi'an* (Old Xi'an) (Nanjing: Jiangsu meishu chubanshe, 1999), p. 48.
67 Sheng Cheng, *A Son of China* (London: Allen & Unwin, 1930), p. 172.
68 Olga Lang, *Chinese Family and Society* (New Haven: Yale University Press, 1946), p. 273.
69 Elisabeth Enders, *Swinging Lanterns* (New York: Appleton, 1923), p. 272.
70 Yang Buwei, *Autobiography of a Chinese Woman* (New York: John Day, 1947), pp. 15–16.
71 Li Hangyu, *Lao Hangzhou* (Old Hangzhou) (Nanjing: Jiangsu meishu chubanshe, 2000), pp. 112–13.
72 Innes Jackson, *China only Yesterday* (London: Faber & Faber, 1938), p. 70.
73 Abel Bonnard, *In China 1920–1921* (London: Routledge, 1926), p. 46; Hu Piyun, *Jiujing shizhao* (Historical photographs of old Beijing) (Beijing: Beijing chubanshe, 1997), pp. 70–3.
74 The evidence presented in this chapter is far from sufficient to reach any viable conclusions, and this section relies heavily on the results presented in Frank Dikötter, *Exotic Commodities*.
75 Joseph J. Tobin (ed.), *Re-made in Japan: Everyday Life and Consumer Taste in a Changing Society* (New Haven: Yale University Press, 1992), p. 26.
76 Gretchen M. Herrmann, 'Gift or Commodity: What Changes Hands in the US Garage Sale?', in Daniel Miller (ed.), *Consumption: Critical Concepts in the Social Sciences*, vol. 2, *The History and Regional Development of Consumption* (London: Routledge, 2001), pp. 72–101, quotation on p. 84.
77 Christine Rush, 'Thrill of the Chase', *Independent*, 15 December 2004, p. 4.
78 Adrian Forty, *Objects of Desire: Design and Society from Wedgwood to IBM* (New York: Pantheon Books, 1986), p. 11.
79 Keith G. Stevens, personal communication, 10 March 2004.

9 Mundane materiality, or, should small things still be forgotten?

Material culture, micro-histories and the problem of scale

Sara Pennell

In 2006, when visiting the *At Home in Renaissance Italy* exhibition at the Victoria and Albert Museum, I was confronted with an object that truly surprised me. At only 12.3 cm long, and made of nothing more elaborate than iron, the object in question was a pastry cutter (also known as a pastry wheel, jagger and spur in early modern cookery books) (Figure 9.1).[1] But what made it remarkable to me was that it closely resembled another pastry cutter I know of, dating to around the same period. This other pastry cutter, now in the collection of the Colonial Williamsburg Foundation, is 2.5 by 14 cm in size, also made of either iron or steel (Figure 9.2). Although they are different in form, they do share another feature, other than their presumed function and dating – they both have names inscribed upon them, 'Allerina' in the case of the Italian example, and 'Ann' on the English/American one. The latter also has a date: '1723'.

Figure 9.1 Iron pastry cutter, Italian, seventeenth century, inscribed on other side 'Allerina', V&A Museum no. 105–1884 © V&A Images/Victoria and Albert Museum, London.

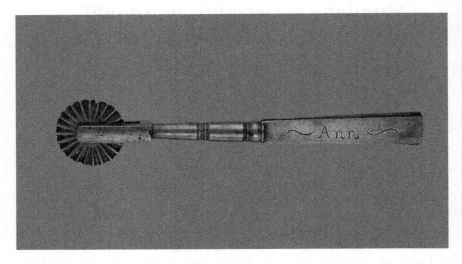

Figure 9.2 Iron pastry cutter, English, dated in inscription 1723, inscribed 'Ann', Colonial Williamsburg Foundation accession no. G1970–3. By permission of the Colonial Williamsburg Foundation. Gift of Mrs Daniel Baker, Jr.

I will return to this 'pair' later in this chapter, but the find of another pastry cutter with an inscribed name allows me to explore the potentially problematic issues of uniqueness, scale and association in the historical study of material culture. In the case of the first two, I will explore how we can use approaches developed in microhistory to think through the problem of the atypicality of the objects central to material culture studies. I will also show how research into the associations of singular objects, especially their material and spatial contexts, can offset the apparent problems that arise when material cultural analysis concentrates on a single object or category of object.

Another purpose of this chapter is to illuminate the potential that material cultural sources bring to the study of that state of being in the past, which is often, rather clumsily, termed 'everyday life'. This was one of the 'virtues' of 'old things' identified by American historians, archaeologists and the like at the turn of the twentieth century. Unlike documentary sources – so often written by 'winners' (and those other 'dead white men' who shaped the sources of academic history as it was studied in the nineteenth century) – material survivals could 'speak' of those in the past who had little or no textual 'voice'. Thus the industrialist Henry Ford, when setting up his museum of American life at Dearborn, Illinois, at the beginning of the twentieth century, praised material culture in its illumination of the everyday and the undocumented: 'By looking at things people used and that show the way they lived a better impression can be gained than could be had in a month of reading.'[2]

The title of this chapter adapts that of a seminal book in the study of material culture in America: James Deetz's *In Small Things Forgotten: The Archaeology of Early American Life* (1977). Deetz was an archaeologist who was one of the early practitioners of what has come to be known as historical archaeology, the study of the material remains of societies since the fifteenth century.[3] In this work he focused on the 'seemingly little and insignificant things that accumulate to make a lifetime' – although one might think his case studies of gravestones and vernacular housing are not really about 'little and insignificant things' at all – and, in the final line of the book, incited his readers to not 'read what we have written', but to 'look at what we have done'.[4]

In arguing for the value of studying material remains as varied as gravestones, Georgian chamber pots and the five-string banjo, Deetz was making the point that while these are remains that may have a textual presence (in inventories, shop or tradesmen's bills, diary accounts), their material features may also tell us something about the society in which they were made, used and (as most archaeological material comes to us as a result of being the past's rubbish, dug up from cesspits and rubbish heaps), thrown away. He was also stressing the value of studying objects that are not museum artefacts, but the 'commonplace objects [consigned] ... to the dump'.[5] As I have already suggested, Deetz's own conception of 'small things' was quite expansive, and one could argue that gravestones were neither 'commonplace' nor even 'everyday'; rather, they were intended as ritual objects, commemorations in stone of the dead. But his was one of the first works to think about how the 'commonplace' material world might hold insights into past practices and beliefs, as well as right the imbalance presented to the visitor in museum collections.[6]

Unfortunately, Deetz's book is little known to historians, not least because it was marketed as a sociology and archaeology textbook by its first American publishers. Thus, 30 years after its publication, it is still common for historians to use material cultural evidence much in the same way as many historians have, until recently, treated the visual image: as simply an illustration (rather than an exploration) of practice, ideology or emotion; objects are used as mute (but often good-looking) 'hooks' on which to hang explanation.[7] One explanation for this is that, as historians, we are insufficiently equipped to 'read' objects, which need the same careful use and interpretation as images. But objects, whether they be 'Capability' Brown landscape gardens or pastry cutters, require more engagement and elucidation, especially if we are to be aware of what they cannot 'say'. The textual trace of objects is to the physical object as musical notation on the page is to the sound of the piece being played – illegible unless one can 'read' the trace and 'know' what it means, and also work out what is going on between the notes. As an opening caution, we should recall the doubts of the landscape historian John Dixon Hunt regarding the potential metaphorical power of objects being limited by their very physicality. Whereas, in linguistic use, the elements of a metaphor – the subject and the metaphorical referent – 'subtly yet crucially modify each other', artefacts cannot easily stand as 'metaphors' for the worlds in which they were created and used; in his memorable phrase, 'teapots as objects stay irredeemably teapotish'.[8]

At the same time, the increasing visibility of material culture within historical studies – both as a subject of study and as informing methodology – can be said to be long overdue. All history depends on material remains for its construction, and those practitioners not attuned to the materiality of their textual sources undertake research myopically and even, on occasion, at the risk of their reputations.[9] Indeed, many ancient and medieval historians, with their closer intellectual and disciplinary connections to archaeology, and the relative paucity of textual documentation are de facto material cultural historians, if not fully aware of that fact. In this sense, it is historians of later eras, the early modernists and modernists, who are late to the material cultural party, and for whom teapots often remain just teapots.

Why material culture is more visible in especially early modern and modern historical studies now, as opposed to 30 years ago (when Deetz was working and writing), is mainly due to the rise in historiographical favour of consumption as a historical phenomenon involved in the creation and sustenance of cultures of (early) modernity. The significance of consumption studies is discussed elsewhere in this book; for my purposes, it is necessary to focus on how analyses of early modern consumption practices and ideologies have created and amplified the problems of typicality in the uses of material culture by historians.

The association between the practice of consumption and the materiality of that consumption for early modern England has depended on viewing material goods at two quantitative extremes: either as the numeric aggregation of probate inventory or trade data presence; or as the singular 'case study' based on a surviving object. In the first instance, the material presence is merely textual (although occasionally supported by an 'example' of the object group in question as an illustrative prop), while in the second the insight is often gained through the survival of the 'case study' object or class of object.

Material culture historians have anxieties about the first approach more than they have the second, seeing in textual quantification of objects a poor proxy for the variety and range of objects. To give an example, 'glasswares' as an entry in an early modern inventory does indicate ownership of what, even in the mid-eighteenth century, was by no means a staple good; but it gives no sense of what those glasswares were – cut decanters, simple water glasses, functional kitchen bowls or decorative parlour items? The location of the glasswares and their valuation might help us tease out a bit more detail of type and usage, but the operative word here is 'might'. As Lena Cowan Orlin has counselled, inventories are texts that, for all their seemingly straightforward listing and enumeration, have the potential to create 'fictitious' accounts of the living standards and spatial arrangements in the households they are taken to represent.[10]

But the second approach is also a compromise fraught with methodological and indeed conceptual difficulties. The surviving object is usually one that has achieved another phase in its 'biography' – to use the common, but far from unproblematic term (see Dannehl in Chapter 6 of this book) – since the phase of the use(s) and meaning(s) we are trying to elucidate; and that phase is often quite specifically the quasi-fetishized state of being a museum artefact, or treasured component of a private collection.

This is not a state of affairs that historians try to gloss over, but after acknowledging the particular circumstances of survival, historians often move on rapidly. As Deetz noted in 1977, what survives in museums and in private collectors' cabinets, is there thanks to a complex set of reasons – taste and connoisseurship, and the development and commercialization of the 'art' market, to name but two – which *in themselves* contribute to shaping a reading of past material worlds. Ignoring or gliding over these factors can lead to a rather romanticized reading of objects that survive precisely because they were not deemed 'commonplace'. A good example of this mode of reading, can be found in Dena Goodman's study of the *bonheur du jour*, a particular type of eighteenth-century desk:

> Our little desk, the one that first caught our eye in the museum, is a *bonheur du jour*. Is it a luxury good? Or is it, rather a commodity, a consumer good? Was its purpose to display the good taste of its owner, or to be useful in her daily practice of letter-writing?[11]

At no time in this analysis does Goodman 'read' the *bonheur du jour* as an object of interest to the historian of eighteenth-century France *precisely because of* its presence in the museum, despite her acknowledgement that it 'exists as the subject of various discourses, past and present, each of which gives it meaning while using it to lay out a certain vision of the culture and history in which it is seen to figure'.[12]

Goodman's interest in the *bonheur du jour*, made explicit in the above quotation, is tied up with a major preoccupation of historical material-culture-as-consumption studies: the shifting discourses of luxury. What 'luxury' was, and who partook of it and its material manifestations, has been the subject of much recent work,[13] but it is telling that our understandings of what constituted the interrelated category of necessity, or at least 'not-luxury', are still under-explored. While obviously implicated in the construction of consumption practices for the long eighteenth century, accounts of mundane goods and their uses have, on the whole, been less materially informed.[14] By 'mundane' I mean those things that have a superficially routine, non-ritual use and locus of use. Such objects can be elite objects – silver basting spoons, for example – in the sense they are made from a valuable material, and used in an aristocratic household; but they are not luxury objects (at least not at the time of use as a basting spoon; they may of course now be construed as antiques, and therefore as luxury items).

This relative paucity of scholarship is surely related not simply to accidents of survival, but rather with the museological priority given to the connoisseurial best (or to put it more pragmatically, the items that are complete, and therefore more easily legible for display purposes). Indeed, I wonder whether the teapots, writing desks, silk mantuas and three-piece suits, Palladian houses, conversation pieces and Wedgwood, Bow and Chelsea china, that have been the material stuff of historical discussions of luxury goods and of discourses of luxury in turn, would have been so prominent had they not also been the stuff of museum and heritage collections.

Of course, museums have storerooms (often off-site, as if to reiterate the lesser importance of the imperfect, lesser or fragmentary) full of pot sherds, knife handles, buttons, and indeed 'brown furniture' that is not by a famed designer such as Chippendale or Hepplewhite.[15] Unless the museum in question has a social history or anthropological remit, such pieces are likely to remain in the artefactual shadows. But even when they are foregrounded in such settings, they are often presented in specific formats: as points on a chronology or typology of forms and manufacturing techniques (for example, clay pipes); as markers of regional diversity, production specialization and distribution (for example pottery sherds, or, at the other end of the scale, the building types reassembled at the Weald and Downland Open Air Museum, Sussex); or as general 'set dressing' for period rooms and 'living history' scenarios (see the 'Bromley-by-Bow' and 'Henrietta Street' rooms at the Victoria and Albert Museum).[16]

In the first two types of study, usually undertaken by the archaeologist or vernacular architectural historian, the scale of survival is important for the comprehensiveness of the sequences that can be achieved, rather more than what quantity can tell us about the meanings of these objects. For the cultural historian – and it is almost always the cultural historian who has taken up material culture as a methodology and a source; the political and economic historians retain their distance, on the whole[17] – the search for the beliefs that frame and condition cultural activity (what is often termed *mentalité*) makes quantity a secondary concern. Thus, the deployment of mundane objects in cultural histories often equals incorporation (and disappearance) into an 'assemblage' where quantity of 'stuff' is believed to have a meaning that is greater than the sum of the individual parts.

Here we can look to the example of clay tobacco pipes, perhaps one of the most ubiquitous archaeological 'finds' of the early modern era, to illustrate these divergent approaches. Although they might seem of straightforward design to the untutored eye, they were in fact subject to changes in form, style and individualized decorative features, including makers' stamps, which mean they can be dated quite precisely and specifically. Their ubiquity coupled with such formal differences, mean that they are perhaps historical archaeologists' most useful material tool in dating the contexts of finds. Yet as such they recede as objects – they become simply a device for dating.[18] Likewise, search for the clay pipe in cultural histories, and you will find it grouped with the other material goods and consumables of an increasingly homosocial public sphere – tobacco pouches and horns, drinking vessels, the accoutrements of the tavern and coffeehouse – considered almost as ephemeral as the tobacco smoke it produced.[19] But in between these two interpretive modes for the tobacco pipe, both of which erase it as an object in its own right, there is a third route, which I would suggest is the approach of the material cultural historian: the microhistorical approach.

As Brad S. Gregory has noted, there are two genres of microhistory that have developed over the past 40 years, mainly at the hands of continental scholars such as Carlo Ginzburg, Giovanni Levi and Guido Ruggiero: the episodic, where examination and elucidation of a particular event (classically, Menoccio's inquisitorial case in Ginzburg's *The Cheese and the Worms* (1980)) supplies novel and, most significantly, alternative or subversive views of contemporary belief structures, power relations and other social networks; and the 'systematic' model, which provides, where possible, a comprehensive account of demographic, social and economic relationships and connections within a given (usually geographical) locus (for example, Wrightson and Levine's Terling in Essex, the focus for *Poverty and Piety in an English Village* (1979)).[20]

Material culture history is clearly more closely related to the 'episodic' variety of microhistory, in its use of the case study focused on an individual object or object group (Goodman's little desk, or Adamson's ottomans in the following chapter). Arguably, material culture historians arrive at this approach by virtue of necessity – the circumstances of survival – whereas microhistorians would argue their analysis of the sixteenth-century miller or the Essex village is not enforced but by design (although Menoccio's inquisitorial records are as unique a survival as an unbroken, complete Georgian tea service). Nevertheless, the material culture historian's task is rooted in the same conviction: that, in Gregory's words, '[a] sufficiently close, detailed examination of a very restricted subject of research calls into question long-term views of historical development and associated conceptualisations of change'.[21]

Now, as critiques of microhistory have argued, there can be good and bad examples of this process, with the very worst helping little, if not at all, to produce in the intensification of focus a shift in understanding of both object and its larger significance.[22] In what we might call 'bad' material cultural history, the circumstances of material survival recede, and 'thick description' or elucidation of the object enables it to seem more meaningful, and thus more relevant – 'bigger', if you will – than it actually is. And I would argue that this is very much the case when it is the material culture of luxury that is the focus of analysis, rather than the material culture of non-luxury.[23] Yet the increasing maturation of material culture history is reflected in the increasingly numerous studies of non-luxury objects and activities, and, in turn, the object as something other than just consumer commodity.[24]

This is all the more crucial in a field where new conceptual 'tools' are being tested and used to elucidate what, to borrow from the title of Muir and Ruggiero's microhistorical anthology, could be called the 'lost practices' of everyday lives. Key among these new 'tools' is the idea of the 'social imaginary' as a process of self and communal location and identification, distinct from more intellectualized and hegemonic forms of cultural identification, such as class identity or ethnic categorizations.[25] In a study of *how* (not why) people read novels in eighteenth-century New England, Robert St George sees objects as essential to the 'material signs' that allow access to 'experimental selves in ... domestic spaces'.[26] To access the 'social imaginary' that shapes and sustains particular practices, especially non-ritual practices, we must use such material signs. Mundane objects are thus not simply the evidence of practices, but the tools by which such practices are enabled, learnt and assimilated, and also by which the value of those practices, which may seem routine and meaningless to the outside world, may be understood as complex, consciously shaped and indeed owned by the people doing them.

In my own research on food practices in early modern England, the mundane object – from bell-metal pots to wooden spoons to cookery books – has loomed as large as (limited) sources will allow. Until recently, however, I had not considered what I was doing as much other than a combination of Riello's first two 'types' of material culture history: history *of* and *with* 'things'. Yet a material cultural approach to the early modern non-elite kitchen is an exercise in mapping the 'living', or what is often more theatrically called the 'performance' of that space. By studying objects associated with the kitchen prescriptively and practically, and their use by the 'actors' both within and without the space of the kitchen, we can hopefully achieve an insightful, rather than purely confirmatory, piece of domestic microhistory – in Riello's category of 'history *and* things'.

Elsewhere I have explored the early modern non-elite kitchen as

> a laboratory in which needs and novelty were experimented with, and coalesced; as the place where female competencies were founded and realised; and [as] the topos underpinning the moral and practical disposition of the early modern household.[27]

And central to this exploration are the 'small things forgotten' until recently relegated to the interests of antiquarian collectors of domestic metalwares, and the growing field of 'kitchenalia' collectables.[28] It is telling that even historians of the household and of gender have rarely strayed into the kitchen much before the twentieth century, seeing it as a colourless place of routinized behaviour, a feminized zone of processing, not transformation, and of extraction, not elaboration.[29] The 'forgetting' of these goods and this space is not merely to do with their size, or trifling value (as we shall see); these things have been forgotten because their associations – with the domestic, with practical skills rather than 'arts and mysteries', with women above all – have rendered them historically 'small' and incapable of carrying explanatory value. As the influential historical archaeologist Anne Yentsch has noted, cooking pots were (and therefore are still) not 'objects to which power accrued'.[30]

But let us think about these powerless pots. Except for the very large metal pots, most kitchen goods were of negligible value, yet documentary sources bear witness to their status as key items of social capital, in household formation and maintenance. Cooking vessels, utensils and hearth goods were frequently incorporated into the 'paraphernalia' – conventionally clothing, linen and jewellery – legally allowed as limited property to married women in the early modern period, and were common bequests between and to female kin and friends.[31] Thus Sarah Boult, a widow of St Lawrence parish, Reading, left to her married daughter, Sarah Clements,

> my largest and smallest brass kettles [,] my largest brass skellett [skillet] one dozen of my pewter plates [,] my iron jack [,] my skreen [firescreen] my largest pair of iron doggs [fireirons] my bell metal pott [,] my limbeck [alembic, a type of still] my chest of drawers and my Bible.[32]

This inventory register of early modern cooking pots and cooking equipment, bequeathed in the same sentence as the Bible, crystallizes the tantalizing promise of the material in studying the 'everyday', as well as its problems. Apart from textual presences like this (and in other textual sources, as diverse as cookery books, court depositions and technological records), the existence of surviving cooking pots and food preparation equipment, scant though they are numerically, allows us to move beyond directly physical issues of form, function and technological development. The saucepan is a useful example, as it is a good constructed by culinary historians as a novelty in the late seventeenth century, associated with the preparation of French-inspired 'made' or composite dishes, like ragouts and fricassees, which were sauce-based.[33] Totting up all items appraised as saucepans in samples of early modern inventories (something I have done in past work) does crudely suggest an increase in the ownership of something called a 'saucepan'. But what sort of saucepan? Such aggregation obscures crucial differences reflected in medium (for example, between an iron and a silver saucepan, the latter a specialist item often identified with heating brandy or butter); number (owning one saucepan compared to owning a set of four or five graduated in volume); and geography (since saucepan is a vessel term well-established in late sixteenth-century Worcestershire probate inventories, but not in those of mid-seventeenth-century London).[34] Sometimes these details do emerge in textual sources, but are these the relevant features of the saucepan we as historians need to know? When confronted with surviving saucepans and other cooking pots what might strike us more than their differing forms, material or volume, is in fact their frequent decoration and person-alization, an element almost never mentioned in textual references to cooking pots (Figure 9.3).

Figure 9.3 Skillet, English late seventeenth century, with handle cast with 'Ye wages of sin is death', Hugh Roberts collection, Bath Preservation Trust, on loan to The Merchants House Trust, Marlborough, Wiltshire. Reproduced by permission of No.1 Royal Crescent, Bath © Bath Preservation Trust.

Why decorate a cooking pot? Casting an improving proverb or biblical exhortation – 'Waste not want not', 'The wages of sin is death' – into the handle of a cooking vessel provides a striking instance of its makers giving it a distinctive, moralistic 'voice', and giving it that voice for a purpose.[35] In the reception of such moralistic cooking pots we do have to take into account practicalities such as literacy levels, but, even so, the inclusion of mottoes and proverbs such as these on functional objects from the mid-seventeenth century onwards, does suggest another role for these utensils, as reminders of and prompts to the necessity of domestic virtue.[36] Otherwise innocuous instructions in domestic manuals for keeping saucepans 'well-tinned' (that is, making sure the tin-coating on copper and brass vessels was refreshed regularly) become more resonant when we realize the consequences of not re-tinning: tainted food and even poisoned eaters – in other words, disorder.

Certainly, axioms such as those found on pot handles reinforced a particularly feminized prescribed set of domestic responsibilities – frugality, philanthropy, patriarchal loyalty – but this does not necessarily mean these objects should be seen as putting the housewife in her powerless place. The cultivation of the virtuous 'good' or 'complete' housewife was a project for the common good throughout the early modern period, and thus the kitchen the locus in which that ideal persona was made visible and accountable. The pre-eminent value of domestic order (what the term 'œconomy', the root of our modern term economy, meant in early modern England), as much as patriarchal order, is prescribed in texts such as Gervase Markham's *The English Housewife* and Richard Bradley's *The Country Housewife and Lady's Director*;[37] but it was realized through using and maintaining cooking pots.

At this point I want to turn to these 'objects', cookery books, the study of which has more conventionally fed into this ideology of domestic competency and ideal housewifery. As texts, such works have their own (until recently marginal) literary status: didactic works that can tell us something about culinary and medicinal and knowledge in the domestic sphere; the interplay of these knowledges with 'professional' expertise in these fields; the state of domestic relations between mistresses and servants; and even the political nuances of such texts.[38] Their materiality has been less visible, however. Scholars using these texts in these ways do not ignore the troubling fact that many of these texts show little acquaintance with the hearthside, and more with the less hazardous surroundings of the studious closet, but they seldom engage with that apparent distance between the 'how-to' book and the circumstances of its use.[39]

When one considers manuscript recipe collections – literally, compilations of recipes written into blank books, or collected as loose leaves, by compilers – the materiality of the text is arguably even more relevant to the motivations of production and circumstances of use than in published cookery books, where publishers and printers surely determined material form as much as authors. Such compilations shed light upon the possibilities of culinary, medicinal and domestic expertise as a form of particularly female knowledge that was neither merely practical nor wholly abstract. But we miss much if we simply look to manuscript recipe books as records of potential/actual culinary and medicinal practice. As objects frequently produced by women (although not exclusively so), manuscript recipe collections also stand as artefacts of identities and relationships that, in the early modern period, were as material as they were textual.[40] They extend the range of materials available for studying female (and indeed male) conceptions of material and moral domesticity, if read in conjunction with other documents and material over which women often exercised some degree of control. Indeed, the compilation of a manuscript could take its makers (and its readers) far from the kitchen hearth – geographically, socially and intellectually.[41]

Turning to the physical object, many questions can be asked of manuscript recipe collections that can shape scholars' understanding of purpose and use. Was the book in which the recipes are inscribed purchased for that specific purpose, or did the project of recipe collection taken over a redundant volume, previously used for other purposes? Is it even a book, or merely a collection of loose recipes? If a book, is it a handy octavo or a more imposing folio, complete with metal clasps; parchment-covered or leather-bound; its use identified in gilded lettering or handwritten script on the cover or spine, or not? The contents too, may be considered materially (as opposed to purely textually); how many blank pages remain, or, if full, what life cycles of possession can be determined from different scripts? How organized is the volume – indexed or not? Has the compiler chosen to write the recipes in a formal calligraphic script or scribbled them in?[42] These may be questions that betray a debt to specialist bibliographic approaches to the text; but the sub-discipline of 'book history', where these issues have been cultivated as serious subjects of study, recognizes in its very name that the material circumstances of the book are as historically resonant as the text within it.

Such rich questions suggest that although these artefacts have a conventional historical 'voice' as texts, they are somewhat limited in their value to historians if we view them only textually. I want to explore this through the manuscript recipe collections of Anne (de) Lisle, which I have used in my research on the acquisition, circulation and applications of domestic culinary and medicinal knowledge. But we can also think about the volumes as part of the complex and sometimes contradictory material cultural residue of a life we would otherwise know very little about.

The two folio volumes comprising the manuscript recipe collection of Anne (de) Lisle are now in the Wellcome Library, London. In the library's online catalogue they are described thus:

> *Description*: Collection of cookery, medical, veterinary, and domestic receipts. The first volume contains cookery receipts, and is in two parts each with an index. The second volume contains 'Physical receits', 'Cattle receits', and 'Curious receits': each of these has its own index. ... *Historical Background*: On the fly leaf of the first volume 'Anne Lisle 1748'. She is perhaps the Ann Cary daughter of Nicholas Cary of Upcern, Dorset, who married Charles Lisle [-1777] of Wodyton and Moyles Court. ... *Physical description*: 2 vols. folio. 31 x 20 cm. Original calf bindings worn.[43]

It is interesting to note that, in cataloguing terms, the physical description is quite minimally concerned with dimensions, quantity and the nature of the binding (it doesn't however mention the watermarked paper within). Yet the rest of the description also tells us something about its material presence; it is very highly organized, into two distinct volumes, and, within that, into indexed sections. It would help us to know, also, that both volumes are written throughout in the same hand, but that the hand is not entirely consistent, suggesting a longer time frame of compilation than the flyleaf date. It is also not the hand of 'Ann Cary, daughter of Nicholas Cary', but of Anne Lisle (*c.*1706–52) of Crux Easton (Hampshire).

That the Anne (de) Lisle who almost certainly undertook the compilation of these books is not the Ann Cary who married Charles Lisle is a fact that only the object/text could reveal to me, rather than any other documentation I have yet found. There is no will, as far as I know, of Anne (de) Lisle, who died unmarried in *c.*1752, and I would probably search in vain for any other documentation that speaks explicitly of Anne's compilation of these volumes. The information of who she is can be worked out from the names of the 'donors' of recipes to the volume, including 'my sister Jane March' (Jane Lisle (1703–74), married Thomas March on 24 August 1734), and 'my mother Mrs Lisle'. Cross-referencing these names with the International Genealogical Index and cross-referencing the information of this source with pedigrees and other information, confirms that Anne was the twelfth child (of 20) and seventh daughter (of 12; 10 survived to adulthood) of Edward (1666–1722) and Mary Lisle (née Phillips, 1672–1749), a family of genteel status, but not enormous wealth, living in northern Hampshire near the border with Berkshire. Anne Cary (1718–81) was indeed a member of this family, marrying Charles Lisle (1708–71), older brother of Anne Lisle, sometime before July 1753; however, there are no internal references in the manuscript to anybody with the family name 'Cary'.

There is no biography of Anne's parents (although her father's work of practical agriculture was published posthumously by her brother, Thomas (1709–67), who was also a minor poet in his own right),[44] and the manuscript recipe collections do not contain any explicit genealogical register. But the circumstances of the family are evident in the text and thus material form of the volumes. The great majority of the donated recipes, both culinary and medicinal/surgical, are attributed to a 'Lady Lisle', who is probably Lady Lucy Lisle (nee Molyneux) widow of Sir Charles Croke Lisle of Moyles Court, Hampshire. Childless at her husband's death in 1721, Lady Lisle's relationship with her cousin-by-marriage's Edward Lisle's family was cemented by the descent of her husband's estates to him and his heirs, after Lady Lisle's death. Edward predeceased Lady Lisle in 1722, and so a fairly common, but by no means straightforward, relationship continued between the two households. How that relationship – between lesser status family and more elevated, with property and its transmission at its heart – worked is literally the stuff of Jane Austen's plots, but in the form of the manuscript recipe collections of Anne Lisle, we might see its workings at a more intimate level.

Unlike several of her sisters, Anne never married, and although the recipe collections may have been started as a pedagogic project for a prospective wife, they are just as likely to be a project of commemoration and deference, with Anne serving as a sort of amanuensis or channel for her childless aunt-by-marriage. That the two volumes are substantial leather-bound folios, rather than more modest quartos, gives them a weight (literally) confirmed by their comprehensive contents; this is a work of record, rather than primarily a work of practice (although there are textual traces of practice within it). That the two volumes came to the Wellcome Library in 1943 via a Sotheby's sale of items from the de Lisle family of Garendon Park, near Loughborough, Leicestershire, goes some way to confirm this: Garendon was originally the home of Anne's maternal grandfather, Sir Ambrose Phillips, who purchased it in 1683, and it remained in the Phillips/de Lisle family thanks to intermarrying again later in the eighteenth century. It seems likely that, following her own death, Anne's recipe collections became family heirlooms, descending within the family very much like Rebecca Price Brandreth's pair of recipe books, described in her 1740 will as 'two receipt books in folio written by myself ... both of the said books being bound with leather and on the inside Lidds of each of them is mentioned that they were written in the year 1681 by Rebecca Price (that being my maiden name)'.[45]

Were the recipe books the only material trace of Anne (de) Lisle we had, then we might conclude that the project of their compilation fits relatively neatly into the model of fairly circumscribed, provincial genteel Georgian womanhood, mapped so convincingly by Amanda Vickery.[46] But Anne Lisle is commemorated (albeit as part of a group) in another text, which in turn tells us of a further, now lost, but far from mundane 'piece' of material culture, the construction of which she was almost certainly involved in. Alexander Pope's poem, 'Inscription on a Grotto of Shells at Crux Easton, the Work of Nine Young Ladies' (*c.* 1734), praises the grotto constructed by nine of Edward Lisle's daughters in these terms:

Here, shunning idleness at once and praise,
This radiant pile nine rural sisters raise;
The glitt'ring emblem of each spotless dame,
Clear as her soul and shining as her frame;
Beauty which nature only can impart,
And such a polish as disgraces art;
But fate disposed them in this humble sort,
And hid in deserts what would charm a court.[47]

The Crux Easton grotto no longer survives, but the construction of this shell grotto – possibly inspired by Pope's own Twickenham grotto, initially completed in *c.* 1729 – and a textual representation that suggests a group of young women whose 'polish' would have not disgraced them at court, makes Anne Lisle's recipe collections into something more than just evidence of domestic aptitude. While the grotto-making was celebrated (albeit in a minor poem), the cookery book was not; but both are testaments to Anne Lisle as clearly a woman of not inconsiderable talents, but one who of necessity, lived a life of a 'humble sort', at the evidential margins of what we know as female gentility. Yet that gentility was not solely bound up with the purely domestic: the recipe books *and* the grotto are material cultural deposits (one surviving, one not) of Anne Lisle's far from idle life. If we can 'write' a life from such deposits, then the life of Anne Lisle was multi-faceted, and perhaps not as confined as that of the figure evoked by the terms under which documentary sources would normally file her: 'spinster', 'unmarried', 'dependant'.

Anne Lisle's recipe books become more 'vocal', if less straightforward, if they are placed in association with other materials – documentary and landscape, in this case. This contextualization is of course common-sense, when we think about our practice as historians (as opposed, say, to the practice of the literary critic); we are academically programmed to establish context for our evidential documents, seek out the links between texts, and provide an account of a particular event or phenomenon based on the assemblage of our textual evidence. But while the 'assemblage' may be a recognizable *material* construct for the archaeologist, such a material assemblage is still a relatively unconsidered one for the historian. By 'assemblage', I mean the physical settings and accompanying objects that provide a framework in which the object(s) of study sit, rather than the more specific archaeological meaning of the context of excavation. Note the plural here; establishing an object's connections, its settings of both normal *and* extraordinary usage and comprehension, is crucial in uncovering the multiple meanings of the mundane object. To return to cooking pots, the association we also need to consider as much as the expected one – a place at the hearth alongside other cooking equipment, or in the store room, awaiting use – is the cacophonic massed use of kitchen pots and utensils ('the harmony of tinging kettles and frying pans' as one contemporary writer sardonically termed it) that accompanied the parading of the cuckolded husband and his bullying wife in the early modern communal shamings known as 'skimmingtons'.[48]

So, finally, what of the pastry cutters of my introduction? How do they move beyond being 'small things forgotten' by most historians other than those interested in the rather niche field of recreating historical pastry work?[49] I hope that the answer 'by association' will not seem too disappointing in its simplicity. First, there is the very obvious association set up by my realization that, on the day of my visit to the exhibition, I now knew of two similar objects both inscribed with women's names. What I had previously known as a unique object now had a sort of 'pair', another example that strengthened some of the suppositions I had had about the (what I had thought of as interesting but problematically unique) Williamsburg example.

Second, the survival of these objects sets up associations with documentary records that contain references to pastry 'spurs' and cutters. Recipes for elaborate pastry work in published cookery books such as Robert May's *The Accomplisht Cook* (London, 1660) told readers that, in order to achieve the fancy lace-like decorations for piecrusts, certain equipment was needed. Such equipment had traditionally been the preserve of the trained pastry cook, depicted in all *his* glory in a frontispiece engraving entitled 'The French Pastry Cook' inserted into 'Monsieur' Marnettè's [sic] *The Perfect Cook* (London, 1656).[50] Yet the professional status of male pastry cooks, with their guilds and trade associations (for example, in France and in England), which stood behind books like *The Perfect Cook*, rather obscures the fact that pastry making was also considered, from the beginning of the seventeenth century at least, as an appropriate female accomplishment; Gervase Markham asserted that 'our English housewife must be skilful in pastry, and know how and in what manner to bake all sorts of meat, and what paste is for every meat, and how to handle and compound such pastes' in his *The English Housewife*. The dedicatory preface to *The Perfect Cook* also rather gushingly claimed that Englishwomen 'are so well vers'd in the Pastry Art as that they may out-vie the best forreign Pastry Cooks'.[51]

But what we do not glean from Markham, *The Perfect Cook* or indeed from the images of professional pastry making is a sense of whether women actually did make decorated pastry goods, for these are prescriptive, didactic texts, not works of record; alongside *The Perfect Cook's* frontispiece cook is a woman assistant, but it is he who is rolling out the pastry. Mary Tillinghast's *Rare and Excellent Receipts* (London, 1678), with its focus on pastry work and confectionery, was published after she had probably circulated them in manuscript 'For the use of my scholars only', as the title page declares, while Edward Kidder – author of *Receipts of Pastry and Cookery, for the Use of his Scholars*, existing in several different versions (including at least one manuscript one), datable to between *c.*1721 and the 1730s – was almost certainly teaching pastry work in the area of Lincolns Inn Fields in the late 1680s and 1690s; he offered classes both at his school, but also to 'Ladies ... at their own Houses'.[52] The existence of such metropolitan schools for teaching pastry making and other culinary specialities by the end of the seventeenth century suggests that the skills outlined in earlier texts were much aspired to, but not necessarily extant. They were to be learnt at a maternal knee (or elbow) only in certain, elite households; the less privileged sought to buy such knowledge.

Yet, although we could make a straightforward association between our pastry cutters and the sort of women who attended such schools, it is not what they are for, but what they say, that makes the relevant association for me. The names inscribed on both cutters might have been a pragmatic mark of ownership; this pastry cutter is Ann's/Allerina's, and used by others at their peril. But I would argue that possession of these objects was not merely a functional act, nor the objects inscribed as such seen as inconsequential. The inscription of possession upon and in items as small as a 14 centimetre-long pastry cutter belies the characterization of these objects as 'utilitarian ... not mysterious ... plain'.[53] Even with the proliferation of didactic culinary texts, much kitchen know-how remained intuitive and implicit. A recipe would provide only partial insight into process, and little information at all as to what utensils to employ, how they worked, how they were to be cleaned, maintained and replaced.[54] Kitchen utensils were thus undoubtedly objects of expertise; women's domestic expertise, so often depicted as rooted in practical, 'how to' information and aptitude, should be seen as far from passive, routinized or 'artless'.[55] The inscription of these female names on pastry cutters was not only a proprietary gesture – it was a register of skill in a culinary field of no little complexity and, moreover, of the gentility that mastery (mistressing?) of such a skill literally engendered. In other words, it was a statement of the depths of meaning residing in these 'small things'.

This chapter does not profess to solve the problem of scale in using material culture in historical research, but it does propose that thinking about objects singly, or in small groups that might superficially strike one as atypical, is an opportunity to claim a place for such material culture approaches in historical research. Instead of fitting the object 'fragment' into the interpretive jigsaw we have assembled from our conventional sources as reiteration of our constructive abilities (what I think of as, adapting Amanda Vickery and others, the 'Delft platter procedure'),[56] we should prioritize examination of the object as a fragment that has no pre-ordained context. Furthermore, investigation of mundane goods in particular can carry us beyond the contexts of familiar engagement with the material world – the stuff of 'splendor' and 'luxury and pleasure'[57] – to understand the roles and multiple registers of the 'everyday', which are in fact sometimes not at all quotidian. The food-related objects I have discussed above were only temporarily commodities (at the moment of purchase or, in the case of the saucepan and the manuscript recipe book, their re-sale as a second-hand good/auction lot) and thus difficult to fit very easily into a discourse of early modern consumption practices based on ideas about luxury and expanding retailing opportunities. Indeed, they can be seen as resisting commodification as Matthew Johnson has defined it – a 'despiritualization' of goods – altogether and are instead vehicles for complex meanings, writ admittedly small, but no less powerfully felt through use, possession and transmission.[58]

Notes

1 Marta Ajmar-Wollheim and Flora Dennis (eds), *At Home in Renaissance Italy* (London: V&A Publications, 2006), cat. entry 96 (also illustrated on p. 248). The object was a little out of place in the exhibition in being at least 100 years younger than the period the exhibition was concerned with (it is assigned to the seventeenth century in the catalogue entry).

2 Attributed to Henry Ford, quoted in David Lowenthal, *The Past is a Foreign Country* (Cambridge: Cambridge University Press, 1985), p. 244.

3 Deetz's own, rather more politicized, definition is 'the archaeology of the spread of European culture throughout the world since the fifteenth century and its impact on indigenous peoples': *In Small Things Forgotten: the Archaeology of Early American Life* (New York: Anchor Books, 1977) p. 5. In Britain, the term used more frequently has been 'post-medieval archaeology', although, recently, this too has been subject to revision; see Sarah Tarlow, *The Archaeology of Improvement in England, 1750–1850* (Cambridge: Cambridge University Press, 2007), pp. 2–4.

4 Deetz, *Small Things*, p. 161 and Chapters 4 and 5.

5 Ibid. pp. 6–7.

6 Cf. earlier texts in a more antiquarian (but no less accessible) vein, e.g. C.H.B. and Marjorie Quennell, *A History of Everyday Things in England*, 4 vols (London: B.T. Batsford Ltd, 1920–34).

7 For a recent example of this in a text declaring itself to be a 'study of the material world of consumption' (p. 13) see Maxine Berg's discussion of English shoe buckle manufacture and the 'illustration' of this trade with an image of two *Irish* shoe buckles: *Luxury and Pleasure in Eighteenth-century England* (Oxford: Oxford University Press, 2005), Fig. 5.4 and pp. 167–8.

8 John Dixon Hunt, 'The Sign of the Object', in Steven Lubar and W. David Kingery (eds) *History from Things* (Washington/London: Smithsonian Institution Press, 1993), pp. 293–8, quote on p. 297.

9 For example, in the case of forged documents, like the so-called 'Hitler Diaries': see Robert Harris, *Selling Hitler: The Story of the Hitler Diaries* (London: Faber & Faber, 1986).

10 Lena Cowan Orlin, 'Fictions of the Early Modern Probate Inventory', in H.S. Turner (ed.) *The Culture of Capital: Properties, Cities and Knowledge in Early Modern England* (London: Routledge, 2002), pp. 51–83.

11 Dena Goodman, 'Furnishing Discourses: Readings of a Writing Desk in Eighteenth-century France', in Maxine Berg & Elizabeth Eger (eds) *Luxury in the Eighteenth Century: Debates, Desires and Delectable Goods* (Basingstoke: Palgrave Macmillan, 2007), pp. 71–88, quote on pp. 82–3.

12 Ibid., pp. 82–3.

13 See Berg and Eger, *Luxury*, esp. 'Introduction'; Berg, *Luxury and Pleasure*, pp. 21–45; and Linda Levy Peck, *Consuming Splendor: Society and Culture in Seventeenth-century England* (Cambridge: Cambridge University Press, 2005), pp. 355–8.

14 Although work on clothing textiles by Lemire and Styles is breaking this mould; see Lemire in this volume, and John Styles, *The Dress of the People: Everyday Fashion in Eighteenth Century England* (London: Yale University Press, 2008).

15 These are rarely open to the public, although the Museum of London Archaeology Service has opened its stores as the London Archaeological Archive and Research Centre, in east London.

16 For a recent critical treatment of this approach from archaeologists themselves, see C.G. Cumberpatch and P.W. Blinkhorn (eds), *Not So Much a Pot, More a Way of Life* (Oxford: Oxbow Books, 1997), esp. the editors' introduction, pp. v–vi.

17 There are exceptions. For example, Styles, *Dress of the People*; Matthew Hilton, *Smoking in British Popular Culture 1800–2000* (Manchester: Manchester University Press, 2000).

18 Deetz, *Small Things*, pp. 18–20. See also the Museum of London microsite, 'Clay Tobacco Pipe Makers' Marks from London', available at: http://www.museumoflondon.org.uk/claypipes/index.asp, accessed 26 March 2008.

19 Tanya Pollard, 'The Pleasures and Perils of Smoking in Early Modern England', in Sander L. Gilman and Xun Zhou (eds), *Smoke: a Global History of Smoking* (London: Reaktion, 2004), pp. 38–45; Brian Cowan, *The Social Life of Coffee: The Emergence of the British Coffeehouse* (London: Yale University Press, 2005), p. 82 and Figs 5 and 8.

20 Brad S. Gregory, '*Is* Small Beautiful? Microhistory and the History of Everyday Life', *History and Theory*, 38, 1 (1999), pp. 100–10, on pp. 102–3. See also Carlo Ginzburg, *The Cheese and the Worms: The Cosmos of a Sixteenth-century Miller*, transl. John and Anne Tedeschi (Baltimore: Johns Hopkins University Press, 1980); and Keith Wrightson and David Levine, *Poverty and Piety in an English Village: Terling, 1525–1700* (Oxford: Clarendon Press, 1979). See also George Iggers, *Historiography in the Twentieth Century: From Scientific Objectivity to the Postmodern Challenge* (Hanover, NH, and London: Wesleyan University Press, 1997), Chapter 9.

21 Gregory, '*Is* Small Beautiful?', p. 104.

22 Simon Schama, 'The Monte Lupo Story', *London Review of Books*, 18 Sept. 1980, pp. 22–3; cited in Edward Muir, 'Introduction: Observing Trifles', in E. Muir and Guido Ruggiero (eds), *Microhistory and the Lost Peoples of Europe* (Baltimore: Johns Hopkins University Press, 1991), pp. vii–xxviii, on p. xx.

23 This in itself differentiates material culture history from microhistory, which grew out of the ideologically charged social history movements of the 1960s and 1970s, and on the whole has laid a just claim to recovering 'lost' voices, or indeed 'lost peoples'; see, for example, Muir and Ruggiero (eds), *Microhistory*.

24 For example, the chapters by Bernard Herman, John Styles and Robert Blair St George in John Styles and Amanda Vickery (eds), *Gender, Taste and Material Culture in Britain and North America, 1700–1830* (London: Yale University Press, 2006).

25 The concept of the 'social imaginary' was developed by the philosopher Charles Taylor

(see Charles Taylor, *Modern Social Imaginaries* (Durham, NC: Duke University Press, 2004)), and is deployed in the recent work of Robert Blair St George; 'Reading Spaces in Eighteenth-century New England', in Styles and Vickery (eds), *Gender*, pp. 81–105, on pp. 83–4.

26 Ibid, p. 84.

27 Sara Pennell, 'Pots and Pans History: The Material Culture of the Kitchen in Early Modern England', *Journal of Design History*, 11, 3 (1998), pp. 201–16, quote on p. 202.

28 Both these terms are neologisms, which suggests the status of kitchen goods as somewhat peripheral to the world of 'true' antiques: see the definition for 'collectable' (n.) in the *OED Online* ('kitchenalia' was not in there as of April 2008, but is used widely by dealers).

29 Anne E. Yentsch, 'The Symbolic Divisions of Pottery: Sex-related Attributes of English and Anglo-American Household Pots', in Randall H. McGuire and Robert Paynter (eds), *The Archaeology of Inequality* (Oxford: Blackwell, 1992), pp. 192–230; Lorna Weatherill, *Consumer Behaviour and Material Culture in Britain, 1660–1760* (London: Routledge, 1988), pp. 150–1. Literary scholars have become more habituated to the domestic, notably Wendy Wall's *Staging Domesticity: Household Work and English Identity in Early Modern Drama* (Cambridge: Cambridge University Press, 2002). For the modern kitchen see June Freeman, *The Making of the Modern Kitchen: A Cultural History* (London: Berg, 2002).

30 Yenstch, 'Symbolic Divisions', p. 212.

31 Amanda Vickery, 'Women and the World of Goods: A Lancashire Consumer and her Possessions, 1751–81', in John Brewer and Roy Porter (eds), *Consumption and the World of Goods* (London: Routledge, 1993), pp. 283, 292–3; Amy Louise Erickson, *Women and Property in Early Modern England* (London: Routledge, 1993), pp. 26, 144–5, 222.

32 Berkshire Record Office, D/A1/49/160, Will of Sarah Boult, dated 11 September 1732.

33 Gilly Lehmann, *The British Housewife: Cookery Books, Cooking and Society in Eighteenth-century Britain* (Totnes: Prospect Books, 2003), pp. 173–93.

34 These shifts are examined in greater detail in Sara Pennell, 'The Material Culture of Food in Early Modern England, *c*.1650–1750', unpublished Oxford DPhil, 1997, Chapter 4.

35 G.K. Chesterton, writing in a letter to his future wife, Frances Blogg, between their meeting in 1896 and their marriage in 1901, might well have been thinking of the same ethos, the loss of which he decried (or mocked?) in his own age: 'There are aesthetic pattering prigs who can look on a saucepan without one tear of joy or sadness: mongrel decadents that can see no dignity in the honourable scars of a kettle. So they concentrate all their house decoration on coloured windows that nobody looks out of, and vases of lilies that everybody wishes out of the way. No: my idea (which is much cheaper) is to make a house really (allegoric) really explain its own essential meaning. Mystical or ancient sayings should be inscribed on every object, the more prosaic the object the better; ... "Even the Hairs of your Head are all numbered" would give a tremendous significance to one's hairbrushes ... while "Our God is a consuming Fire" might be written over the kitchen-grate, to assist the mystic musings of the cook': see http://www.cse.dmu.ac.uk/~mward/gkc/books/to-frances.html, accessed 16 January 2008.

36 Andrew Morrall has drawn similar conclusions in his study of the use of Protestant texts and imagery on sixteenth-century Northern European ceramics, but his focus is on goods I would term 'luxury', rather than 'mundane'; 'Protestant Pots: Morality and Social Ritual in the Early Modern Home', *Journal of Design History*, 15, 4 (2002), pp. 263–73.

37 Gervase Markham, *The English Housewife* was first published in 1615 as Book II of *Countrey Contentments*, but later as part of *A Way to Get Wealth*; see Michael Best, 'Introduction', in *The English Housewife*, ed. Michael R. Best (Montreal/Kingston: McGill University Press, 1986), p. liv; Richard Bradley, *The Country Housewife and Lady's Director*, 2 parts (London, 1727 and 1732).

38 See, for example, Lehmann, *The British Housewife*; Sandra Sherman, '*The Whole Art and Mystery of Cooking*: What Cookbooks Taught Readers in the Eighteenth Century', *Eighteenth-Century Life*, 28, 1 (2004), pp. 115–35; Laura Lunger Knoppers, 'Opening the Queen's Closet: Henrietta Maria, Elizabeth Cromwell, and the Politics of Cookery', *Renaissance Quarterly*, 60, 2 (2007), pp. 464–99.

39 Natasha Glaisyer and Sara Pennell, 'Introduction', in Natasha Glaisyer and Sara Pennell (eds), *Didactic Literature in England, 1500–1800: Expertise Constructed* (Aldershot: Ashgate, 2003), pp. 1–18.

40 Katherine Sharp, 'Women's Creativity and Display in the Eighteenth Century British Interior', in Susie McKellar and Penny Sparke (eds), *Interior Design and Identity* (Manchester: Manchester University Press, 2004), pp. 10–26.

41 A fuller introduction to manuscript recipe texts is provided in Sara Pennell, 'Introduction', in *Women in Medicine: Remedy Books, 1533–1865* (Woodbridge, CO: Primary Source Microfilm, 2004).

42 Ibid.

43 Wellcome Library online catalogue, consulted 16 January 2008.

44 Edward Lisle, *Observations in Husbandry* (London, 1757).

45 Madeleine Masson and Anthony Vaughan (eds), *The Compleat Cook, or Secrets of a Seventeenth Century Housewife, by Rebecca Price* (London: Routledge & Kegan Paul, 1974), p. 345.

46 Amanda Vickery, *The Gentleman's Daughter: Women's Lives in Georgian England* (London: Yale University Press, 1998).

47 Alexander Pope, *Minor Poems*, ed. Norman Ault and completed by John Butt (London: Methuen & Co., 1954), p. 353.

48 R. Cotgrove, *A Dictionarie of the French and English Tongues* (London, 1611), quoted in E.P. Thompson, 'Rough Music', in *idem, Customs in Common* (London: Penguin, 1993), p. 467, n. 1.

49 They do exist: for example, see Ivan Day's website: http://www.historicfood.com, accessed 16 January 2008).

50 'Monsieur Marnettè' [sic], *The Perfect Cook* (London: Nathaniel Brookes, 1656), frontispiece. This can be viewed on Early English Books Online at: http://gateway.proquest.com/openurl?ctx_ver=Z39.88–2003&res_id=xri:eebo&rft_id=xri:eebo:image:1 70273:3, accessed 6 June 2008.

51 *The English Housewife*, ed. Best, p. 96; Marnettè [sic], *The Perfect Cook*, sig. A4r.

52 For Kidder's biography and complicated text history of his recipes, see the summary in Lehmann, *British Housewife*, pp. 431–2. The quoted material comes from the title page of the (undated) engraved edition of the recipes in the British Library, shelfmark 1037.e.34.

53 Cf. Yentsch, 'Symbolic Divisions', pp. 206, 212.

54 Pennell, 'Material Culture of Food', Chapters 2 and 3.

55 For a further discussion of this, see Sara Pennell 'Perfecting Practice? Women, Manuscript Recipes and Knowledge in Early Modern England', in Victoria Burke and Jonathan Gibson (eds), *Early Modern Women's Manuscript Writing: Selected Papers from the Trinity/Trent Colloquium* (Aldershot: Ashgate, 2004), pp. 237–58.

56 Amanda Vickery develops the idiom of the 'intact Delft platter' to signify the atypicality of the complete object/text survival, but its utility in making sense of the 'shattered fragments' traceable in other sources: Vickery, 'Women and the World of Goods', p. 29, n. 118. Here, I use it slightly more critically, to suggest how historians have tried to 'fit' the material culture fragments into the reconstituted evidential 'platter'.

57 Alluding to Peck, *Consuming Splendor*, and Berg, *Luxury and Pleasure*.

58 Matthew Johnson, *An Archaeology of Capitalism* (Oxford: Blackwell, 1996), pp. 87–90, 163–78, 200–1.

10 The case of the missing footstool
Reading the absent object

Glenn Adamson

One of the key problems in the study of material culture is the phenomenon of loss. Indeed, when it comes to the material past, disappearance is the norm, and preservation is the exception. This fact is widely recognized by historians, who have tried to study the way that uneven rates of survival create a false picture of the past – in terms of class, gender, geography and ethnic identity – often working with archaeologists and literary scholars in order to draw a more accurate picture. Alteration, a subcategory of loss, also presents many obstacles for interpretation. Surviving objects may have acquired new parts or a new surface; and of course by the time we come to study any material thing, it will invariably have been recontextualized. Even in those rarest of circumstances when an object still sits in the very spot for which it was originally intended, perhaps in the perfectly intact room of a magically well-preserved country house, in the moment when we walk into its presence we have created a new encounter.

These various forms of absence are central to the study of material culture, and it is imperative to bear them in mind. But there is another sense in which historical objects may be 'missing'. This is when they are absent not only in the present day, but seemingly in the historical record as well. When scholars look at the past, they look above all for patterns – shapes that are disposed across time, space and cultures. Much of modern museology has been premised on the reconstruction of such patterns. Here a point made to me by Craig Clunas, formerly a curator of Chinese art at the Victoria and Albert Museum, is worth relating. He was describing to me the creation of the ceramics collection at the museum, which today numbers in the many thousands of examples. The strategy employed by the institution's early curators was a comprehensive one, so that (for example) they set out to collect a sample of every significant porcelain manufactory in England. This accomplished, they then began to gather examples of each manufactory's early, middle and late periods where possible, and then every form known to have been produced by each manufactory. Clunas drew the story to a close by pointing out the obvious: every time the curators made an acquisition, they made their job exponentially more difficult, for in filling the 'hole' in the collection with a new object they succeeded only in creating new 'holes' on every side of it.

The moral of this story is that discerning patterns in history is an act of selective will. But there is also a narrower, and perhaps more useful, point to make: isolating the gaps within a pattern is a vital part of the process of writing history. While the V&A's curators thought they were constructing a complete history of English porcelain through the acquisition of objects, it was actually in identifying the salient 'holes' in the collection that the curators really made their decisions. With this in mind, we might ask: 'What if absence in the historical record were to be treated not as a problem to be overcome, but rather as a matter of historical interest in its own right?' This chapter will consider this possibility through the consideration of one example: the eighteenth-century British domestic footstool, an object that seems to have gone missing in a most suggestive fashion.

Setting the scene

We know for certain that the eighteenth-century British public was aware of such a thing as a footstool for domestic use. A particularly prominent depiction of one appears in 'The Tête à Tête', the second painting in William Hogarth's famous satirical cycle of paintings *Marriage à la Mode* (1743) (Figure 10.1). The scene is set in the lavishly decorated home of a young Viscount and his new wife, who are seated to either side of a fireplace liberally decorated with Chinese ornaments. All is not well. A distraught servant exits to the right carrying a bill of expenses that one senses may go unpaid, but the couple are unconcerned. It has clearly been a hard night of carousing and gambling (to judge by the dishevelled card table in the background). The nattily attired Viscount stretches out his legs disconsolately, his

Figure 10.1 William Hogarth, *Marriage a La Mode*, Plate II. 1745. Etching and engraving on paper. H 38.1 cm × W 46.3 cm. V&A F.118:21; Forster Bequest. Courtesy of Victoria and Albert Museum, London.

sword lying in pieces at his feet and a lady's cap (presumably not his wife's) peeking out from his pocket. We notice the cap thanks to a sniffing dog, who is perched on a small gilt footstool with red upholstery. The Viscount does not actually prop his feet up on the little piece of furniture but, like every other detail in Hogarth's painting, it helps to underpin a narrative of impending disaster: even as these young people's affairs are spinning dangerously out of control, all they want to do is put their feet up.

'The Tête à Tête' serves as an apt introduction to the study of the footstool, which, as this chapter will go on to argue, was no less important to eighteenth-century Britain for being absent. After seeing Hogarth's painting, we might, as historians of material culture, want to find a real footstool of the period, to see if it bears any similarity to the one in the image. We might want to find out who owned such objects. Were they, as Hogarth implies, signs of conspicuous consumption and excessive spending? Or were they more common than that, a fixture of the middling British home? How were they made? Were there various levels of expense and refinement available to the prospective footstool owner? Such questions are routinely asked of other object types, often with a great deal of success. But in the case of the footstool, one comes up empty. It has proven impossible (for this writer, anyway) to locate a single surviving British domestic footstool that can be securely dated much before 1800. This could be because of their small size and seemingly marginal role within the interior, of course – perhaps their scarcity today is a straightforward case of attrition. But there are also surprisingly few references to footstools in period documents. Samuel Johnson's 1755 *Dictionary of the English Language* duly defined the term – a 'stool on which he that sits places his feet' – but usage in texts of the period is limited almost entirely to a religious context. The resonant Biblical phrase 'sit thou on my right hand, until I make thine enemies thy footstool' (Psalms, cx. 1) was cited and paraphrased extensively in the period, as was a figure of speech in which the earthly world was described as God's footstool.[1] But there is scarcely any evidence in inventories, diaries, fiction or published descriptions of homes that makes mention of the form in use.

The only context in which the footstool was used consistently in Britain prior to the nineteenth century was at court, particularly in royal and ecclesiastical ceremonies. Several important examples survive, such as the throne and footstool of the Archbishop William Juxon, who was canonized in 1661, which are preserved with their original upholstery in the Victoria and Albert Museum; or a similar set for the coronation of Queen Anne in 1702, which survives at Hatfield House.[2] (In some cases a simple cushion, rather than a piece of furniture with a frame, was used for the purpose.) Courtly usage, however, might best be considered as the exception that proves the rule. In the artificial, ritualized and historically resonant surroundings of an event like a royal coronation, the footstool could take on an emblematic role precisely because it was distinctive. A description dating from 1727 gives the flavour:

> In the meantime the King rises from his Devotions, and goes to the Altar, supported as before, and attended by the Lord Great Chamberlain ... And King

Edward's Chair, with a Footstool before it, being placed in the midst of the Area or Sacrarium before the Altar, and being covered over with Cloth of Gold, his Majesty seats himself in it.[3]

The tradition of using a footstool to signify rulership goes far back in history, and is not limited to European cultures. As the Biblical passages cited above suggest, the presence of a footstool suggests domination – the symbolism is only a short step away from a medieval representation of an angel with his feet upon a devil, or St George standing triumphant atop a dragon. Such long-standing symbolic use of footstools could be said to make the domestic footstool only more conspicuous by its absence.

This absence is doubly remarkable because, just after the turn of the nineteenth century, footstools seem to have suddenly become nearly omnipresent in the British interior. Jane West's prescriptive book *Letters to a Young Lady*, which offered instructions on matters ranging from etiquette to morality, inveighed against the 'folly of fashionable ostentation' that seemed to her to have become all too common of late among 'the middle classes of life':

> [I]t becomes an undertaking of no little skill, to conduct one's person through an apartment twelve feet square, furnished in style by a lady of taste, without any injury to ourselves, or to the fauteuils, candelabras, console tables, jardiniers, chiffoniers, &c. Should we, at entering the apartment, escape the workboxes, footstools, and cushions for lapdogs, our debut may still be celebrated by the overthrow of half a dozen top-gallant screens, as many perfume jars, or even by the total demolition of a glass cabinet stuck full of stuffed monsters.[4]

West might not be a reliable source, since she is writing in a censorious and exaggerated tone. But inventories also attest to the presence of footstools in British and American homes during the first decade of the nineteenth century, occasionally located in the dining room but most often in the drawing room, itself a new type of space within the middle-class home.[5] There are other types of evidence, too: letters, like one written by Theresa Villiers to a friend in 1805, expressing thanks for the present of a footstool;[6] images, like Andy Buck's sentimental 1808 print 'Darling Awake', which shows a woman in an Empire dress dandling a child on her knee, and employs a footstool as a synecdoche (that is, a metaphorical stand-in) for the domestic setting itself.[7] And there are plenty of surviving objects as well, mostly in the neoclassical Regency style that flourished in the early part of the century. Some of these, like a pair of footstools (now in the Metropolitan Museum of Art) made by the leading New York cabinetmaker Duncan Phyfe, were made *en suite* with a matching sofa and chairs, suggesting that the footstool was becoming a standard part of the well-appointed home. After 1800, then, the footstool seems to have been a common enough feature of the British domestic interior. Why was it missing until then – and what might account for its sudden arrival on the scene?

A short history of putting one's feet up

Methodologically speaking, the best thing to do when faced with an unexpected 'hole' in the historical record is to look at the edges of the perceived gap, in the hope of delineating its precise contours, and thus some way of guessing at the reasons behind it. As it turns out, there are several interesting discoveries to be made about the missing footstool through this strategy – each of which makes the case seem even more intriguing.

A first step might be to consider objects that are similar to our absent object, but lack its precise use or connotations. So, what other small-scale items populated the floor in an eighteenth-century household? The most common forms of seating in the seventeenth century, and in some rural areas well into the nineteenth, were the form (a long, simple bench) and the joint or board stool (not to be confused with the footstool, this was a low, backless seat, usually lacking upholstery). In wealthier interiors, seating was again mostly backless, with an upholstered seat and sometimes a separate cushion. The French referred to this form as a *tabouret*, and the English simply called it a 'stool' (meaning 'seat', and etymologically linked to the German *Stuhl*). Until the late seventeenth century, only the most significant person present in a gathering – perhaps the patriarch of the household – would be seated in a chair as we would now use that term. This would have been a substantial piece of furniture with a high back and arms, either turned or carved, and often upholstered. In a courtly context such a seat might be described as a throne, but typically it was called a 'great chair,' and most homes would have had only one. It was not until the proliferation of cheaply built caned chairs in London and the Netherlands in the late seventeenth century that households tended to have multiple seats with backs. Though lightly and quickly built, these caned chairs were an improvement in terms of comfort, because they raked slightly backwards and often had cushions tied on to their seat frames. Thus our own idea of sitting as an activity that involves reclining to a degree, and certainly as a posture that would permit resting one's feet upon a lower stool or cushion, is actually of relatively recent vintage.

Does this mean, then, that people did not put their feet up before the beginning of the nineteenth century? This is exactly the sort of question that written documents tend not to answer for the historian, but we can resort to the examination of surviving artefacts; for, despite the missing footstool, there are convincing material indications that people did indeed sit with their feet up off the floor. The most pervasive such evidence is the presence of wear on the front stretchers (the horizontal braces that run sideways between a chair's front legs) on seventeenth- and eighteenth-century seating (Figure 10.2). This is particularly striking to the modern viewer because few chairs nowadays have stretchers at all – they began to disappear from seating in the middle of the eighteenth century (an elimination made possible by improvements to the strength of the joints of chairs at the seat). When chairs did have stretchers, however, we should imagine that people tended to sit with their knees lifted, heels tucked securely on a wooden perch. This attitude was suggestive not so much of relaxation as activity. With the knees drawn up, the lap was rendered a convenient surface for eating, sewing or reading.

Figure 10.2 Armchair, England, 1675–1700. Oak and elm, with carving and turning. H 115 cm × W 57 cm × D 55.5 cm. V&C CIRC. 214–1911. Courtesy of Victoria and Albert Museum, London.

A similar point might be made about another type of object that comes quite close to the footstool: the footwarmer. This was a common domestic accoutrement in the seventeenth century and seems to have seen continued use in the eighteenth. It developed first in the Netherlands, and many Dutch genre paintings show footwarmers in use. One travelling British writer, clearly unfamiliar with the form, found it to be worthy of extended comment:

> The portable Stoves universally used both by the Men and Women of these Provinces, are extremely convenient. It is a little square wooden Box, within which there is a small earthen Pan with a Bit of lighted Turf in it. The Stove has a Door, which is shut when the Pan is put in it, and Holes on the Top, on which People place their Feet by way of a Foot-stool. By this contrivance they keep themselves gently warm the whole Winter's Day either by Land or Water; for with this little portable Equipage they travel, sit behind their Counters, and at Church, from which the coldest Day in Winter does not detain them. If the Turf be good, it keeps in two or three Hours, and when it is burnt out, they renew it.[8]

As this passage indicates, the footwarmer, like a chair's front stretcher, was not used in a spirit of relaxation but rather to better enable the sitter to work or perform some other activity, such as riding in a carriage or sitting quietly in a stone-cold church.

A final form that should be mentioned in relation to the footstool is the charmingly named 'cricket' (or sometimes 'cricket stool'), a small piece of furniture with a round top and turned legs. These must have been extremely common in the eighteenth century, but they were so small and inexpensive (and so dispensable) that few securely datable to the period survive. In any case, despite their small scale, crickets seem to have been used almost exclusively to sit upon rather than to rest one's feet. They are recorded as seating for children, after they had outgrown high chairs, and also being used by clerks and servants while at work.[9]

'Be always ashamed to catch thyself idle'

The foregoing discussion of cognate forms amounts to a historical argument – tentative, as arguments built largely from surviving material evidence tend to be – that a form of seated posture that we now consider to be absolutely conventional (and comfortable) was unusual and perhaps even unknown until about 1800. What might explain this surprising fact? Here we might return to Hogarth's painting 'The Tête à Tête', and reconsider its moralizing aspects. The eighteenth century was, like most periods in history, a great time for moralizers. A brief tour of the era's prescriptive literature establishes an interesting context for the Viscount's splayed-leg posture. Idleness and indolence were criticized constantly by writers of the period. A text from earlier in the century (sometimes attributed to Daniel Defoe), for example, offered cautionary advice that might almost have been written to caption Hogarth's painting: 'Idle Excursions, vain Diversions, or what's worse, may give a temporary Relaxation; but if God intend them good, they'll find their Troubles recur with Force; as a Current dam'd up a while, rushes with redoubled Violence, the Obstruction once master'd'.[10] The misogynist aspect of Hogarth's painting, too, was reflected in a wide range of texts in the period, in which women's supposed tendency towards excessive consumption was held to place both the household and the national economy at risk. And the *chinoiserie* elements of the interior in 'The Tête à Tête' were meant to read as signifiers of foreign luxuries – a point to which we will return.[11]

Another great moralizer of the eighteenth century was Benjamin Franklin, whose prescriptive *Poor Richard's Almanack* was first published in 1732, when the future great statesman was still establishing himself as a printer. The *Almanack* became one of the most popular books of the era despite – or perhaps because of – its stern, mordant tone. Aphorisms (some of Franklin's own composition, others borrowed from previous publications) such as 'Trouble springs from idleness and grievous toil from needless ease' and 'Be always ashamed to catch thyself idle' were typical of a text that hectored its reader to remain ever vigilant in the struggle against temptation, idleness and luxury. It so happens that Franklin suffered from gout later in life, a fact that makes another aphorism in the *Almanack* somewhat poignant: 'O Lazy-Bones! Dost thou think God would have given thee Arms and Legs, if he had not design'd thou should'st use them.' This line seems as though it could have been written specifically to chastise the Viscount in 'The Tête à Tête', but it takes on nearly premonitory dimensions when one considers a much later writing of Franklin's entitled *Dialogue Between Franklin and the Gout*. This short, funny text pits a defensive and hapless Ben against his own painful illness. The personification of gout addresses him in a critical tone not too different from that which Franklin himself had adopted in the *Almanack*:

FRANKLIN. Eh! Oh! Eh! What have I done to merit these cruel sufferings?

GOUT. Many things; you have ate and drank too freely, and too much indulged those legs of yours in their indolence.

Today, with the benefit of modern medicine, we know that gout is caused not by 'indolence' but a build-up of uric acid around the cartilage of the joints. The result is excruciating pain, stiffness, and swelling – nothing to laugh about, really, though this did not prevent eighteenth-century caricaturists and satirists from doing so, mainly because they saw the disease as afflicting the lazy rich who ate too much and exercised too little.[12] Franklin was not above teasing himself on this point:

GOUT. It is a maxim of your own, that 'a man may take as much exercise in walking a mile, up and down stairs, as in ten on level ground.' What an opportunity was here for you to have had exercise in both these ways! Did you embrace it, and how often?

FRANKLIN. I cannot immediately answer that question.

GOUT. I will do it for you; not once.

FRANKLIN. Not once?

GOUT. Even so.

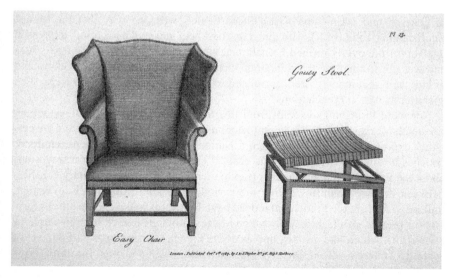

Figure 10.3 George Hepplewhite, *The Cabinet-Maker & Upholsterer's Guide*, 1787, Plate 15. Courtesy of Victoria and Albert Museum, London.

Gout is a useful point of reference for our story about footstools, in part because it served as the basis for moral invective against inactivity, but also because the only time that putting one's feet up *was* considered appropriate in the eighteenth century was when one suffered from the affliction. The 'gouty stool', a simple wooden frame with a moveable square top, was developed specifically to aid in the comfort of those who suffered from the disease (Figure 10.3). In a neat coincidence, it was only when one brought misfortune upon oneself through idleness that a piece of furniture specifically designed for propping up the feet came into use. (A similar but less morally freighted case is that of the winged or 'easy' chair, which was not used for relaxation when it was first introduced, but rather was intended to support the head of an invalid.)[13] Indeed, in the first painting in Hogarth's *Marriage à la Mode*, entitled 'The Marriage Settlement', we find the Earl of Squander (the Viscount's father) with a bandaged foot propped up on a gilt and upholstered footstool closely comparable to the one in 'The Tête à Tête'. Through the language of objects, Hogarth is foreshadowing the inevitable results of high living.

An aspect of Hogarth's footstools that deserves consideration in this connection is their boldly scrolled Baroque style, which in the 1740s and in the context of this series of paintings would likely have been perceived as French. This is not the only nod to fashions from across the Channel: the Viscount sports shoe-heels made of dyed red leather, which were a sartorial privilege afforded only to the nobility in France. The ridiculous, overly ornamented clock on the wall, which incorporates the figures of a cat, a monkey and a fish, must also have been intended to evoke the elaborate creations of Parisian *mécaniciens*. Hogarth was famously anti-Gallic and lampooned French manners and mannerisms mercilessly in other works (most memorably the print 'A Taste in High Life', in which a skinny gentleman and his portly wife thrill to the delights of a tiny, exquisite teacup). Disapproval of luxury in general, and taking one's ease in particular, was one way that the honest Englishman ('John Bull'), who dined on roast beef and spoke his mind, expressed disdain for the overly refined Frenchman, who ate strange things like frog's legs and was constrained by the ridiculous dictates of fashion.[14] The 'supineness and effeminacy' that many writers correlated with indolence and ill health were often specifically cast in French terms.[15]

Nor were furnishings exempt from this logic; as the prominent Bluestocking Elizabeth Montagu wrote in a letter to her husband, 'the manners of an age are certainly expressed by furniture. When a Nation grows effeminate Beds, chairs & couches are made fit for luxurious ease.'[16] Given all these British reservations about the French national character (not to mention the frequent military conflicts between the two countries during the period), it is interesting to discover that, unlike the British, the French did indeed have footstools in the eighteenth century. No less prominent a fashion victim than Marie Antoinette herself is known to have owned one, which like most examples of the French footstool was part of a set of seating furniture made *en suite*.[17] The French also developed other furniture forms specifically dedicated to putting one's feet up, like the 'fauteuil de commodité en bergère' – an armchair with a matching footstool to extend its seat, a form that was also called a *duchesse* or *chaise longue brisée*.[18] Another form called the *récamier*, a couch with an asymmetrical scrolled arm, came to be a prominent symbol of French classical style and luxury at the end of the century. It was named for Madame Jeanne Françoise Julie Adélaïde Récamier, who favoured reclining in such a piece of furniture. The couch and the woman alike were immortalized in Jacques-Louis David's 1800 portrait, now in the Louvre.[19]

Thus it appears that while the British were assiduously avoiding putting their feet up, the French (the aristocratic French, at any rate) were conceiving varied and novel means of doing just that. While this divergence in the matter of personal comportment seems hard to credit, it is worth noting that travellers often remarked upon differences. British travellers to America, for example, pronounced themselves amused by the habit they observed there of tipping back in a chair, which seemed to them curious and possibly dangerous.[20] But such encounters with difference were much more striking to Englishmen when they went further afield, culturally speaking, and this brings us, finally, to the emergence of the British domestic footstool.

The term 'ottoman' was often applied to a low seat – not unlike the ones once described as tabourets – but was also used to describe the footstool. The employment of this exotic word may betray a continuity of the unspoken assumptions about luxury, decadence and foreignness that we have explored thus far. The first mention of an ottoman listed in the *Oxford English Dictionary* is in a memorandum book of Thomas Jefferson, who listed payment for an 'ottomane of velours d'Utrecht', a phrase that encapsulates the complex geography of objects at this time – a French form that had acquired the name of the great Near Eastern empire, and was covered with a fabric made in the Netherlands. Like the 'sofa' and the 'divan', two words of Arabic derivation that (like the forms they describe) date earlier in the eighteenth century, the ottoman's introduction to the British interior circa 1800 announced a more horizontal approach to seating. In their early years, all these forms were conceptually tied to dubious French luxury. The sofa, in particular, was associated with moral as well as physical relaxation, having been brought to the attention of many Britons by the English translation of Crébillon fils's scurrilous novel *La Sopha* (1742), set in the Orient, in which the hero is transformed into a piece of furniture and relates the various assignations that he observes as a result.

British writers seized upon the connection between the sofa and sexuality, using it much as Hogarth used his prop footstools to create an atmosphere of impropriety. In 1773, for example, the novelist Richard Graves opened a scene in his novel *The Spiritual Quixote* (a scene, incidentally, also entitled 'Tête à Tête') with the lines: 'The Lady received him in a genteel dishabille [sic], sitting, or rather leaning, on a rich sofa, in such a posture as necessarily displayed an handsome foot, somewhat above the instep.'[21] It is worth noting that women's shoes, too, were changing at this time, in line with this spirit of alluring display: new 'neoclassical' styles of footwear often revealed the shape of the ankle and foot to an unprecedented degree. The rigidly constructed woman's shoe of the eighteenth century typically had a high heel, a pointed toe and a buckle to fasten it. In the 1790s this style was displaced by a narrower, much more lightly built shoe that tied with laces, and was made with a silk or satin upper. These shoes were so flimsy that they were often bought six or twelve at a time, and could only be worn a few times before being worn out. As Giorgio Riello has written, 'the famous red heels of Louis XIV gave way to elegant flat shoes, unsuitable for walking but very demonstrative'.[22] An 'ottoman' would have performed much the same role as the sofa described in Graves' novel, acting as a platform for the showing off of the newly unconcealed foot.

Three hypotheses

The American art historian Jules Prown, one of the pioneers of material culture theory, has suggested that artefacts from the past might best be interpreted as a psychiatrist would interpret a patient's dreams: 'Perhaps if we had access to a culture's dream world, we could discover and analyse some of [their] hidden beliefs. In the absence of that, I suggest that some of these beliefs are encapsulated in the form of things.'[23] This argument has a certain persuasive force. What a culture takes for granted, or will not allow itself to speak aloud, might be found precisely in those areas that are less self-conscious. But if we are to take Prown's argument seriously – that the material culture scholar is something like an analyst burrowing into a patient's unconscious – then surely what will be most revelatory is that which is literally repressed. A teapot or a table is likely to 'match' written texts of the same period. Connecting the two is never likely to be easy. The German art historian Heinrich Wölfflin wrote over a century ago that 'we have yet to find the way from the scholar's pen to the mason's yard'. All these years later, scholars still struggle to find the links between intellectual and material history.[24] The areas of greatest success have normally relied on period discussions about the world of material goods: economics, consumption, taste and aesthetics. This essay adopts a different approach. I have tried to take to heart Prown's contention that the study of material culture, in its purest form, is not simply an adjunct or support for the history of such fields of thought, but is rather a means of getting at cultural content that could be recovered in no other way. Put simply, if we want the study of material culture to unlock the secrets of history, then surely we should be analysing what people of the past did *not* make, what they did *not* do, with as much care as we examine their surviving material traces. Behind every object that has 'gone missing', there is a hidden cause. If we have done our detective work well, then at the bottom of the case of the missing footstool should lie something like a motive.[25]

Despite the clues we have assembled thus far, it may not be elementary to find this motive. Moving from the specific to the general, finding reasons behind the pattern of material evidence (or absence), requires a leap of induction no easier than the deductive feats of Sherlock Holmes. While I will now be offering three possible explanations for the footstool's absence and its subsequent fashionability, it should be stressed that these are a series of informed guesses – hypotheses – rather than an open-and-shut case.

We might begin with the issue of class. It was a commonplace in the eighteenth century that the lower sorts did not seek to improve their lot when they had the opportunity. Once labourers had enough to subsist on, the conventional thinking ran, they did not seek additional work or income, but rather directed any excess income they might have into 'luxuries', drink, or other forms of indolent behaviour. This argument was used by economic theorists to justify workers' low wages, and was also consistent with a generally suspicious view of leisure. That suspicion was equally prevalent among the 'polite' or middling sorts, and as we have seen in the example of Hogarth (and, indeed, in the merciless satire of wealthy, overstuffed gout sufferers), such disapprobation was also levelled at the more well-to-do. It was not until the beginning of the nineteenth century that this set of convictions began to reverse itself. In these years, moralizing rhetoric was more likely to present the British proletariat as the hard-working pride of the nation, perhaps deserving of a rest at the end of a long day. This change in attitudes towards luxury was inextricably bound up with the ongoing progress of the Industrial Revolution and the rise of machine-powered manufacture. These processes had begun long before the late eighteenth century, were unevenly distributed across various industries, and were understood very differently by observers at the time.[26] Yet it would be difficult to deny that labour's relation to the economy transformed radically during this period. The shift was reflected in many ways: in economic theory (most famously in the work of Adam Smith), which began to frame 'surplus' income and luxury consumption as benefits to the broader society, rather than moral ills; in business practice, which became increasingly orientated to questions of organization as well as production; and, most importantly for our purposes, in changes of attitude towards issues of class and work.[27] The sudden fashionability of the footstool, and its implication that relaxation was a normal part of domesticity rather than a privilege of the few, must be seen against this backdrop of change.

Changing attitudes towards sexuality might also help us to understand the emergence of the footstool. As we have seen, despite its seeming innocuousness, the footstool served as a display for a revealed, sexualized foot. This fact takes us in a different direction from that of class, in that the footstool seems to cut against (rather than confirm) our initial expectations about the shift from the eighteenth to the nineteenth century. Michel Foucault has written of a 'repressive hypothesis' that tends to guide thinking about sexuality during modernization. According to this theory, the Victorian age was a period of denial, a moment in history in which the body and its needs were shunted to the side of culture. Thus, the Victorians could see sexual desire as occurring only within contexts then considered to be deviant, such as homosexuality, prostitution and pornography. The exception to the rule was marital sex, which still caused embarrassment for the culture but was religiously sanctioned and expressly devoted to reproduction of the society through childbirth. Foucault disputes this 'repressive hypothesis' by showing the ways in which sexual discourse flourished during the period: in the gendered organization of institutions such as schools (which imply a recognition that desire is ever-present); in the development of medical literature; and in moralizing literature. If the Victorians were so repressed, Foucault asks, why did sexuality perform such a key ordering role in their society? In fact, the Victorians talked and thought about sex all the time. They were not 'repressed', exactly, but rather *displaced* sexual desire continually, most importantly through institutions, as a means of articulating power relations within culture.[28] The footstool can be profitably viewed as a detail within this Foucaultean reading of sexuality. Its staging of an erogenous zone, the foot, at the very heart of the parlour (itself the symbolic centre of the domestic interior), suggests that a displacement is at work. Sexuality is emphatically *not* repressed here, as it arguably had been in the eighteenth century – when the footstool was present only through its conspicuous absence, as a cautionary talisman. In the nineteenth century, by contrast, the play of desire has been brought front and centre, only to be controlled: as if to demonstrate the efficacy of the familial order in managing a potentially destabilizing force.

A third and final context in which the footstool might be placed is that of Britain's changing relations to the foreign. As in the case of sexuality, the case of the missing footstool may surprise us initially, given our intuitions about the presence of the exotic within British culture. We tend to think of the mid-eighteenth century, the moment of the high rococo, as the apex of orientalizing style, and indeed there is good reason to. The presence of porcelains, japanned furniture and fanciful depictions of Chinese subjects on everything from wallpaper to spice boxes suggests that Britain in the 1750s and 1760s was a culture completely in thrall to the Other. The difference between such rococo *chinoiserie* and the 'luxurious' ottoman, however, is palpable: the difference between the symbolic and the submerged. Though some Chinese forms were taken up by the British in the eighteenth century, mostly for taking tea, they were also seen as expressly, demonstratively Chinese (as the use of the term 'china' to mean porcelain attests). In this sense, tea wares were an extension of the more purely representational approach to the exotic. As David Porter has argued, this moment in the history of orientalism should be seen as a deployment of 'hybrid' forms, which were attractive precisely for their incoherency and sheer difference from prevailing classical norms of taste.[29] The footstool is a completely different kettle of fish. It implies a more casual and less fascinated relation with the Other. By 1800 Britain was an imperial power, with extensive and growing holdings around the world. It is clear that the footstool was associated with French (and perhaps kingly) culture, which was perhaps the most important reason for its absence in the eighteenth-century British household. But does the term 'ottoman' signal an Eastern association with the footstool as well? It may be noteworthy that many chairs made in India (Britain's largest colonial possession) during the late eighteenth and early nineteenth centuries were accompanied by matching footstools. But 'ottoman footstools', despite the name, were not designed in an exoticizing manner; they were comfortably in line with the neoclassical style of the time. Perhaps the fact that the ottoman was implicitly associated with Eastern luxury, but was not designed in such a way as to dramatize that relationship, suggests a process of normalization. The footstool, in this case, could be seen as exemplifying a diminishing of anxiety and curiosity alike, a smoother and less troubled integration of the foreign into the domestic.

Conclusion

Our three hypotheses suggest not only readings of the footstool in the early nineteenth century, but also its absence in the eighteenth. Collectively, they tell a story about the inability of a culture to come to terms with certain disquieting phenomena: class struggle, sexual desire, the foreign. This brings us, however, to a final dilemma. Assuming that the contexts just described do help to illuminate the case of the missing footstool, can we say the reverse? Does the footstool's absence, and its subsequent emergence, really help us to understand the currents of history that swirl around such issues as class, luxury, sexuality and the exotic? A historian might say no. After all, these larger developments are already well understood. One hardly needs to look at footstools, which offer only tantalizing flickers of resonance with broader historical dynamics, when one can look at Adam Smith and Michel Foucault. And indeed, if one can only make sense of the footstool's fortunes with reference to such 'master' texts, then what is the point of making sense of the footstool at all? What expectations should we have of material culture, as a subject area and as a discipline?

One answer, I think, lies in the issue of *register*, a term with a useful double meaning for the study of material culture. To say that an object 'registers' the larger patterns around it, as a seismograph registers an earthquake, is a nicely open way of suggesting our quarry as historians. The term 'register' also captures the social range of material culture: the fact that it is distributed in shapes that extend across multiple levels of society, and thus permits us to draw interpretive connections across hierarchical boundaries. It is the job of one kind of historian to define the past in terms of ideas and large-scale transformations. Concepts like the Industrial Revolution, discourses of sexuality, exoticism, even 'modernity' itself, are useful because they do have explanatory force. We cannot, in a sense, do without them. Without large-scale conceptual tools, history would be reduced to a stream of mutually unintelligible data points, anecdotes and individual biographies. Yet the Big Ideas also need to be tested constantly, and in every way available. And perhaps this is the job of the material culture historian. Something like a footstool brings history literally down to earth. It is encouraging to find that some of the momentous moral and economic currents of the early nineteenth century were registered within the zones of comportment, of domesticity, of furniture production, and indeed the body itself. Such confirmation helps us to have faith in the Big Ideas, which impose order on the past. But material culture can do more than affirm metanarratives. It also helps us to create a more nuanced picture of history, one with multiple registers – something more like a full symphony than a single line of melody. To return to the metaphor of the detective story, we might say that without the study of material culture, we would have nothing but a series of final, culminating scenes, the bits in which we find out 'whodunnit'. But, as any reader knows, the pleasure of Sherlock Holmes' adventures is not just in the revelation of the solution to the mystery, but also in the details: the accumulation of not-quite-explicable facts along the way. It is detail that material culture provides in infinite variety. Though the significance of a clue like the missing footstool may never be decoded conclusively, it might nonetheless exert a salutary influence on the process of writing history. As Holmes himself put it, 'perhaps when a man has special knowledge ... it rather encourages him to seek a complex explanation when a simpler one is at hand'.[30]

Notes

1 A typical poetic example is the couplet, 'Natures's cast fabrick he controuls *alone;*/This globe's his footstool, high heaven his throne.' Thomas Amory, *The Life of John Buncle, Esq; containing various observations and reflections, made in several parts of the world* (London, 1770).

2 James Yorke, 'Archbishop Juxon's Chair', *Burlington Magazine,* 141, 1154 (May 1999), pp. 282–6; Anthony Coleridge, 'English Furniture and Cabinet-makers at Hatfield House, I: *c.*1600–1750', *Burlington Magazine,* 109, 767 (Feb. 1967), pp. 63–70, 72: 67. Documentary evidence related to this set attests that, as one might expect, the expense of a royal footstool was mostly in the fabric used to cover it. The furniture maker in this case was the royal supplier Thomas Roberts, who charged £17 for the throne and £3 for the footstool, while merchant Anthony Ryland received £72 for the 'eight yards of rich gold and blue brocade' used to cover them.

3 *A complete account of the ceremonies observed in the coronations of the kings and queens of England* (London: printed for J. Roberts, 1727).

4 Jane West, *Letters to a Young Lady* (London: Longman, Hurst, Rees and Orme, 1806).

5 Stana Nenadic, 'Middle-rank Consumers and Domestic Culture in Edinburgh and Glasgow 1720–1840', *Past and Present,* 145 (Nov. 1994), pp. 122–56;

6 Theresa Villiers to Parker of Saltam, 23 December 1805. Plymouth and West Devon Record Office, ref. 1259/2/759. Another mention of footstools as a gift appears in a letter from Thomas P. Robinson, Third Baron Grantham, to his aunt Katherine Gertrude Robinson, 23 July 1804. Bedfordshire and Luton Archives and Record Service [L 30/16/17 – L 30/28/2, ref. 30/16/18/23]. That it was appropriate to give such an apparently functional object as a gift may suggest a degree of novelty or curiosity in the form.

7 The Buck print and its pendant 'Darling Asleep' were reproduced in Ackerman's *Repository of the Arts* and were popular enough to be reproduced on tabletops – an example in scagliola is in the Museu Nacional de Arte Antiga, Lisbon.

8 *A Description of Holland: or, the present state of the United Provinces* (London: J. and P. Knapton, 1743), pp. 212–13. Dutch paintings showing footwarmers in use are fairly common in the seventeenth century; a good example is Egland Van Neer (1635–1703), *The Visit,* 1664 (Museum voor Schone Kunsten, Antwerp).

9 Nancy Goyne Evans, *Windsor Chair-making in America: From Craft Shop to Consumer* (Hanover and London: University Press of New England, 2006), p. 344; *Oxford English Dictionary,* 'cricket.'

10 *An account of some remarkable passages in the life of a private gentleman; with reflections thereon* (London: Joseph Downing, 1708).

11 David L. Porter, 'Monstrous Beauty: Eighteenth-century Fashion and the Aesthetics of Chinese Taste', *Eighteenth-Century Studies,* 53, 3 (2002), pp. 395–411; Elizabeth Kowaleski-Wallace, *Consuming Subjects: Women, Shopping and Business in the Eighteenth Century* (New York: Columbia University Press, 1996).

12 Roy Porter, *Gout: The Patrician Malady* (New Haven: Yale University Press, 1998).

13 See John E. Crowley, 'The Sensibility of Comfort', *American Historical Review,* 104, 3 (June 1999), pp. 749–82, at 756–7. For a further history of reclining furniture in relation to invalidism, see Margaret Campbell, 'From Cure Chair to *Chaise Longue*: Medical Treatment and the Form of the Modern Recliner', *Journal of Design History,* 12, 4 (1999), pp. 327–43.

14 In 1770, for example, John Andrews wrote that a 'scrupulous Conformity to established Manners and Customs constitutes indubitably, as essential a Difference as any subsisting in the Character of the French, when compared with that of the English: no People acting more from pure, native, unrestrained Impulse than we do, without inquiring about the Ways of others; and no Nation, on the other Hand, more tamely submitting to the Guidance of the Mode, in every Respect, than the French.' *An Account of the Character and Manners of the French* (London: E. and C. Dilly, 1770), p. 75.

15 L.M. Stretch, *The beauties of history; or, pictures of virtue and vice, drawn from real life; designed for the instruction and entertainment of youth* (London: Charles Dilly, 1780), p. 17.
16 Elizabeth Montagu to Edward Montagu, 10 August, 1769. Huntington Library ms. 2713. My thanks to Elizabeth Eger for this reference.
17 The footstool, made by Jean-Baptiste-Claude Sené in 1788, is in the collection of the Metropolitan Museum of Art, New York.
18 Penelope Hunter, 'A Royal Taste: Louis XV, 1738', *Metropolitan Museum Journal*, 7 (1973), pp. 89–113.
19 In America the *récamier* became immediately popular as a 'Grecian sofa'. On the introduction of the form see Dean Lahikainen, *Samuel McIntire: Carving an American Style* (Salem, MA: Peabody Essex Museum, 2007).
20 Nancy Goyne Evans, *Windsor Chair-making in America*, pp. 131–2.
21 Richard Graves, *The Spiritual Quixote, or, The Summer's Ramble of Mr. Geoffrey Wildgoose* (London, 1773), p. 284.
22 Giorgio Riello, *A Foot in the Past: Consumers, Producers and Footwear in the Long Eighteenth Century*. Pasold Studies in Textile History 15 (New York: Oxford University Press, 2006), pp. 205ff.
23 Jules David Prown, 'The Truth of Material Culture: History or Fiction?', in Steven Lubar and W. David Kingery (eds), *History From Things: Essays on Material Culture* (Washington, DC: Smithsonian Institution Press, 1993); reprinted in Kenneth Haltman (ed.), *American Artifacts: Essays in Material Culture* (Ann Arbor: Michigan State University Press, 2002), p. 14.
24 Heinrich Wölfflin, *Renaissance and Baroque*, transl. Kathrin Simon (Ithaca: Cornell University Press, 1967), pp. 76–7.
25 Charles Rice has written suggestively about the study of the domestic interior as a form of detective work in 'Evidence, Experience and Conjecture: Reading the Interior Through Benjamin and Bloch', *Home Cultures*, 2, 3 (2005), pp. 285–97.
26 Maxine Berg, *The Machinery Question and the Making of Political Economy 1815–1848* (Cambridge: Cambridge University Press, 1980).
27 See John Hatcher, 'Labour, Leisure, and Economic Thought Before the Nineteenth Century', *Past and Present*, 160 (August 1998), pp. 64–115; Maxine Berg and Elizabeth Eger, *Luxury in the Eighteenth Century: Debates, Desires and Delectable Goods* (Basingstoke: Palgrave Macmillan, 2002).
28 Michel Foucault, *The History of Sexuality: An Introduction, Vol. 1* (New York: Random House, 1990); orig. pub. as *La Volonté de Savoir*, 1976.
29 Porter, 'Monstrous Beauty'.
30 Arthur Conan Doyle, 'The Adventure of the Abbey Grange', in *The Return of Sherlock Holmes* (1904).

Index

advertising 129, 130, 132, 151, 165
'Aerial Steam Carriage' 38, 39–41, 42
agency 5–6
America *see* United States of America
Annapolis, Maryland 144
Anthonisz, Cornelis 57, 58
anthropology 3, 6, 7, 26, 139–40, 142–3
'antiquarianism' 142, 150
archaeology 7, 140, 141–2, 143, 144, 176;
    historical 5, 174–5, 178; methodologies
    26
architecture 10, 54, 75–6, 103, 117–18,
    166; *see also* buildings
art 48, 127, 151, 152
art history 3, 4, 10, 47, 48, 63–4

Baroque style 200
baskets 91–2
Baxandall, Michael 53, 54, 55
bedrooms 87–8, 90
Beilby glass 145–53
biography 123–4, 126, 128, 133–4, 176
body 31, 89, 90, 99, 130, 203
boundaries 73–4
Bourdieu, Pierre 53–4, 62
Brett, David 61–3
buildings 10, 11, 75–6, 103–22; China
    159; concealment 27–8, 31; country
    houses 117–18; defence and security
    110–15; as display 115–17; 'Great
    Rebuilding' 31, 103–5; sources 106–9

cabinets 59
calico 86–7, 88, 89, 90–1, 93
calligraphy 55, 167, 168
cameras 166, 167
capitalism 24, 32
Catholics 105, 110, 111
Central Park 76, 77
ceramics 34–6, 192–3

chairs 196
china 34–6, 162, 204
China 5–6, 35, 158–72; copy culture
    160–2; glass 162–5; photography 165–8
chintzes 88, 89, 91, 93
class 202–3; *see also* social status
clothing 9, 85, 89, 91, 93–8, 99;
    concealment 27–8; stomacher 26–32
collections 127, 176–7; costume 96;
    glassware 152; recipes 182–6
colonialism 160
comfort 89–90, 91
commodification 31–2, 125, 188
concealed objects 26–8, 30, 31, 32, 144
consumption 8–9, 11, 25, 32–3, 176, 188;
    consumer revolution 33, 35; cooking
    pots 129, 130; global 34; life cycle of
    objects 123, 127; women 198
context 11, 13, 15, 125–6, 127–8, 133, 142
Conzen, Michael 69, 70, 71, 77
cookery books 129, 182–7, 188
cooking 131, 181, 182–6
cooking pots 127, 128–32, 133, 180–2,
    186, 188
cottons 86–7, 88, 89, 90–1
craft 48, 127, 151
'crickets' 198
cultural history 6, 7, 93, 178
cultural provinces 141, 143
'cultural turn' 7–8, 9
curtains 88–9, 90, 91

De Certeau, Michel 159–60
decoration 9; cooking pots 181–2;
    glassware 149; ornament 48, 50–2, 61
Deetz, James 174–5, 176
design 4, 10, 25, 53, 142; glassware 147,
    148, 149–50; life cycle assessment 125;
    ornament 49, 53; Plain Style 61–3;
    stomacher 30; textiles 88

dining 104, 150
domesticity 180, 182, 183, 185–6, 203, 205

England 35, 158, 176; buildings 10, 103,
105, 106–7, 110, 116–18; footstools
193–5, 200–1, 203–4; glass 9, 145–53;
regional identity 140, 141
Erasmus 52, 53, 55, 56–7
'everyday' 9, 153, 160, 174, 180, 188
exceptional objects 126–7
exoticism 158, 204, 205

farms 78–80
fashion 91, 95
floral culture 88
Flötner, Peter 49–52, 53, 56
footstools 193–205
footwarmers 197
footwear 201–2
Foucault, Michel 33, 160, 203, 205
France 35, 105, 158, 177, 200–1
Franklin, Benjamin 198–9
Fugger, Hans 59, 60

galleries 12, 14, 15–17
garage sales 168–9
gardens 69, 88, 166
gender: housewives 182; kitchens 180;
stomacher 30; textile workers 95, 96,
97–8; *see also* women
Germany 35, 49–50, 53–4, 55, 152, 158
Girouard, Mark 117–18
glass 9, 11, 141, 145–53, 162–5, 176
Glassie, Henry 3, 11
globalization 24, 35–6, 159
Goodman, Dena 177
Grassby, Richard 7
'Great Rebuilding' 31, 103–5
grottos 185–6

habitus 47, 53–4, 56, 58, 61–2, 63
hats 141
Henson, William Samuel 39–41, 42
heritage 109, 118–19, 153
Herman, Bernard 2, 3, 11
historical archaeology 5, 174–5, 178
history 6–13, 42–3, 144, 175–6, 202, 205;
biography and life cycle model 133;
gaps in 192–3, 196; identity 139–40;
landscape 69–70, 77, 81–2; types of
25–6, 179–80
Hogarth, William 193–4, 198, 200, 203
home 57, 61, 86–7, 89–90, 195; *see also*
domesticity

Hood, Adrienne 7, 92–3
Hoskins, W.G. 103, 104, 105, 143
Hunt, John Dixon 4, 6, 175

identity 139–41, 143–4, 146, 153;
boundaries 74; photographic images
167; 'social imaginary' 179
Industrial Revolution 10, 24, 26, 37–42,
203, 205
innovation 89–90, 108, 145, 148
interdisciplinarity 3, 6, 8, 10, 25–6, 32–3,
139–40
internet 39
inventories 85, 87, 107–8, 176, 195
Ireland 10, 103, 105, 106–9, 110–11, 118
Irish Georgian Society 118
Italianate style 49, 53–5

Jackson, John Brinckerhoff (J.B.) 70, 74,
75, 77, 80
Jamestown 34, 35, 36
Japan 158, 168
Johnson, Matthew 105, 106

Kingery, W. David 3–4, 8
kitchens 123, 131, 132, 179–80, 182

land 70, 71, 77, 78–9, 140, 143
landscape 5, 12, 67–84; boundaries 73–4;
economic markers 77–8; pathways
74–5; reserves 76–7; scale 71–2;
structures 75–6
Le Corbusier 48
Lewis, Peirce 72, 73, 76
life cycle model 123, 124–5, 126, 128–9,
133–4
Lisle, Anne (de) 183–6
local history 143, 153
Loos, Adolf 48
loss 192
luxury 9, 161, 177, 179, 188, 200, 203

Machin, R. 103–4, 106
maps 81
Martin, Ann Smart 3, 7
Marxism 32
material culture studies 2–3, 4–5, 6–7, 93
Mauss, Marcel 53–4
meaning 6, 53, 56
Meinig, D.W. 70–1, 72, 81, 82
metalware 128–32
metaphor 4, 56–61, 175
methodologies 1–13, 24, 26, 32, 41, 43
microhistory 174, 178–9

mirrors 163–4
Modernism 48
modernity 53, 54, 158, 159, 205; China 6,
    160, 166, 169; consumption 176
morality 56–7, 58, 60–1, 198, 200, 203
mundane objects 126, 127, 177–8, 179,
    186, 188
museums 12, 14, 15–17, 42, 176–8, 192–3;
    Dearborn 174; exhibition cases 127–8;
    glassware 152–3; 'living history'
    131–2, 178

narratives 24, 29–33, 36, 37–9, 41, 43, 205
National Trust 118
nature 71, 77
'new historicism' 140
Newcastle 145–7, 150–1, 152

'object-centred' approach 2, 5, 7
'object-driven' approach 2–3
'ordinary culture' 159–60
ornament 47–66; buildings 115–16; as
    metaphor 56–61; spectacles 165; as
    structural principle of style 49–56
'ornatus' 52, 53, 56
ottomans 201, 202, 204

pastry cutters 173–4, 186–7
pathways 74–5
petticoats 95, 96–8
photography 165–8
Phythian-Adams, Charles 143
Plain Style 61–3
pockets 93–4
poetry 52–3
porcelain 34–6, 158, 162, 192–3, 204
postmodernism 37, 139, 144
preservation 127, 129, 131, 144, 192
production 123, 124–5, 159; cooking pots
    128, 129; glass 145–50, 151
Protestantism 61–3, 105, 111
Prown, Jules David 2–3, 4, 6, 12, 13, 202
Puttenham, George 52–3

quilts 86, 89, 90–1
Quintillian 52

recipe books 182–7, 188
recycling 31–2, 86, 98, 115, 129, 162
re-enactment 131, 132
regions 140–1, 143, 153
religion: ornament 57, 58, 59–60; Plain
    Style 61–3
Renaissance 24, 52, 88

retailing 130, 133, 188
ritual 11, 167, 175
rococo style 149, 204
Roeck, Bernd 53–4

Salmon, Lucy Maynard 67–9, 70, 71, 72,
    74, 80
Science Museum 39
Scotland 10, 105, 108, 110, 111–15, 118
script design 55–6
sculpture 55
secondhand objects 168–9
senses 12, 31, 85–6, 130
sexuality 30, 201, 203–4, 205
shoes 201–2
'social imaginary' 179
social status 142, 150; buildings 110, 111,
    114, 115, 117; China 161, 167
sofas 201, 202
sources 3–4, 6, 11, 13, 14, 25; buildings
    106–9; integration of 29, 32
spectacles 164–5
Stilgoe, John R. 70–1, 76
stomacher 26–32
stoves 58–9
style 10, 49–56, 142, 149, 152, 200
supply/distribution 128–9, 132

taste 2, 9, 54–5, 63, 150, 167, 176–7
technology 37, 130, 132, 145, 152, 160–1
textiles 9, 11, 30, 85–102
texts 3–4, 139, 140, 176, 182–7
Tilley, Christopher 4
tobacco pipes 178

Ulrich, Laurel Thatcher 91–2
United States of America: Annapolis 144;
    garage sales 168–9; housing 76;
    landscape 70, 72, 74–5, 77, 78–80;
    porcelain 34, 35, 36; textiles 92–3

Virtues 57–8, 59–60, 61
visual evidence 129, 166
Vogtherr, Heinrich 49

Wales 105, 110
West, Jane 195
Westernization 159
women 85, 92, 198; clothing 93–5, 96–7;
    cooking pots 180, 182; pastry making
    187; recipe books 183, 185–6; shoes
    201–2; textile workers 95, 96, 97–8
written sources 3, 5, 11, 29, 71, 81, 99,
    107–9, 128–30, 139, 174–6, 182–3, 186

CPSIA information can be obtained
at www.ICGtesting.com
Printed in the USA
LVOW04s1423140116

470656LV00013B/93/P

9 780415 459